Journeyman Warrior

Journeyman Warrior

✦

A Soldier's Story of WWII and Korean Police Action

Clifford William Morrow

iUniverse, Inc.
New York Lincoln Shanghai

Journeyman Warrior
A Soldier's Story of WWII and Korean Police Action

iUniverse books may be ordered through booksellers or by contacting:

iUniverse
2021 Pine Lake Road, Suite 100
Lincoln, NE 68512
www.iuniverse.com
1-800-Authors (1-800-288-4677)

ISBN-13: 978-0-595-42152-7 (pbk)
ISBN-13: 978-0-595-67977-5 (cloth)
ISBN-13: 978-0-595-86492-8 (ebk)
ISBN-10: 0-595-42152-0 (pbk)
ISBN-10: 0-595-67977-3 (cloth)
ISBN-10: 0-595-86492-9 (ebk)

Printed in the United States of America

Contents

PREFACE

This is an account of one civilian soldier's experiences beginning in the early thirties. The account is of civil disorders, two operations in the Solomon Islands, the pursuit of defeated German Armies across Southern France and the Rhineland, the final defense of the Korean MLR before the truce and the training of ROK units subsequent to the signing. Included is some but not all of the life experiences in following the dictates of a part time military career.

From hindsight it is hard to imagine an operation more poorly designed, resting on flawed assumptions and filled with more secular concessions than the mission assigned to the Northern Landing force on New Georgia's Dragon's Peninsula operation. The South Pacific was a Navy command and Guadalcanal had been a Marine operation until the final stages when the American Army 25th and Americal Divisions reinforced and relieved Marine units. The Army 43rd and 37th Divisions had been moved to Guadalcanal in preparation for the next stop on the South Pacific Island hopping campaign, the 37th Division was short one combat team, the 129th that remained on the New Hebrides Islands.

The plan called for the 43rd Division to take Munda Airport on the southern shore of New Georgia. Preceding the assault on Munda, the first Marine Raider Regiment consisting of the 1st, 2nd and 4th Raider Battalions would seize three, small lightly held, by the Japanese, islands off Munda where all the Artillery of both Army Divisions plus some Marine Artillery units would be emplaced to support the assault.

After seizure of these Islands the Raiders were to return to Guadalcanal, regroup and embark for New Georgia and secure Bairoko Harbor on Dragon Peninsula. Their mission was to block Japanese reinforcement of Munda from the island of Kolbangara, some fourteen miles south of Bairoko. Only the Raider's regimental Headquarters and the 1st Battalion were able to extricate themselves from their first mission in time to take part in the second. At that point new orders were cut assigning the third Battalions of the 145th and 148th Infantry Regiments to the First Raider regiment. Things went downhill hill from there but didn't stop. It was something like a football coach on the eve of the homecoming game learning that his entire offensive team had come down with measles and that the Athletic director had replaced them with the Soccer team.

Intelligence reported the Bairoko Garrison to be five hundred members of Japanese Imperial Marines, officially referred to as Special Naval Landing Force. Intelligence didn't know or report the day before the Northern Landing Force arrived at Rice Anchorage the Japanese put ashore at Bairoko an additional three thousand Army troops designated for the defense of Munda.

The monsoons came early and by the third of July what had been reported, as passable native trails were water soaked and turned to waist deep quagmires with the passage of large bodies of troops. Presence of Japanese Naval units in and around Kula gulf, the fifteen-mile passage between New Georgia and adjacent Kolumbangara prevented surface re-supply of the Northern Landing Force for two weeks. Bairoko did not fall nor did the Northern Landing force succeed in closing the supply and evacuation routes between Munda and Bairoko. However, they did succeed in reducing the movement of reinforcement and supplies to the point that greatly reduced the time that the Japanese were able to hold onto Munda.

American troops from the 3rd Battalion 145th infantry walked into Bairoko unopposed on the 24th of August 1943 fifty-two days after landing in what was planned as a ten-day operation.

The second Solomon Island Operation covered was more conventional. The First Marine Amphibious corps made the initial assault on the Japanese garrison at Empress Augusta Bay on the Island of Bouganville. The Army's 37th Division landed a few days later followed by the Americal Division. The Marines cleared the beach head and with the help of the 1st BN 145th Inf. reduced the Japanese garrison to isolated units without communication or command structure who continued fight. The Americal Division relieved the Marines and drove the remnants of the Japanese garrison back into the hills. The 37th Division established the left half of a perimeter defense anchored on the beach and extended into a low range of hills some fifteen miles from sea. The Americal Division completed their half of the perimeter creating a secure base for the airfield Seabees were carving out of the jungle. This completed the operation's objective. Nearly three months later the Japanese Sixth Division reinforced, crossed the Empress Augusta Mountains, a volcanic range that ran down the spine of the Island and were annihilated in two weeks of bloody fighting.

The scene shifts to experience with the Armies replacement system and the initial US Air/Ground Liaison School and Continues with the author's travel through the wartime replacement pipeline and assignment to the US Seventh Army's Liaison Section.

This portion details the cooperative efforts of American air and ground forces, the part played by Fighter/bomber pilots of the 324th US Fighter/Bomber Group in the pursuit of the defeated German Armies across the Rhineland.

Portions relating to Korea cover some of the bloodiest fighting in the final half-year of that war particularly around Old Baldy and Porkchop Hills. S.L.A.Marshall in his book Porkchop Hill presents a more detailed and objective view of the fighting. The author sat in on portions of Marshall's painstaking interrogation of four of the seven surviving members of B Company's 3d platoon, 31st Infantry Regiment, 7th Division. Marshall transcribed verbatim in long hand the scenario of the action as related in sequence by each starting with the question; "Who was the first to be aware of the attack?" interrupting only to bring in the next man at the point he entered the battle. Korea is classified as a limited war by having an objective less than the defeat of the Enemy. While such an objective might make sense to many, the policies put together to achieve that objective were in many instances counter productive. Rotating men out of combat reduces the casualties among those being rotated out but the argument that it increases casualties among those being rotated in is persuasive. Rotation policy is only the beginning; there are many more examples. These are my observations with a narrow up close view of specific campaigns or portions of campaigns fought in the Solomon Islands, Rhineland and Korea. The account would be incomplete without a stateside view of Army life between deployments. Somebody else can judge the epic proportions of the battles, their importance and their impact on history. When you are in the middle of a two-minute firefight, believe me, it is epic. Having said all that, there always was a lighter side that erupted at the least expected moment. With out them more participants would have lost their sanity.

1

AUTOLITE

The spring of 1933 brought a smoldering dispute between the Autolite Corporation and the fledgling CIO union to a head and erupted in flames. Cars were overturned and set afire. Strikers bloodied non-strikers. Police broke heads, strikers and non-strikers alike. Strikers stoned and clubbed, and were clubbed by police. Ohio's governor declared an emergency and called out the National Guard to deal with the mayhem.

Company G 145th Infantry and Company B 148th Infantry were the first two units to arrive on the scene, rather the first and second units to arrive on the scene. Company B from Fremont Ohio, some thirty miles closer to Toledo arrived by interurban streetcar an hour ahead of Company G.

Company B battled its way two miles into the Autolite plant suffering several casualties from flying bricks and other debris. Except for one broken leg none were incapacitating. Company G, an hour later followed a different route and escaped opposition until they broke through the ring of strikers surrounding the plant.

The following morning G's supply truck items arrived to find the plant secured. The workers who had holed up in the plants were out and the area was relatively quiet. All the windows in the plant were broken. Several hulks of burned out cars remained in the parking lot. Inside the plant several hundred guardsmen, most in their late teens or early twenties were stowing gear and converting the plant into temporary living quarters and looking forward to collecting three dollars a day state pay as long as the strike lasted.

Half dozen guardsmen wearing helmets, armed with bayonet fixed-rifles and carrying gas masks held each street intersection outside the plant. On the opposite side of the street a number of pickets carrying signs held sway. Between the plant and intersection a platoon of guardsmen, similarly equipped, under the command of a lieutenant, relaxed and watched from beyond thrown missile range. One of the squads carried batons and tear gas grenades instead of rifles and bayonets.

During training sessions on riot control our instructors had made it clear that their role was neutral. Their sole concern was protecting life, property and restoring civilian authority. It did not take long to learn that they were also fair targets for whatever missile came to hand or foul-mouthed expletive to mind of their opponents. After one shift on an outpost men lost all inclination to turn the other cheek. Instead they learned to dodge stones, bottles and bricks ignoring the foul-mouthed insults. They would get their licks in when part of the support platoon.

For the first two or three days manning forward outposts took a lot of fortitude. Rocks and bottles could be dodged but the verbal abuse was difficult to get used to. The men on forward outposts had the tough duty so members of the support relieved them frequently, sometimes as often as every half hour. At first tours were four hours on; four off later when more troops arrived they went to four on, eight off. Pickets on their side of the street, except for occasional taunts avoided confrontation with us.

They were there for the duration. In fact over time they became quite familiar, in fact friendly enemies. Mornings were usually quiet, as the day wore on crowds increased and tension mounted. The larger the crowd made up of striking Autolite Workers, Union Organizers, imported "goons", sympathizers, thrill seekers, reporters and spectators the more restless they became.

As crowds gathered, became louder and bolder. Pressure from the rear would force the mob into the intersection. Flying debris, mostly broken bricks and bottles but some more exotic items such as eggs, tomatoes and other garbage would rain down on the outposts. The Support Platoon in wedge formation and wearing gas masks would charge into the mob lobbing tear gas grenades into the rear ranks of the crowd. In the ensuing confusion the platoon would penetrated the mob and the baton armed squad passed through the front of the wedge and dragged conspicuous members of the mob back inside the wedge. The support would withdraw back inside the outpost and turn their prisoners over to the police.

The police loaded them into paddy wagons and took them downtown for booking where they were processed and turned loose in time to take part in the next day's riot. Some were detained longer but guardsmen came to know the regulars quite well.

Riot control followed the pattern most of the time. There were some failures that developed into exciting melees but none serious enough to call for emergency rescue by the troops resting off shift inside the plant. Usually the mob collapsed in pandemonium with those in front fleeing to the rear to escape bayonets and those in the rear pushing forward to avoid tear gas. Strikers falling over strikers incurred most injuries. The only bayonet wound publicly claimed was by Heyward Braun. He reportedly claimed a brutal guardsman stabbed him in the butt. The guardsman in question admitted; "Aw, I might have goosed him with my baton a couple of times to make him keep up with the rest of the bunch we were taking back to the cops. Braun was a well-known, recognizable, flat-footed, overweight, pro-labor columnist from New York City.

The support platoons were issued "guard ammunition" before going on duty but were under strict orders not to load their weapons without a direct order from the lieutenant in command of their platoon. The platoon leader drew and signed for the ammunition just before going on duty and turned in the precise number of rounds signed for upon coming off shift. On one occasion a lieutenant who failed to turn in one five round clip barely escaped court-martial but was reprimanded and sent home for dereliction of duty. "Guard ammunition" was standard thirty Caliber cases loaded with a reduced powder charge and a short round nosed bullet designed for indoor target practice but abandoned for that purpose because the rounds developed so much smoke that the targets on a well ventilated and lighted range became invisible after only a few shots were fired. Army Disciplinary Barrack guards were issued this less lethal round while guarding prisoners, hence the designation "guard ammunition".

On the whole the demonstrators were well armed with profane vocabularies, particularly the distaff side. The guardsmen were no strangers to profanity and scatology, but totally unprepared for the depth, breadth, volume and source of delivery. What they heard exceeded barnyard or locker room talk. These were dirty fighting words, not just tactical insults. Strikers knew this. Their objective was to enrage the men on outposts to the point they lost their cool and left their posts to take on the hecklers on the heckler's side of the street where the odds were not in the guardsmen's favor. Patience was the guardsmen's ally; dodge the rocks, ignore the words, wait until you are part of the support then sweet revenge is yours.

The atmosphere inside the plant was not entirely serene either. Enlisted men were billeted under one of the plants overhead carrier systems used to move batteries from one work station to the next which and made excellent clothes hangers, that is until someone discovered the control box and started the line up, moving clothes into the next room.

Uproar erupted threatening a donnybrook surpassing any of the brick throwing, gas dodging, and filthy talking melees taking place outside. Fortunately Buck Waters, the six foot two, two-forty pound first sergeant of G Company successfully reasoned with his peers from the vantage point of seniority, physique and bellicosity to reverse the carrier, return our clothes and appoint him sole custodian of the keys to the control box.

The assembly room, enlisted men's home away from home was filthy. The floor, workbenches and tables were oil and acid soaked. They stayed that way in spite of best efforts to tidy up. So storerooms were raided for cardboard and paper packing material for floor covering and tablecloths. Showers and toilets, meager to say the least, were even worse. Sergeant Waters virtually kidnapped his daily latrine detail. Units pooled their kitchens and mess personnel into one big cafeteria that served chow morning, noon, night and midnight. Very confusing made it difficult to differentiate between night and day from the inside.

2

NO RISK HERO

Company G 145th Infantry was called to state duty during two other strikes during the thirties, most notable was the Little Steel Strike in 1937. This strike developed quite differently from the earlier Autolite Strike.

The union walked out of the mills and management replaced them with non-union workers and locked the strikers out. Strikers picketed the mills and confrontations between strikers and workers occurred but because of the larger area occupied by the steel mills compared to the Autolite plant there was much less organized violence. Instead there were occasional fights between workers and strikers, bombings and sniper fire.

The Ohio Governor called a composite force of guard units including Companies E and G of the 145th Infantry to state duty. Billeting was in the Warren National Guard Armory some distance from the mills. Instead of physically securing the mills Assembly Areas were set up in the mill complex and manned by tactical units. Trucks were used to move troops quickly wherever needed for response to disturbances. Command maintained liaison by radio, phone and personal contact with the local police, who patrolled the area and provided information. This exercise was much better organized, more exciting and less stressful than the hand-to-hand combat of the Toledo experience three years earlier.

On one occasion a police car began a chase of a car of a suspected dynamiter. A squad from Company E in a two and a half ton army truck attempted to intercept the chase only to fall in behind the police car in time to witness the back end of the bomb car disappear in a cloud of smoke and debris. The would be bomber dropped a short fused stick of dynamite through a hole in the car's floor boards intending to have it explode under the police car. His miscalculation let the dynamite explode under his own rear axle. Injuries to the bombers were minor; those to the car were not. The police car suffered a broken windshield, the Company E truck barely escaped back ending the police car and members of the squad were left with a story that escalated daily.

A few days' later circumstances put me in a hero's role; not really, it only looked that way. For two evenings prior to the incident a sniper had hidden at the edge of a wood and fired several shots at the yard engine delivering a string of flat cars to the rolling mill. His hideout was some six hundred yards from the railroad track into the mill. The morning following the second shooting we discovered the snipers nest with a handful of thirty-thirty shell casings on the ground. Our Commanding Officer after council from the local police set a trap for the sniper.

The plan was to put two teams of riflemen in hidden positions that covering the sniper's nest and take him under fire when he shot at the train again. If he did not shoot as the train passed troops would converge on his post and capture him. The plan sounded good but had a gaping hole. No one let the train crew in on the plan. They had decided on their own that being shot at twice was enough and the rolling mill could survive without an evening delivery of flat cars. So when the train failed to appear on schedule I volunteered to walk the track and draw the sniper's fire.

What looked like a foolhardy risk was no risk. A rifle platoon had tramped all over the woods leaving many footprints and other visible signs. Several officers and some uniformed policemen surveyed the scene, all very visible. Any one who valued his hide enough to snipe at a yard engine from a hidden vantage point would suspect that his secret now was out and a trap was being prepared for his benefit. It was doubtful that he would show. If he was stupid enough to try again there were a lot of facts on my side.

The shells we found were thirty-thirties most likely fired from an open sighted deer rifle. The alleged marksman was not very accurate; he had hit the yard engine only once out of a half dozen tries. I was much smaller than a yard engine and determined not to give him a second opportunity. Never the less I stayed on the side of the tracks away from the woods, and kept watch on the edge of the woods in case a puff of smoke suddenly appeared. The shells we picked up were of a relatively low velocity that would take about a second and a half for the bullet to cover six hundred yards, ample time for me to drop behind the railroad berm before the bullet arrived. I was young and foolish but not crazy; I did not dawdle on my stroll across that stretch of track. The Little Steel Strike continued for some time but the threat of violence eased after another week or so and we were sent home.

In 1938 while we were in training at Camp Perry a general strike of the rubber industry in Akron was called with an objective to shut down the entire city not just the rubber industry. Again Company G 145th Infantry was part of the force trucked to Akron and billeted in the Akron National Guard Armory. We were back in Camp Perry a week later without leaving the Akron Armory on official business. Many left on unofficial business, mostly at night.

Company G suffered the only casualty of the strike when Emery Preston (allegedly) tied Supply Sergeant A.G.Smith's puttee tapes together. Sergeant Smith was resting his eyes. A.G. was also known variously as Silver, George and Cannonball (from his gory accounts of exploits as an artilleryman in WW I). George awakened. Emery fled. George, who was barefoot, pursued but not for long, he fell and broke his big toe. Fortunately for Emery, George didn't learn the identity of the knotter until a long time after we returned to Camp Perry. We returned to Norwalk on schedule without completing the final week of field training. Spending a week at Camp Perry over the following Thanksgiving holiday made up the missed week of summer field training.

As a foot note small town units such as ours were favored over big city units for strike duty by the Ohio Adjutant General on the premise we were less likely to be contaminated with union dogma. Perhaps so, that policy earned us the unsavory title of "strike breakers" in the press and among union sympathizers. We didn't care; we were pretty good at our assignment. People swearing and throwing rocks at us were easy enough to dislike and quieted qualms over exerting violence on one's fellows for three dollars day.

3

KILPER'S REVENGE

Pre WW II Ohio National Guard summer camp was mainly devoted to marksmanship training and what else could be worked into a two weeks schedule. That was fine with me. Hunting was one of my hobbies. Among farmers Guns were just another tool. Wild animals fell into three categories, beneficial, bad and food. The last two were hunted, the first (mainly song birds) protected. My father was a good shot and very strict about gun safety. He encouraged me with patience and persistence, gathered from his vantage point of dealing with the peccadilloes six younger siblings, to become safely proficient in every undertaking. My first rifle was a twenty-two Hamilton purchased by mail order for the princely sum of three dollars and fifty cents. The money was earned picking strawberries shortly after my eighth birthday.

Instead of being intimidated by the issued model 1903 service rifle I qualified as sharpshooter on my first try, the next year at Camp Perry I made expert. That accomplishment brought an invitation to a try out for a place on the Ohio National Guard Rifle Team. An unsuccessful attempt that never the less led to promotion to Corporal.

The following year, 1935 I made the State Rifle Team Squad and remained at Camp Perry for further competition for a place on the team that would participate in the National Matches. I survived until the final cut to ten firing members and two alternates. That earned me a promotion to Sergeant and assignment as first platoon guide. First platoon simply because I was taller than the other platoon guides. Summer camp in 1936 the 37th Division trained as a unit for the first time since WW I. The training site was Fort Knox Kentucky.

Fort Knox was a huge change from Camp Perry. Fort Knox spreads some two hundred square miles over Appalachian foothills. Camp Perry occupies less than one square mile of drained Lake Erie marshes, in fact Camp Perry was created for the purpose of hosting the National High Power Rifle Matches and only incidentally as a training site for the Ohio National Guard. National Guard summer camps were mainly devoted to extended order drill and marksmanship training. Fort Knox has room for several Armored and Infantry divisions to train at the same time.

At Fort Knox we were housed in eight man tents adjacent to some of the post's permanent training facilities. There we received more sophisticated training than possible at Camp Perry or home armories. Most noteworthy was a session at the Chemical Warfare Center. We were taught the correct method of putting on a gas mask in the presence of gas. Then we went through the gas chamber where an instructor pulled the pin on a tear gas grenade and yelled "gas". We then put on our gas masks and left the chamber. For veterans of the Toledo riots this was old hat, we had put on gas masks while dodging rocks. Some of the recruits got pretty weepy, though. Then we were passed sniff bottles of diluted war gasses such as mustard, phosgene and chlorine.

Sergeant Jim Esker Company G's designated CW (chemical warfare) NCO decided his drill night classes in CW would be jazzed up if the students got a whiff of the most noxious of the real gasses. He coaxed a little of the mustard gas out of the bottle onto his handkerchief. Wrapped the gas impregnated handkerchief in a candy wrapper then stowed it in his barracks bag for later use. Of course the candy wrapper leaked and the gas migrated to the collar and shoulders of a clean shirt. A shirt he wore the next week when we left the cantonment for a division field exercise, Murphy's Law prevailed.

By mid Monday morning, under the weight of a full pack Sergeant Esker was sweating profusely and very hot under the collar. His neck and shoulders were covered with water blisters. Our battalion medical detachment gained valuable experience in evacuating a real mustard gas casualty even if Jim's wounds were not diagnosed correctly until after he was admitted to the post hospital. He spent the next two weeks there recovering. Jim was released and returned home only after signing a disclaimer releasing the U.S. Army of blame. He was not awarded a purple heart for his wounds either.

Jim Eskers misfortune was the beginning of a week of adventure during the 37th Divisions first since WW I field exercise, a maneuver, affectionately known by members of Company G as the Fort Knox Manure. The 145th Infantry Regiment was the lead element of the division's route march to the maneuver area. G Company was the advance guard. My assignment was to lead a flank patrol on a route parallel to that of the main body. The mission was to guard against a surprise flank attack by an imagined aggressor force.

The going was pretty rough until we discovered a dirt road going our way, so we took it. The main body was also on a dirt road. The dust raised made it easy to keep track of them.

Mid morning we discovered a flock of turkeys and decide to shoot one just in case we ran out of food. A distinct possibility, our one per man, one cheese, and one bologna sandwich lunch was already eaten. The romantic vision of a roast turkey feast with we gallant soldiers around a campfire, Civil War style, was pleasant to contemplate. Details could come later, at the moment we were busy converting a lead pencil into bullets to load ahead of the blank cartridges we were carrying. That plan received a dose of cold water when PFC Don Robertson reported a house just ahead of us. We abandoned the project on the theory that these might not be wild turkeys after all and the likelihood that their owners might take umbrage to our appropriation of their property and their guns might not be loaded with blanks. We kept the wooden bullets just in case one of the birds might follow us out of earshot of the house.

By mid afternoon and much meandering of the dirt road we noticed there were no longer plumes of dust rising on our left where the main body should be marching, so we made a ninety-degree left turn. An hour later we came to another dirt road unmarked by marching feet and made a ninety-degree turn back in the direction from hence we came. Light and hope were fading when we came to a fork in the road marked by many footprints pointing down the left fork. It was well after dark when we stumbled into Company G's bivouac, not lit by campfires just flashlights and our comrades in arms were not singing. We did not need General Sherman to tell us "War is Hell"

Our main lesson from this division field exercise was that the Infantry walks a lot carrying all the comforts of life on their backs and where ever they may go trucks filled with jeering Artillerymen riding in the opposite direction will force them off the road. The division revue that concluded our stay at Fort Knox was a boring anticlimax.

Shortly after returning from Fort Knox, to my father's disgust, the Ohio Adjutant General directed me by letter to report to Camp Perry to try out for the state rifle team. This time I was successful, partially successful. I was an alternate. My reward was that the state paid my entry fees into the National Rifle Association Matches plus three dollars a day and keep. As an alternate my duty during the National Trophy Team Match was to serve as our team's official witness to the scoring of targets in the pits. I could have shot on the team if some body broke a leg or something but nobody did.

Captain Ben L. Kilper, from Massillon Ohio, commander of Company C 145th Infantry was the Officer-in-charge and coach of the Ohio National Guard Rifle Team. A fearsome and feared by my peers figure, he ran the Ohio National Guard competitive marksmanship program with an iron fist and imaginative some times profane vocabulary. He was a Distinguished Marksman in his own right; having won that distinction at the end of WW I. Eighteen years later he was an imposing figure. Six feet tall, military bearing, piercing blue eyes and aquiline nose gave him a presence that denied crossing. That is with his campaign hat on. Off, his naked pate fringed with graying hair softened his persona with a hint of a grandfatherly mien. His vocabulary did not; Ben was fluent in the King's English, the Bastard King of England's English.

Ohio's Adjutant General, Emil Marx owed Ben a political debt that he paid by having constructed permanent billets for Ohio's National Guard Rifle Team. The other hundred plus teams that competed in the National Matches were housed in eight man squad tents. We lived in the luxury of a mosquito proof concrete block barracks with a separate mess hall, with additional squad tents for team candidates and pit detail.

Ben had a unique advantage over other team coaches. By assigning his team Adjutant, one Captain Black to the room adjacent to the rear door of the building and occupying the room next to the front exit, he controlled nighttime traffic to and from the barracks. So he thought. He overlooked the windows in the long common bunkroom occupied by the enlisted team members. He not only conducted team meetings on the range he also critiqued his team nightly immediately after turning the lights off in the bunkroom. His nightly lecture not only covered shooting lore but also his wide range of worldly knowledge, military philosophy and experiences. Ben was well-versed and held strong opinions on every note and stanza.

There was a night that our day's efforts had not pleased Ben, so he massaged our egos with a sprightly vitriolic lecture, no individual or performance was spared. After Ben finished, gloom descended on the room and a squeaky floorboard signaled his departure. Fred Shafner spoke up; "Now, he's a pleasant old son-of-a-bitch, isn't he?" "Yes I am and I can back up every Damned word I said," Ben answered from the foot of Fred's bunk. The silence was electric, punctuated by a floorboard squeak. Fred did not say anything, neither did any one else. We weren't cowards, just cautious in the face of Ben's omnipotence.

Ben used the NRA team matches to test various combinations of team members for selecting the ten firing members of his National Match Team and relays on which they would fire. The all-important National Rifle Team Match consisted of sixty shots fired by each member of a ten man team. Barring serious injury to a team member all ten firing members listed on the entry form were required to fire each of the five stages of the match.

The stages were ten shots standing offhand, rifle supported only by two hands and one shoulder, neither elbow touching the body, slow fire at two hundred yards, time limit ten minutes per man.

Ten shots sitting, rapid fire, at two hundred yards, time limit sixty seconds. Ten shots prone, rapid fire, at three hundred yards, time limit seventy seconds. Ten shots prone, slow fire, at six hundred yards, time limit ten minutes per man. Twenty shots prone, slow fire, at one thousand yards, time limit thirty minutes per man. Slow fire time limits were combined to a team time limit of one hour forty-five minutes at the two and six hundred yard stages and five hours fifteen minutes at the thousand yard stage including three minutes preparation time per relay. Rapid-fire time limits were the length of time targets were exposed for one shooter to fire ten shots.

The match was fired over two days; two through six hundred yard stages the first day and the thousand yard stage the second. The rapid-fire stages were fired one man at a time with a coach seated on a stool with a large tripod mounted telescope. The coach directly behind the shooter observed the strike of each bullet on the target as it was fired. During the slow fire stages two shooters, coach and telescope were allowed on the line. The shooters fired alternately starting with the team member on the right. During both slow and rapid fire stages the coach was permitted to talk to the shooters but not touch them or their rifle. He could direct sight changes but not physically change their sights, legally, that is.

During the NRA Herrick trophy team match, Ben found out how well Glen Lakes worked with me and vice versa. The Herrick was a ten-man team match slow fire, prone at a thousand yards. Hitting a thirty-six inch bulls-eye at over a half-mile distance requires a combination of skill, good eyesight, steady nerves, unflappable emotions, applied knowledge of ballistics, observation, and a touch of luck.

A high power rifle bullet leaves the muzzle of a thirty-caliber service rifle at a velocity of 2700 feet per second give or take a few hundredths of a second. Because of wind resistance the bullets speed over a distance of a thousand yards diminishes to a little above the speed of sound. Roughly it takes a thirty-caliber service bullet a little over a second and a half to reach the target over a half mile away. In that time it falls about eighteen feet and a twenty mile an hour wind moving at a right angle to the bullets path will move it sideways about twenty feet. Light waves are distorted by air born water vapor so that the target is seldom where it appears to be. Further complicating the problem rifles are fired from an unsteady platform, the human body.

In team shooting accounting for and computing changes in sight settings to hit the center of the bulls-eye is the coach's responsibility. These changes he calls to the shooters who adjust the sights on their rifles accordingly. The shooter whose turn it is to fire retreats into a semi-somnolent state, holds his rifle steady as his physical condition will allow, holds his breath, aligns the rifle sights on the bulls-eye and applies increasing pressure on the trigger until the rifle fires. If all goes well the bullet hits the center of the bulls-eye and the coach tells the second shooter to do likewise. If not the coach taking all facts into consideration starts the same process all over again with the second shooter, Coach Kilper called Glen and me up on Camp Perry's thousand-yard range as the second pair in the 1936 Herrick Trophy Match. Sergeant Nelson Voight and Lieutenant Don Grim, the first pair, had fired passable scores, not their best but passable. That left us scant room in our class, scant but some. Ben gave us the variation from normal data due to the day's temperature, humidity, light and wind conditions to hit the center of the bulls-eye. We adjusted our sight settings and Glen on the right fired the first shot. Ben watched the vapor trail of the bullet, visible in his spotting scope. The target went down, a sign that it had been hit. In seconds the target reappeared with a black spotter in the four ring on the three o'clock side of the bulls-eye. The team had lost one more point.

Ben concluded that he had missed a change in wind velocity and gave me a correction from Glen's shot. I fired. I got a three at nine o'clock. Down two more points. Ben gave Glen a correction from my shot. Glen fired and the target did not go down. Ben fumed a bit and called for a mark, promptly relayed by our team scorer to the pits via telephone. The target went down and remained down in the pits for a long time.

When it reappeared there was no spotter in it and we received the ultimate insult, a red flag affectionately known to shooters as Maggie's Drawers passed slowly, so very slowly, across the face of the target signifying the target had been completely missed. Down five more points. Every one else on the line knew Ohio's reputation for straight shooting was being impugned. Ben suspected the truth; he got up from his coach's chair behind the scope, knelt down beside me, took off his glasses and squinted through one lens at the windage gauge on my rifle. Grunted put his glasses back on, suspicions sustained, reached down and turned the knob to a new setting. Obviously, I had been turning the knob in the wrong direction. He got back on his chair, peered through the scope, got up, walked up and kicked me in the butt, returned to his coaching station, looked through the scope and said, "There Dammit, shoot." I did. The target went down and came up with a spotter in the center of the bulls-eye. Then I knew what Ben just learned. Glen and I were not suitable pair mates for the National Team Match.

4

STEADY JOB AT LAST

My attempts to make the Ohio National Guard Rifle Team in 1937 and 8 failed, but that of 1939 was successful. Governors had changed and so had Adjutant Generals. Captain Perry D. Swindler replaced Captain Kilper as OIC of the Ohio Team. Perry was six inches shorter than Ben, had a high squeaky voice. He earned his Distinguished Marksman Medal in the A.E.F. matches at the end of WW I. During those matches he won the individual championship as a nineteen-year-old PFC and returned Prisoner of War. Twenty-six years later near the end of WW II Colonel Perry D Swindler, was again captured and later returned to the Americans earning an unwanted, by Perry, distinction of being captured in two separate wars by the same enemy.

Perry's casual and relaxed approach to shooting was a welcome change for the veteran squad he had inherited from Ben Kilper. Ben schooled us in the fundamentals and discipline of shooting, set high goals and demanded dedication. Perry taught us how to relax and enjoy competitive shooting.

Prior to the beginning of the National Matches, Perry arranged for us to train with the U.S. Army Infantry Team. The experience of training with professionals who did little else than hone their skills as marksmen raised our level of expectations and changed our view of acceptable performances. What we had considered excellent was downgraded to mediocre and mediocre to unacceptable.

During the NRA Matches I equaled the 600-yard Members Match record only to have Lieutenant Hamilton of the Marine Corps Team set a new record; but I won the reserve component money pool of about forty dollars as well as placing in the money in several other matches. Sergeant Coats Brown of the Infantry Team and my shooting partner during our joint training sessions won the National Individual Service Rifle Championship.

The Ohio National Guard Team with Sergeant Fred Schaffner and me shooting as the lead off pair won the Hilton Trophy awarded the high National Guard team. Placing Ohio fourth over all behind our old shooting buddies, the Army

Infantry team, followed by the Marine Corps and Army Cavalry Teams. Our finish was the highest recorded by a National Guard team since the National matches were first held at Camp Perry in 1906. At the Ohio National Guard Association Banquet held in Columbus Ohio we were The Adjutant General's guests and introduced from the head table.

Field training in 1940 was extended to three weeks and the training site shifted to Camp McCoy, Wisconsin. We maneuvered at McCoy, as the Queen of Battles always does, by walking and sleeping out a lot. We also fought mosquitoes, lots of mosquitoes, big mosquitoes. In fact the only thing bigger than Wisconsin Swamp Mosquitoes was the stories our men wrote home about them.

For me Wisconsin was a blast, I was the company's First Sergeant and now held a position not an assignment. As long as the company's internal affairs moved smoothly and few complaints reached Captain Keene's ears, my major problem was being able to provide our Battalion Commander, newly promoted Major Ben L. Kilper, with an occasional night cap. Being a veteran of Ben's leadership of the Ohio National Guard Rifle Team therefore one of "his boys" he felt free to impose on me at any time. Battalion Sergeant Major Bertram made nightly rounds of "Ben's Boys" to cadge Ben's nightcap, extracted his own tot, too. "Ben's Boys" considered this routine a small price for the privilege of Ben's recognition.

Now competitive shooting had me hooked and again my efforts were successful and the veteran Ohio Team won the Hilton Trophy, another first. Never before had a team repeated as the Hilton winner. Ohio's Adjutant General convened a board of Officers to examine candidates for commission in the National Guard as Second Lieutenants. The board endorsed mine and forwarded it to the War Department for approval. On the 21st of September General Light received an order from the War Department to induct the 37th Division into federal service effective the 15th of October.

Our allocation of drill dates was increased to use up those remaining in the current fiscal year and our strength authorization was conditionally increased to full Table of Equipment and Organization for rifle companies of some 200 enlisted men. The condition was that the strength of National Guard units being called was frozen at the strength obtained by midnight of the day prior to induction.

We increased our strength from about sixty to ninety plus. Eighty-three passed physical exams and were inducted. Don Robertson ate bananas and drank all the water he could hold to meet the minimum weight requirement for his height and barely passed, "Weinie" Herbe put two inner soles in each sock to increase his height to over the five foot minimum and failed passing. The doctor made him take off his socks to check for flat feet.

We took him along as a mascot anyway. Captain Bernard Keane failed and didn't go along as a mascot. He stayed in Norwalk and organized the home guard, ending the Keane family tradition of service in Company G at three generations. First Lieutenant Alfred E. Westrick assumed command of Company G, 145th Infantry, 37th Division, United States Army.

Paper work during the induction process was no mean task. National Guard records were in the Dick and Jane level of sophistication compared to Active Army standards. Everyone had to fill out questionnaires containing a multitude of personal questions like. "Who is your next of kin? What is your occupation? Have you ever been arrested?" Some others were down right personal. It didn't make a lot of sense to men who had just been indoctrinated with the intricacies of the Geneva Convention's Rules of Warfare, which clearly stated that a soldier was not required to give interrogators information beyond his name, rank and serial number. Anyone asking questions that personal was suspect besides serial numbers were yet to be assigned.

In spite of these complications with the help of the Army Instructor's staff and former Administrative Officer, Company Clerk, and First Sergeant, not necessarily in that order, Del Crawford, the task was accomplished. Those not engaged in shuffling papers and packing gear was treated to an assortment of exceedingly dry and boring subjects while waiting to be immunized by Doctor Battles. Doc's office was several blocks away from the armory and following Army tradition of not trusting a private to do anything on his own until he was being shot at, twice daily a noncom would march a ten man shots detail to Doc's office and return.

One morning exercising my newly developed first-sergeant's-suspicious-nature, I watched the ten-man shots detail leave. It seemed to me that the column was a mite long. The last two men were privates Faulhaber and Hillman.

When the afternoon detail returned I counted and there were twelve, not ten and the last two men were privates Hillman and Faulhaber. I pulled them out of the formation. They reeked of sour mash and their eyes were a bit unfocused and blurry. They had been falling in with each morning detail and falling out at Lobey's saloon two blocks short of Doc Battles office to get their shots and returning to the armory with the afternoon detail. Three years later when I returned to Company G on Bougainville in the South Pacific Private Hillman was a Lieutenant with another unit and Faulhaber was Company G's First Sergeant.

Two days before our departure for Camp Shelby Mississippi Two boxcars were spotted on the local railroad siding, one for our use as a baggage car and the other to be converted into a kitchen car. Under the haggling direction of Supply Sergeant Smith and Mess Sergeant Berdue our newly issued liquid fuel field ranges were installed on sand box bases. Sergeant Berdue knew how to operate the new ranges from reading the instructions and Sergeant Smith had helped install an old model sheet Iron field range in a box car during WW I. No matter that in an earlier version of George's exploits the boxcar caught fire and burned to the wheels. Artificer Plue knew how to drive nails and did the work.

5

NEW POST

The train ride from Norwalk Ohio to Camp Shelby Mississippi lasted the better part of four days and three nights or was it five days and four nights? Much stopping, backing, jostling, direction changes and the inevitable question, "are we there yet" at each delay punctuated it. Our cars were joined en route with cars carrying other units of the 2nd. Battalion, 145th Infantry. We arrived at our destination, Camp Shelby Mississippi, on October 22nd 1940 at 0800 hours. The regimental band and our new Battalion Commander, Major Rudy Ursprung, met us. Major Kilper also failed to pass his physical and Rudy had been given command of the battalion. However, Ben was not one to give in easily, fully aware of the queasiness of Army Bean Counters caused by Congressional Inquiries, he filed an appeal with a notation of a copy being sent to his Congressman. His appeal was granted and he received a six weeks leave for a minor hernia operation and recuperation.

We debarked from the train and under Major Ursprung's command, followed the band playing "The Beer Barrel Polka" to our new home. The Beer Barrel Polka was the regimental anthem in deference to a large Slavic presence on our regimental roster. We Non-Slavs liked the tune and we had several non-printable and insulting sets of lyrics to keep the Slavs in their place. As we entered the 145th Infantry cantonment area Colonel Luke Wolford took our salute as we passed in revue. All very military and militarily impressive for a group who had been, derisively known by regulars as "Corn Stalk Militia", "Weekend Warriors" came later.

More impressive was the fact that we marched into an organized and setup temporary cantonment area complete with squad tents, kitchens, mess tents, showers and latrines. Our baggage soon followed and by the end of the day we were settled into our home away from home. My tenure of First Sergeant was short lived, before the day was out Division directed that all Officer Candidates whose applications for commission were pending in the War Department would assume the rank of Second Lieutenant and be assigned to fill vacancies in their current units. This was great news, Lt Westrick, at the conclusion of the evening retreat ceremony ordered Sergeants Morrow, Schwenn and Robertson front and center and with the help of Lt. Orr ripped off our stripes and pinned second lieutenant bars on us. After the euphoria settled over the next few days facts began to emerge, all negative.

The first question from the new Second Lieutenants was, "When do I get my first clothing allowance payment and can I draw an advance?" Commissioned Officers in our Military services have a long-standing honor predating the Declaration of Independence of buying personal weapons and uniforms of own liking. The founding fathers abandoned the liking part about the time they declared independence. They wanted everyone to be independent but military officers not that independent. Government issue of personal weapons, except for General George Patton came later.

The second and most of the following questions involved "when and how much money"? The answers were, "wait, we're working on that, we expect the War Department to issue a directive momentarily," and finally the correct one, "The War department lost your records and answer will be forthcoming as soon as your records can be reconstructed." Shortly after the first of 1941 we were officially commissioned Second Lieutenants in the Army of the United States with rank dating from January 1 1941. No back pay, no back uniform allowance, no apologies. "You're in the Army Buddy, zip up, shut up and get with it." To add insult to life on sergeant's pay with lieutenant responsibilities we gained the dubious unofficial sobriquet of "Third Lieutenants. The Army was right we were in and we go with it.

Dick Herbe, Louis Kuhnle and Rhett our Irish Setter pup arrived with our baggage. Dick and Looey made themselves useful and Rhett did pretty much the opposite, ingratiatingly. However, she had one big hang up that led to her undoing or perhaps a second life without martial music. From the sound of the first note from the regimental band until the last drumbeat she was an object of abject terror. Dick who was her guardian had to make sure that she was securely confined before the band tuned up to play the troops to quarters from the training area, a daily occurrence. Just once he was a step late and the last sight of Rhett was as she disappeared through an open door into carload of civilian workmen leaving for the day. The door closed and so did life in the military for Rhett. Dick was upset. I was upset. Betty was more upset when she arrived a few days later.

Betty, Gladys Westrick and Gladys` infant son Tommy arrived in Camp Shelby on the Tuesday before the third Thursday of November. Lt. Bob Scott also from Norwalk newly married and commissioned as our Battalion Surgeon volunteered to put Betty up temporarily with his bride Hannah. We accepted without knowing whether or not Hannah had been consulted before hand, it is most likely not. Bob was inclined toward impromptu off the top of his head decisions and Hannah was too much of a lady and too newly married to publicly embarrass her husband, privately is a matter of pure speculation. Within a week, through the good offices of a housing bureau, sponsored jointly by the Hattiesburg Chamber of Commerce, and 37th Division Headquarters, Betty found a room in private home and a new chapter in our life opened.

6

SPIRIT OF 76

President Roosevelt declared the fourth Thursday of November 1940 Thanksgiving day, the Governor of Mississippi not to be outdone by a Yankee Democrat declared the third Thursday of November 1940 Thanksgiving day. Nominal Republican, officially neutral Major General Robert Beitler, Commanding General of the 37th Division upstaged both and declared two Holidays. The Army Commissary at Camp Shelby opted out of the exchange and provided for one holiday dinner with a special issue with a ten percent excess of turkey.

Astutely grasping opportunity, Sergeants Sattig and Battles and I conspired with Lt Westrick to promote a turkey with some gently implied blackmail of Mess Sergeant Berdue. Then with turkey in hand we prevailed on Lieutenant Scott to host a Thanksgiving dinner for a few close Norwalk friends, namely Lieutenant Westrick, (acting) Lieutenant Morrow, Sergeants Sattig and Battles. Bob added Lieutenant Jim Mays, 1st Bn 145th. Inf. Surgeon, to the guest list.

Thanksgiving morning dawned bright and early, the four of us with turkey arrived at the Scott quarters. Jim and Betty Mays, Al and Gladys Westrick, arrived soon after. We quickly reverted to a traditional first name basis as a token to our recent civilian past. Hannah, Gladys and the two Betties assembled all the fixings that go with Thanksgiving dinner while Tom Battles and I stuffed and roasted the turkey. Meanwhile in the living room the two surgeons, with Scott's Irish Setter, Pat, underfoot, provided a skeptical audience for Al's rambling explanation of Military protocol while Willy Sattig tended bar. Fixing the fixings went well while Tommy and I put together a creative dressing combining our mothers` recipes from memory. Jim Mays contributed a mason jar of colorless liquid as a sample of the results of his private survey of the quality of the product of a Mississippi cottage industry, bootlegging.

Mid afternoon under a deepening alcoholic haze and thickening atmosphere of distaff disapproval the party sat down at the diner table while Tommy and I repaired to the kitchen to bring in the piece de resistance. We opened the oven and slid the turkey out however something misfired because the turkey kept right on sliding it hit the oven door and I gabbed for it and succeeded in hitting it hard enough to increase its speed. Tom dived for it and succeeded in putting it in orbit. The turkey slid across the kitchen linoleum and into the dining room with Tommy and me in hot pursuit on our hands and knees where we recaptured the beast and retreated to the kitchen.

The ladies followed and assessed the damage, the turkey was pretty well intact and except for an accumulation of dog hair and grit appeared eatable. They banned Tom and me from the kitchen on the undisputed charge of male incompetence, removed the skin and grime, carved and served the turkey very careful of the selection of their own portions. The rest of us didn't care we were just thankful.

1st Lt Joe Brooks, 148th Infantry Dental Surgeon, was recently commissioned without the slightest inkling of what the United States Army held in store for him. His duty station was just one regimental street away from me and his wife Ruth Anne had a room in the same residence as my wife. A very convenient arrangement since Joe had a car and I didn't.

I offered him all sorts of advice on matters military from my vast knowledge of military lore gleaned from eight years of National Guard service. In exchange he provided transportation to and from Camp Shelby.

Due to the lack of patients Joe's main duty evolved down to sanitary inspector. Army Regulations required routine inspections of mess halls and latrines by medical personnel. Joe qualified. Joe's feet hurt, too, and that didn't help his morale. It was very hard for him to elevate his love for his country above the pain in his pride and feet.

Joe's big beef was that his dental clinic consisted of one room in the 148th Infantry Dispensary equipped with an army dental field set. The Army dental field set was surely a relic from the First World War or maybe the Civil war. It consisted of a kit of hypodermic needles, scrapers, probes and sundry other dental hand tools plus a foot powered dental drill.

Foot powered in the sense that the machine that drove the flexible shaft that drove the drill bit looked a lot like a modern exercise bicycle. It had pedals, a drive chain to a large flywheel, a belt driven power head. It also had a bicycle seat above the pedals and a set of handlebars all on a stationary mount. Joe's dental technician (not yet assigned) was to sit on the seat and pump the pedals up to speed, mainly determined by the whine of the drill while Joe did his dental magic on the patient. That is if the patient had not escaped before hand. That was the long and short of Army field dental care of that time and Joe didn't take kindly to it. It also was the reason soldiers favored extractions over fillings ten to one.

The incursion of Ohio National Guard into Hattiesburg was not the town's first brush with Yankees. Setting the War Between States aside, some twenty-three years earlier Camp Shelby had been the training site of the 38th Infantry Division made up of units from Indiana and Kentucky National Guard.

The town had greeted enthusiastically the flow of dollars into Hattiesburg but the effect of several thousand young eligible bachelors on local society was most disturbing to the regents of Mississippi Southern Women's College if not the student body. This time, on the eve of the announcement of Camp Shelby as the training site for the Ohio 37th Division the regents announced the closing of the Women's College for the duration.

All members of the 37th Division may not have welcomed the town's population reduction by several hundred southern belles but to the married junior officers of the division it proved to be a blessing. An advance party from the division visited Hattiesburg in September to meet with local authorities including the Chamber of Commerce to discuss many things including off base housing. An outcome of the conference was the formation of a nonprofit corporation that leased the campus of the Mississippi Women's College for off base officer family housing.

The only reason Betty was the Scott's houseguest and Davis` upstairs renter was that the college dormitories were not yet ready for occupancy and therefore our reservation could not be honored. It was about three weeks later shortly before Christmas of 1940 that Betty moved in. That remained our home, except for a thirteen-week school tour at Fort Benning Georgia until the division shipped to Indiantown Gap Military Reservation, Pennsylvania, in January of 1942.

During that year we both did a lot of growing up. The Army offered security and structure; no longer did we worry about the next day or the next job. Our family suddenly increased to several thousands of people with the same goals, responsibilities and frustrations. The Army also placed a heavy load on both of us. Duty came first, everything else trailed away in a diminishing queue of importance including income.

The Pre-WWII army tolerated married life for junior officers and first three enlisted grades, just barely. Married junior officers received quarters and subsistence allowances offset by having to buy their uniforms and pay for their meals. Second Lieutenants monthly pay gain over First Sergeants was thirty-seven dollars, Mess bills varied but thirty dollars was a fair average, net gain seven dollars.

The up side was that in spite of the rigidity of structure no one was ever a stranger among strangers. No matter where one went within the structure there was someone to offer a leg up and in Hattiesburg there was life in the Women's College.

Quarters in the College were fifteen by twenty foot rooms separated by a shared bath. Lt. and Betty Gephart were our bath cohabiters. Furniture was twin beds, a dresser and a pair of chairs plus what could be scrounged from the storage room.

In addition to the dormitories the Association operated the kitchen and dining room. The time husbands could spend with their wives was ruled by the omnipresent "Duty." Company grade officers assigned to troop units could expect to spend some Sundays and possibly a night or two a week in town. Field grade and staff did a little better.

To make up for those shortcomings most Regimental Officer's Messes welcomed guests at evening meals at the host's expense and held a weekly family night when `Duty" permitted. Weekly, at least one of the Officer's clubs in the division held a Saturday night party. Enlisted men were less fortunate, family members were always welcome as guests at evening meals and there were non-commissioned officer clubs. Weekend and after duty passes were available for one third of unit rosters at a time.

Between thanksgiving and the years end, the 37th Division and Camp Shelby prepared to receive selective service draftees and also moved out of the "old" area into a much better organized "new" cantonment area.

Monday through Friday, at 0730 hours we assembled and marched to the training area where we reviewed basic training. Privates played the role of recruits, Noncoms and Junior Officers honed instructional skills. Senior Officers directed, observed and evaluated. All this very military correct, critical and soon boring. At 1130 hours we returned to the cantonment for mess, at 1300 hours back to the field for more basics. At 1600 back to quarters, only this time the band came out to play the troops back to the cantonment area where Colonel Wolford the regimental commander, with his staff arrayed behind him took the troops salute as we entered. The band continued to lead the march some distance after passing the Regimental Commander before turning left and counter marching to play the troops past and to their Quarters.

Major Rudy Ursprung commanded the 2nd Battalion 145th Infantry. Rudy left with one leg shorter than the other from a wound and a Distinguished Service Cross for Bravery earned in WW I had a reputation for eating disingenuous Lieutenants alive, he also lisped, slightly. Daily, Major Ursprung, well aware of his position, selected three lieutenants to march behind him as his staff for the evening's return to quarters. This was not a welcome assignment. Rudy's limp made his pace hard to match and out of step lieutenants drew senior staff officer's attention not to mention regimental commanders. While the latter might not mention the deficiency one of the former was sure to let the miscreant know the Colonel noticed.

One afternoon Lieutenants Lady, Maloney and Morrow were Rudy's victims. We managed to maintain decorum and step past the reviewing stand. Shortly thereafter Maloney lost cadence and regained it by mocking Rudy's limp. Lady countered by limping and turning his "go to Hell" cap side ways. Not to be outdone I limped, turned my cap sideways and pantomimed a flute player. Now filled with the Spirit of Seventy-six Maloney turned his cap sideways, pantomimed a flag bearer and Lady pantomimed a drummer.

Thus we passed the band, in perfect cadence with Rudy long hup, short two, long hup short two. All would of ended well except the band broke up in laughter and the discordance caused Rudy to turn and catch our act. He said; "Gentlemen, I will sthee you in my quartersth immediately after thisth formation". He did and removed our hides in long, thin, bloody strips, verbally. A long time later I learned he relished telling the story particularly the part where Lieutenants Lady,

Maloney and Morrow appeared shaken, hat in hands at his doorstep.

7

REINFORCEMENTS

Shortly after New Years Day, 1941, Division Headquarters received from the War Department a list of applicants, my name included, who had been appointed Second Lieutenants in the Army of the United States. However, in time tested tradition of seldom ever solving a personnel problem without a glitch or two, rank was dated January 1 1941. Thus with the same stroke of the pen elevating me to the status of Officer and Gentleman by Act of Congress and robbing me of two and a half months pay.

As a slightly less important act, Congress also had invoked the first peacetime draft in the nation's history. The initial honorees of this distinction began arriving in Camp Shelby shortly after the first of the year. The War Department spared them the stigma of draftee by dubbing first victims of the Selective Service system, "Selectees" also they denied them the privilege of being processed by trained reception center personnel. They left it to the National Guard divisions being brought to full strength the task of processing, equipping and assigning Selectees to units. Then too, in deference to concerned citizens, Selectees were assigned to National Guard divisions from their home states with a commitment to place them in hometown units. However, the system did not take into consideration that In 1941 about half of Ohio's population and two thirds of the 37th Divisions former home armories were concentrated in five major metropolitan areas. That left fifty units scattered over eighty counties with a lot of good sized towns without claim to a 37th Division unit, thus creating a lot of orphans including those who declined to serve with home town units.

Out of a recipe for disaster a minor miracle happened more or less. Some ten thousand Selectees joined the division without a major disaster, it wasn't my fault though. Somebody volunteered my services as the 145th Infantry regiment's assignment officer. When I reported to Captain Norman Finney the regiment's Personnel Officer he handed me a Military Occupation Specialty catalog and told me to report to Division Headquarters with the detail of men waiting outside in a weapons carrier and Division would tell me what to do.

They did, they told me to take this roster of arriving Selectees and go over to the building with a 145th Infantry sign over the door and set up shop with my crew of assignment specialist, that is when I learned who rode to Division in the weapon carrier with me and that is how I became an expert Military Occupation Specialty Assignor.

Lady Luck smiled. The detail turned out to be a half dozen-clerk typist including First Sergeant Thomas from L Company. With his penchant for details and mine for getting the job done in due course the project fell into a routine and the regiment's strength was brought up to full table of organization and equipment.

We gained some interesting trivia, many Selectees claimed to be truck drivers. Obviously someone had spread the rumor that Infantry, Queen of Battles gained that title on her feet with her home on her back but used trucks to bring up the ammunition. American youth of our generation were not stupid.

Not one to overlook our company interest, I snared Pete Petrides the scion of a well-known Columbus Ohio restaurateur for my unit's mess hall. I learned that machinists make good antitank gunners because operating lathes and such they need to rotate their hands in opposite directions on the controls, the same requirement applies to antitank guns when tracking a moving target. All very useful information never used again.

While all this was going on a contingent of reserve officers reported for duty with the 37th Division from the Fourth Corps Area. Most were Second Lieutenants on their first duty assignment since graduating from an ROTC program. Many of the 37th Division units had military histories reaching back into the Civil War, War Between the States to our new assignees. These Officers were filled with foreboding since they hailed from the cradle of the confederacy.

On arrival they were assigned quarters and introduced to their new units. The next morning, at reveille the regimental band instead of the customary march and countermarch down the regimental street, marched and counter marched through Officer's Row playing Dixie. The area resounded in rebel yells from jubilant Southerners. The following morning the band played a return visit to Officer's Row playing Marching Through Georgia. This time the Yankees danced and cheered. One Unreconstructed Rebel refused to leave his bed.

The following morning Colonel Wolford the regimental commander met with the newcomers and informed them that for the next two weeks for their benefit and to avoid embarrassment from their lack of experience they would have the opportunity to bring their basic military skills up to speed. They would attend a refresher course supervised by the regiment's Executive Officer Lieutenant Colonel Whitcomb.

He did not tell them that their senior instructor was the Regimental Sergeant Major and their instructors would be a group of sergeants whose approved applications had been forwarded to the War Department for appointment as Second Lieutenants. The Regimental Sergeant Major was a West Point graduate who had served as a captain during WWI, resigned at the end of the war and had enlisted in the Ohio National Guard a few years later.

The avenues leading to the objective of this plot were varied and several. The Sergeant Major was a soldier's soldier completely unimpressed by second Lieutenants. LTC Whitcomb had never ruled in favor of an appeal of The Sergeant Major's decisions. The Sergeant Instructors were in full accord with The Sergeant Major's dictum "In this school there are two ranks in the following order, Instructors and students, I am the chief instructor."

When the Sergeant Instructors received commissions as Second Lieutenants every one of their current students out ranked them. Instructors, except for The Sergeant Major, and students shared vulnerability. There was one instructional failure. Lieutenant Campbell, one of the student officers, on his first day of duty with G Company put his canvas leggings on with the laces inside his calves and fell flat on his face in front of the company at reveille as his legging laces and hooks snagged each other.

Otherwise Colonel Wolfords strategy worked well. In a matter of weeks the regiment had a cohesive compliment of junior officers who served the regiment well during three years of overseas service.

The physical organization of the "new" area was much more conclusive to the social organization of both enlisted and officer cadres. Mess halls were larger and better arranged. Pyramidal tents were framed and each had an infamous Sibley stove mounted in a sand box. Companies had day rooms in addition to mess halls and sufficient tentage for full TO&E strength at a rate of one pyramidal (eight man) tent for every six men. Officer rows provided for one pyramidal tent, occupied by the company commander and executive officer plus four individual A tents for platoon leaders. Regimental areas had an officer's mess, an Officer's club, an NCOs club and a chapel all in separate buildings. From a chaplain's view the latter should be at the head of the list, although at times Chaplain's influence was more theoretical than practical.

Private First Class Ralph Riley Captain Bill Morr`s orderly learned about the bitter taste of best intentions gone wrong from a Sibley stove. Bill and I learned to approach high expectations for Riley with caution. The Army provided Rifle

Company Commanders with an orderly in the Table of Organization. The purpose was not to provide a perk as a reward for escaping the rank of Lieutenant as many like to believe but rather to free the Company commander from details of caring for his own creature comfort. His responsibility is the task of caring for the comfort, well being and soldierly productivity of the some two hundred plus men assigned to his command.

Little did Captain Morr know how much of a burden that one TO&E slot could be. Riley, AKA Ripper, started military life as an orphan that hung around the Ashland Ohio Armory and went to summer camp with Company E as a mascot. There is some question as to Ripper's chronological age in 1941 but his gullibility lingered in the age of innocence.

One Friday afternoon, at recall, Bill and I rounded the entrance to Officers Row after a hard day in the field intent on a shower, clean clothes, and a refreshing drink, to see the spark arrester and a length of stove pipe erupt with a bang from our tent top followed by a cloud of smoke and soot. Seconds later a second cloud enclosing Riley erupted from the tent door. "Riley, what in Hell have you done now?" yelled Captain Morr, being very commanding. "Nothin`, not me, captain. I did not do it," replied Riley, his white teeth showing through a very black face, "it was Ernie Barrick`s fault, that old Sibley wasn't drawing worth a damn on account of all the soot in the stove pipe so I asked Ernie what to do and he said if I threw an M80 in the stove and held my foot against the stove door it would sure as Hell clean out the soot and look what happened." We had our drink without a shower and dined dirty that night.

Louis Kuhnle, G Company's stow away found a home as the Steward of the 145th Infantry Officer's Club and Mess. The 37th Division was fortunate in its commanding general who put high emphasis on morale and esprit de corps. The 145th Infantry was fortunate in its commander who emphasized cohesiveness of its officer cadre.

Colonel Wolford conducted a formal mess every evening, in his absence the senior officer present presided. Shortly after five o'clock retreat the Colonel would appear at the club have a cocktail and visit with various officers until Steward Kuhnle informed him that dinner was ready to be served. Colonel Wolford then led the way to the officer's mess hall adjacent to the club, followed by the rest of us.

The table in the mess hall was U-shaped and covered with oilcloth except for more formal occasions. The seating arrangement was by rank with the Colonel seated in the center of the head table and the Regiments field grade officers seated by rank alternately right and left of the Colonel. Company grade officers were seated by rank alternately down the outside of the flank tables. Over flow followed the same pattern inside the table. Guests sat with their sponsors. Dinner began with a blessing by one of the chaplains, moved to serving of food in courses, highest rank first and ended with remarks by the senior officer present.

In between many unusual things happened. Thomas "Doc" Battles first appearance after being commissioned from the ranks of G Company created a sensation not of his doing. Harold Conrad, G Company's best intentioned, most unaccomplished soldier and greatest challenge to former DI Sergeant Thomas Battles was a regular detailed to duty as an Officer's mess orderly. On this occasion, immediately after grace and before polite conversation could begin, Private Conrad entered the Mess Hall bearing a large medium rare steak, rightfully the Colonels and served it to Tommy loudly remarking; "There Doc I brought you the best damned steak in the house." While Doc slowly melted into the floor, figuratively, the Colonel recovered and said; "That was an auspicious start, young man. Titters grew to snickers to guffaws. 2nd Lieutenant Battles was the first officer out of the mess hall when the Colonel said, "Dismissed."

Lieutenant Jules Brazil brought the after dinner conversation to silence one evening by tapping his water glass with his knife as the Colonel's normal procedure before making an announcement. He also created a panic among his tablemates by continuing to butter his palm after the slice of bread formerly there slid off.

Some unknown Lieutenant invented a most noxious practical joke. He folded the overhanging oilcloth table covering into a trough slanted toward his table mate on the head table side then poured a half glass of water into it. If his tablemate was alert he picked up the edge of the cloth and continued the flow toward the head of the table, if not he found himself cradling half a glass of water in his lap. This practice came to a screeching halt one evening when the water migrated to the head table and dumped into Major Kilper`s lap. Ben was not one to suffer in silence or not retaliate to injury. The flow of water was matched by the flow of invective. That practice ran its course, abruptly.

One Lieutenant after imbibing unwisely wakened Sunday morning sharing his A tent with one of the yearling heifers that wandered through the area courtesy of his cup companions of the night before. Sherman was right; War is Hell, without lighter moments getting ready for it no one would go.

8

ASS DEEP GENERAL, ASS DEEP

The 37th Division took part in two famous Louisiana Maneuvers in 1941 the first, "wet", one in June notable for editorial comment by Mookey Adams and that of another unknown GI. Mookey and his tent mate Greeny Allen made apprehensive by his companions conversations about snakes during the first day truck ride to the maneuver site decided to remedy the situation.

The following morning at reveille when G Company 145th Infantry's Sergeant Faulhaber counted noses, privates Adams and Allen were conspicuous by their absence. Further investigation revealed a note in their unoccupied pup tent, stating "Sargant Faulhaber, you tell Lootenant Westricks me and Greenie, we dont like snakes so we went home." "Me and Greeny we don` like snakes" became a password for G Company veterans of the Louisiana Maneuvers for the duration of the war.

The other occurred later and expressed the entire division's opinion of Louisiana, Maneuvers and generals boosting GI morale. It happened on a day that E Company of the same regiment had slogged all morning and half the afternoon down a narrow rain soaked dirt road with bayou waters lapping the berm on both sides when a call was relayed from the rear of the column; "Make way for General Bietler`s jeep!" E Company men had no choice but to step of the road berm. The jeep stopped between the two files of men in water swirling around their hips and the Division Commanding General making pleasant conversation undoubtedly with the intent to raise enlisted morale, inquired of one:

"How deep is that water, Soldier?" The soldier looked up at the general, noted his shiny brass, dry uniform, polished boots, sighed with disgust at the obvious and replied; "Ass deep General, ass deep. The General spoke to his driver and the jeep resumed its journey without further raising morale between two files of soldiers standing "Ass deep, General, ass deep."

The Louisiana Maneuvers were declared a great success by those in charge others entertained their own views. My parents were Democrats and so were most of my associates. I was aware of politics, slightly. During the fall exercise the provisional unit I was serving with bivouacked on a Friday evening outside of Alexandria Louisiana. We had been in the field for three weeks without respite. The prospect of a night on the town raised morale to a new high.

Saturday morning brought word that all passes were canceled and our efforts would be directed to making the bivouac presentable for a Sunday visit by the Nation's First Lady, who would tour the area and raise our morale. We labored diligently Saturday and stood by patently Sunday until evening when Eleanor rode by in a staff car on the main road outside the bivouac scarcely visible to us morale raisees. About midnight we struck camp and rolled west bound for Texas. I have been a Republican ever since.

There is no question that the tactical exercises during the summer and fall of 1941 saved countless lives during WW II. Army Materiel, Tactics, Command and Logistics of the "hollow" Army of the thirties had long been mired in the lessons of WWI trench warfare. If nothing else the problem of moving large bodies of troops pointed up the inadequacies of the organization of American "square" divisions much weaponry remained of WWI vintage. U.S. army doctrine lagged behind that of our future allies in Europe and that behind Axis doctrine.

Communication relied on telephone and hand delivered messages. Commanders were reluctant to relinquish control to subordinates. The Louisiana maneuvers were a step to rouse us out of lethargy. Improvisation was the order of the day. Saw horses with signs became artillery pieces, soldiers with flags became all sorts of things from machine guns to tank barriers. Change was in the pipeline. Half-ton 4x4 trucks had just been introduced as weapons carriers. Half-ton 4x4 truck chassis with a soft top bodies featuring cut outs in lieu of doors to the front and rear seat compartments served as command cars forever removing mules and horses from infantry Tables of Organization and Equipment.

Formerly a Company Commander's command vehicle was a horse and weapons carriers were either mule or hand drawn carts. Quarter ton 4x4 general-purpose vehicles were still being tested by the U.S. Army Infantry Board at Fort Benning Georgia and soon replaced half-ton command cars but inherited the sobriquet "Jeep". Half ton Weapons Carriers were eventually replaced with similar but heavier three quarter ton vehicles. Other Materiel along with Tactics, Command and Logistics were in a similar state of flux.

However, the Cavalry retained a relic of the old west; the black 9th and 10th Calvary regiments bearing the traditions of famed "Buffalo Soldiers", remnants of the Indian wars retained their horses.

The value of the experience from the 1941 maneuvers split equally between Command and Troops. It set a point of departure for the task ahead. Commanders learned the inadequacies of the tools they had at hand. Their Staffs learned the complexities of their functions. Troops learned to endure. Endure they did with a little added ingenuity here and there. In June Troops learned to endure mud in August and September to endure heat and dust. In both to endure boredom, exhaustion and orders that made no sense at all to their little picture. Possibly in the big picture but who looked at the big picture, how could they? They were in it.

For me the June Maneuver was all hearsay. In April I passed the board for promotion to First Lieutenant and was sent to Fort Benning, Georgia to attend the Company Officers Course of the Infantry School. August was a different matter. By the time I returned from school the Division was adjusting to new age Weapons, Materiel and Training. We were now retraining to correct deficiencies noted by senior commanders in the first exercise. Nobody asked the GI's` opinions likely because no one wanted to know. "Me and Greenie, we don' like snakes." and "Ass deep, General, ass deep."

9

TIS

In late March my mother fell ill and we returned to Ohio on a short emergency leave. On our return we found orders to the Infantry School's Company Officer's Course waiting at regimental headquarters. Still smarting over a bus station manager's decision to route our return from Ohio over a longer and more costly route we decided to try rail travel to Fort Benning GA.

Captain Norman Finney entered the picture and offered to drive us in interest of absorbing more southern culture. We made the three hundred mile trip quite comfortably by mid afternoon on the fourteenth of April. Norm had previously attended the Infantry School so he gave us a guided tour of the post before returning to Columbus and finding a place to spend the night.

There was no room at the Inn or Hotel or Motel or Hostelry or Hospice or anything resembling any of the above. Finally, at three in the morning of the next day we found vacancies at a hotel, eighteen miles back in Opelika Alabama. Later that day we found Betty a room in a private home through the classified section of the local paper and signed me in the Infantry School Bachelor Officer Quarters. The Finneys departed to continue their search for absorbable southern culture.

That evening I discovered that three of my classmates were Lieutenants Johnny Norris, Pat Patterson and Bud Russell all from Seattle Washington and the 40th Infantry Division. Their wives lodged near Betty in Columbus so we became immediate fast friends out of need, my need for transportation. Five days later we moved Betty to a room nearer the Seattle contingent for obvious reasons;

Reason one; Betty's landlady did not like Yankees.
Reason two; she did not approve of any religion, other than her own.
Reason three; she did not permit women to entertain men in her house without first seeing their marriage certificate.
Reason four; she did not permit renters to sit on the bed and there were no chairs in the room.

Reason five; Renters were not allowed to rinse sox or underwear in the bath.
Reason six; Renters were not allowed to use electric iron.
Reason seven; Betty did not like the landlady.

To prove her point the landlady declined to refund any of the weeks rent paid in advance. The move worked out well, our school schedules were identical there was one more expense sharer in the car pool. All four wives got on together and Mrs. Johnson, Betty's new landlady shared her washing machine and kitchen including a shelf in the fridge. She and Betty became fast friends.

About a week later Lieutenant Don Robertson from G Company 145th Infantry and Norwalk OH showed up to attend the Communication Officer's Course. Followed in turn By Lieutenant and Mrs. Art Richwine and Major Ben and Gladys Kilper from our regiment. The latter to take the Field Grade Officer's Course and the former the next Company Officer's course.

After The Infantry School I saw Norris, Patterson and Russell on Guadalcanal. Now assigned to the 25th Infantry Division, the three were returning to Fiji for rest and recuperation. Patterson and Russell again on New Georgia where they were part of the party who relieved the Northern Landing Force at Biaroko Harbor at the end of the Dragon's Peninsula action. Johnny Norris had been severely wounded during the Munda Operation and neither knew whether or not he survived.

10

CURRICULUM

Fort Benning is the site of the Infantry Board that has the final responsibility for enunciating doctrine and determining the suitability of equipment, weapons and tactics for infantry combat. Coping with TIS jargon was an early lesson. One of the more important bits was the noun "blivet". Blivet was used to describe a wide range of unpleasant or impossible situations or things. We were hit with Blivets, described as Blivet gunners, ran into stacks of Blivets, loaded Blivets, and were forced to attend Blivet classes. A Blivet was defined in more polite terms as two pounds of excreta stuffed into a one pound bag.

A new quarter ton, four-wheel drive general-purpose vehicle was undergoing tests at TIS. Later, assuming the role and name of "Jeep" from the current half-ton command car that users had dubbed "Jeep." The original version of the new Jeep not only was four-wheel drive, it also was four-wheel steer. An interesting feature that often left front seat passengers seated on thin air in the midst of a left hand turn. It also was much easier to tip over than the accepted standard steering version but you sure could turn it around and get the Hell out of there fast, a capability sorely missed by some during combat.

TIS taught the profession of soldiering, starting with hand-to-hand combat and small unit leadership through regimental staff operations and tactics. Students received hands on experience with every Infantry weapon from hand grenades to 37 millimeter anti tank guns and filled the role of squad leaders through regimental staff positions. We witnessed dozens of demonstrations, took part in more exercises, passed still more quizzes and endured examinations practical and theoretical with logical solutions and school solutions of which only the later was acceptable.

Perhaps the most impressive demonstration was "The Mad Minute" where all supporting weapons of an Infantry Battalion fired for one minute on a facsimile of a typical organized defense manned by silhouettes. The rolling cloud of dust, angry red punctuated black smoke, the cacophony of sound and fury from the exploding shells is as if the gates of Hell had been swept open for sixty seconds. After all weapons were cleared the audience moved forward for a close up view of the carnage and two things became apparent. The silhouettes on top of the ground were riddled and about sixty percent of those in hasty fortifications were intact. We gained a healthy respect for firepower and learned that a hole in the ground was the infantryman's best friend. The course in Hasty Field Fortification had us digging and occupying fox holes run over by a light tank with the digger in it. It gave us a lot of blisters and confidence in entrenching tools.

My old friend, Coats Brown from Camp Perry days, with two added stripes was part of TIS Rifle Committee and performed many roles both as an instructor and as a demonstrator but our personal relationship had changed. We no longer were teacher and pupil or friendly competitors; we were Lieutenant and Sergeant at Coats` insistence.

Not that we were strangers, we still enjoyed reminiscing over shared incidents and were proud of each other's successes. Our regard for each other was as strong as ever but now we belonged to different worlds separated by the responsibility of command. It was Sergeant Coats Brown U.S.A. who brought the separation home to me.

Map reading was a must pass course, no one left TIS without passing the map reading course including recognizing all the technical characteristics of a map and all practical uses of maps except perhaps fire building and sanitary. Students soon learned that any class in map reading that had PE following the title was not, pretty easy, more likely it was positively exhausting.

The second part of the Map Reading exam was a practical exercise that loaded the class into trucks at dusk and drove the students at least five miles out into the reservation.

Groups of four were dropped off at numbered stakes placed at hundred yard intervals along a dirt road handed a map, a compass, a flash light and a list of directions consisting of azimuths and distances in yards between checkpoints. Students were required to write in the number found on a stake marking each checkpoint. The route plotted by direction and distance covered several zigzag miles of Fort Benning terrain to a numbered stake on a parallel dirt road.

The country covered was run of the mill Georgia reclaimed farm land beaten up by years of military exercises including shelling, construction and abandonment of hasty field fortifications such as barbed wire not to mention an occasional kitchen sump rooted open by feral pigs. The diabolic thing about this exercise was two fold first there were several different routes plotted of which students had no way of identifying the correct check point or destination number and the trucks carrying the class back to barracks left promptly at midnight. The horror was that the exercise was graded fail/no fail and the bright spot failing students got to take it over until they passed.

It was widely rumored that only three of the issue flashlights had batteries replaced with new between classes and that an occasional Union Army Veteran wandered into camp. Definitely not Confederate Veterans, They were Southern Boys too astute to get lost in a Georgia swamp.

Just so we wouldn't become overly impressed with our own importance students learned the pleasures of carrying 81-millimeter mortar base plates and heavy machine gun tripods in gun drills. We also had the opportunity to qualify with every weapon organic to an Infantry Battalion.

We were treated to an all time low scam in the class on hand grenades. The instructor set us up in the opening session by displaying a set of all types of hand grenades currently in the army arsenal each variety easily identifiable by its color, black for inert dummy grenades, blue for practice, yellow for live grenades on down the list. He then demonstrated the correct form of throwing a grenade with the dummy grenade. Next he demonstrated pulling the safety pin from the practice grenade while holding the handle tight against the grenade while throwing it. He then gingerly picked up the yellow grenade, warned us again of its lethality, grasped the grenade in his right hand and told us that he was going to pull the pin and throw it over a log barricade that would contain the fragments from the exploding grenade.

Keeping tight grip on the grenade he pulled the pin. Then almost as an after thought turned to the class and said; "If ever you find yourself in this position with a live grenade in one hand, the pin in the other and your target disappears just keep a tight grip on the grenade handle and reinsert the pin." and proceeded to do just that.

Grenade Pins are cotter keys with a ring through the eye of the pin and the split end crimped open to retain the pin in place and virtually impossible to reinsert. The class grew more restive as he changed the grenade to his left hand and the pin to his right, then he said; "not to worry, even if I drop it there still is a five second delay after the striker detonates the grenade, time enough to pick up the grenade and throw it behind the barrier." At this point he dropped the grenade, the detonator popped, he casually stooped down picked up the grenade, tossed it over the barricade and with a wide grin said: "it was only a practice grenade painted yellow."

At that moment there was a terrific explosion and a mushroom cloud of smoke and debris ascended from behind the barricade. Those of us caught in middle of the bleachers realized that we had been had. The explosion was from a quarter of pound of TNT in the bottom of a pit filled with lime, dirt and leaves touched off on cue by a co-conspirator.

Several of the students, in the front of the bleachers had open escape routes left when the detonator popped and were still running when the explosion occurred. They walked back, red faced to the cheers of their deserted comrades. One seated in the top row was not so fortunate; he jumped off the back of the bleachers and quite unintentionally cushioned the fall of a seatmate. He suffered a broken leg in the process. Ours was the last class to witness that particular demonstration.

We watched the epic "Crossing the Chattahoochee" courtesy U.S.A. Engineers, narrated by Burgess Merideth on NBC radio. The audience of invited guest included dignitaries, members of the Press, TIS student's wives and admirers.

The spectacular began with simulated artillery fire on the far bank of a bridge site followed by an assault crossing of infantry under the cover of machine gun fire (blanks) in rubber assault boats and more explosions simulating artillery. This was all very noisy and realistic causing me to make a firm resolve not to ever attempt to engage the enemy from a rubber boat. They are too big a target and water is not conclusive to digging foxholes.

After the Infantry secured a foothold on the far bank the engineers moved pontoons into the river, anchored them in place and linked them together with steel planking. As tanks began moving into place to cross the river a pontoon on the far side of the river was blown out of the water to simulate a shell hit. Engineers replaced the bridge section, several tanks and trucks crossed over the floating bridge to the acclaim of the crowd and end of the demonstration. Since it was a Saturday morning demonstration guests departed for the Officer's Club swimming pool and bar.

Perhaps the most spectacular of all demonstrations I missed by not being at the right place at the right time. My disappointment heightened when I learned that Betty co-starred in the production although she was a victim of circumstances, more or less.

She with her friends from Seattle joined a recreational riding club on the base and progressed nicely advancing by the time the course concluded to the point where she stayed in the saddle with her mount at a trot. At the final session she joined the most advanced group on invitation. She fared well as the group began their ride over the bridle trail, kept her elbows tucked in, reins in her left hand, erect and leaning forward in the saddle.

Trotting proved jolting and regrettable, when they moved to a gallop her mount recalled his post colt-hood days when as a Cavalry Captain's steed he led the charge and once again he did scattering a class unloading trucks on return from a field exercise.

I was not among them but by the time our car pool left for home that evening I had heard several versions of this mad woman on horseback trying to run down a group of defenseless Infantry Officers. Fortunately our room at the Johnson's included a fireplace so Betty could eat off the mantle for the next few days.

The Bixbys, Mother, Father, Grandmother and Alice lived next door to the Johnson and soon Betty became good friends with Alice and her friend Claire Hamil. Alice and Claire needed an in to Fort Benning social life and Betty needed an in to southern customs, there were absolutely no ulterior motives involved.

On Memorial Day weekend Betty and I chaperoned Alice, Claire and their boy friends, who by pure chance happened to include two of my classmates, on a three-day excursion. Our first attempt at chaperoning was successful, no broken romances or shogun weddings we all parted friends.

Alice's Grandmother, who was both blind and a victim of Sherman's march through Georgia provided Betty an unusual thrill by relating her experiences with "those murderous Damn yankees from Ohio who burned her Mama's home and stole her Papa's live stock and drove off "theyah niggahs". A few days later after Grandma's emotions subsided Alice diplomatically let Grandma know that Betty was married to one of those northern soldiers out at the fort. Grandma said; "I like that little Yankee girl next door you just bring her over any time you like." Alice did not mention Ohio.

11

TANK KILLERS

On August 12th the 145th Infantry left Camp Shelby by truck and closed in the 37th Division's base camp at Gillis, Louisiana on the 14th prepared to take part in "The Great Bloodless War between the Shirtless Wonders and the Yoohoo Boys."

A unit of the "Blue" Army was severely chastised by General Krueger for riding through Baton Rouge shirtless and General McNair raised Hell with units of his "Red" Army for yoo-hooing at girls while passing through Alexandria. In the mean time a Life reporter coined OHIO as an acronym for "Over the Hill In October and credited it to an unnamed member of the 37th Division as a response to the division's federal service being extended eighteen months.

Not that the unnamed disagreed with the response, a reporter inventing news denied him the opportunity of voicing it.

One obvious shortcoming of force organization uncovered in the June Maneuver was a lack of an active defense against Armor. The Army's defense against armor doctrine was passive relying heavily on tank traps and field barriers. The June exercise confirmed what the Allies in Europe had recently learned.

No matter how impregnable a fortification, field or otherwise a mobile force can go around, under, over and through it. Newly formed provisional antitank units were to be tested in the forthcoming exercises to see if they could counter the "go around" bit.

On August 16th the fickle finger of fate reached out and touched me again. I liked to think that my keen intellect and inquisitive mind persuaded my immediate senior commanders to select me for this experimental mission but perhaps there was a propensity for standing around looking stupid that caused them to rationalize; "Now there is a lieutenant we can very well do without, let's send him."

Regardless, regiment ordered me to report with a reinforced platoon from E Company to Division for further orders. I did and I got them along with two more platoons with attached machine gun sections one each from the 147th and 166th Infantry also three platoons from the 112th Engineers, all mounted on trucks and ready to roll. I don't know why I was apprehensive rather than flattered to discover that I was honored with the command of this outfit since I was the only Officer included. We were to report forthwith to a General March at Camp Claiborne Louisiana.

Soon after arrival at Camp Claiborne we learned we now were a part of a new "Tank Killer" Group consisting of three provisional antitank battalions. All of the battalions were from an anti aircraft artillery group made over from a coast artillery regiment of the Louisiana National Guard. My "Command" of Infantry/Engineers converted the group to a combined arms unit. My delusions of grandeur evaporated with my "Command" as General March forthwith assigned one reinforced infantry platoon to each artillery battalion while keeping the engineers at group headquarters.

The E Company platoon, me included was assigned to the 73rd {prov} Antitank Battalion. The Battalion Commander exercised his sense of proportions and further assigned each of the three rifle squads to one of the three firing batteries, retaining the machine gun section with Battalion Headquarters and Service Battery for defensive purposes or so he claimed. I was easy to see that H&S Battery was short handed and ten more duty soldiers eased housekeeping problems. Thus I became a thorn. To keep me out of his side he made me the Battalion Operations Officer sharing a command car and driver with the Battalion Intelligence Officer, one Lt. Richard also a thorn.

Our staff section was the command car driver. We rode unencumbered. We rode all over Louisiana and a lot of East Texas. We found places where the enemy might attack and didn't. We got lost behind enemy lines and faked our way out by wearing white armbands.

We also were caught by a hurricane and barely survived. It rained all afternoon while our convoy splashed through Louisiana mud to a new position Richard and I found three other officers camped under a tarpaulin slung by its corners to trees and joined them. Rain and wind intensified until one corner of the tarp by now resembling a suspended Olympic swimming pool tore loose and cascaded several hundred gallons of cold water flushing me completely out of my bed roll scattering sodden belongings over a sea of mud. My companions gave me absolutely no sympathy; "God finally got that Dam Yankee."

One midnight we were awakened in our hastily set defensive position by the sound of hoof beats and creaking saddles as the 10th Cavalry moved into bivouac in our rear. Before daybreak they passed through our lines to attack "Blue" Army positions to our front. When they arrived they had been in the saddle for ten hours and they left a clean campsite on departure. They were soldiers.

On the first of September I passed through "enemy" lines under a white flag to pick up the 37th Division troop's payroll from Division Rear at an unknown location in Texas. Two days later I found the lost Division Rear, they did not know where they were neither did most of the people I asked. "Nah Suh, I aint seen no Yankee soldiers ridden in no trucks with 37 on they bumpah`s". After I received and signed for six separate payrolls and bags of cash totaling several thousands dollars I spent the next three days locating and paying the 37th Division troops and returned the executed payrolls to the divisions Finance Officer. His comment was; "Where in the Hell have you been Lieutenant? You are expected to make payroll returns within twenty-four hours." I said; "Yes sir, Colonel, war is Hell." I waited standing at attention while he counted the returns, very slowly, each in turn, checked each payroll for signatures, very slowly, each in turn. Another lesson learned; do not get flip with paymasters ever.

The 73rd [prov] AT Bn had a lot of problems. Living in the field, Infantry style, roughing it, wasn't their bag, but their food was good. Their practice of field sanitation was casual at the best and several times they had to send details back to abandoned campsites to clean up the mess they left behind. Military skills common to Infantry units such as camouflage, security and march discipline were lacking.

As guardsmen they had trained on coastal defense guns designed to engage battleships from permanent emplacements only to be equipped with out dated 37-millimeter antiaircraft guns and now, obsolete "French 75s" in lieu of a 90-millimeter high velocity gun still being tested. The antitank tactics being tested were defensive and built around the concept of building obstacles to funnel armored attacks into the field of fire of emplaced truck towed high velocity guns capable of penetrating tank armor. Our efforts in the exercises were futile in spite of setting up many road blocks and ambushes not once did we intercept the "enemy." Tank Destroyers were still to come.

12

GOOD-BY BEN

During the next two months while practicing what I learned at Benning in the famous Louisiana Maneuvers, Betty practiced for the war years that she did not know were coming, by worrying about me and fighting off bouts of home sickness.

The middle of October brought the 37th Division back to Shelby and the first anniversary of our induction into federal service passed being hardly noticed. We had come a long way. We weren't combat ready but now we knew how to get that way.

Between the Octobers end of the Louisiana maneuvers and December seventh the flow of new equipment into the Division continued. Command relationships were solidified; most of the Division Officer Corps was now graduates of their respective service schools. Enlisted replacements were being provided by replacement training centers freeing the Division from the responsibility of basic training. Now we could concentrate on molding cohesive fighting units out of squads, platoons, companies, battalions and all other division elements.

The executive order that extended our period of service had enough loopholes so that everyone who had reason and desire to be discharged were. Some who did not were. Among the latter was Major Ben Kilper caught in the age-in-grade crack.

Ben was well past fifty not even a pending promotion to Lieutenant-Colonel could save him, to further complicate matters he failed his final physical examination and was sent to the New Orleans General Hospital for evaluation. The regiment lost one of its most colorful officers, not quite at least not yet. He returned on November eleventh to await result of the evaluation board's disposition of his case and moved into the room just vacated by the Frank Landes` who recently transferred to the Army Air Corps.

Ben turned me into his private conduit of information from the regiment. Whenever I spent the night at the Women's college Ben would be waiting for me, empty glass in hand, to hear the latest "poop from the troops". Then he critiqued all he heard. Kept me up late and he never did shake that Nineteen-Forty Wisconson Summercamp bad habit of drinking my whisky. Eventually he returned to New Orleans for further treatment.

His remarks at the end of his last meal at the 145th Infantry Officer's Mess were vintage Ben. He regaled us with a pithy assessment of the progress the 145th had made since he first came on board claiming copious credit for turning the outfit into possibly a credible fighting unit from a disorganized bunch of "corn stalk militia", his favorite term for poorly trained pre-induction units, pointed out shortcomings of various individuals sparing few, none because of rank. He expressed his concern for our welfare in the days ahead without his steadying influence. He railed at the injustice of his being left behind. Declared his undying devotion to his "boys", the Officers and men of the 145th and ended it all with; "Don't worry about Ben Kilper; I'll live to piss on all your graves."

Eight A.M. December Seventh Nineteen-Forty-One Betty and I were having a leisurely cup of coffee at the Women's College, at eight P.M. that same day she watched as I loaded trucks at Camp Shelby to embark on an unknown mission at an unknown destination, very dramatic.

Ten that morning we were on our way out to Camp Shelby. My intent was to sign the morning reports for both Companies E and H. Captain Bill Morr, my boss was still at Fort Benning Lieutenants Stover and Clark the other two officers assigned to E company were on leave. Lieutenant Tom Battles acting CO of H Company was freshly married and spending the weekend incognito on an abbreviated honeymoon in Gulfport. I signed for him with the Battalion commander's consent.

Half way to camp Betty turned on the car radio and we heard the announcement of the Japanese attack on Pearl Harbor. Betty dropped off at the Officer's Club and I continued on to E Company's orderly room where the duty NCO was unaware of the Japanese Pearl Harbor attack.

By the time I checked and signed the morning report and had done the same for H company word was down from regiment that all leaves were canceled, absent members were to be contacted by phone, directed to report to their unit as soon as possible and there would be an Officer's call at 1300 hours. The 37th Division had taken its first step down the long road that ended in the Philippines when General McArthur accepted Japans surrender in Tokyo Bay.

The second step began immediately after Officers call where we learned a little more of the attack and were sent back to our units to continue the process of getting all of the troops on pass and leave back under control. About 1500 hours we received word to prepare to leave with all present and accounted for. Regiment, in Army tradition, would tell us when they were. By 1600 hours trucks were spotted at company kitchens and supply rooms loading equipment, a little later regiment issued an order attaching H Company to E company. My problems just doubled. About 1930 E and H companies were assembled with full field equipment men fed, supply trucks loaded, kitchen trucks loaded with newly drawn five days of emergency rations when a convoy of empty trucks pulled in to deliver us to an unknown destination.

The lieutenant in charge of the trucks did not know either while we were discussing our options (he opted for Gulfport, I favored New Orleans) when Major Parker the battalion CO drove up handed me a sealed envelope and said; "Morrow, here are your orders, open them after you leave camp." I saluted, said; "Yes sir" gave the order to mount trucks and we left camp.

The envelope contained a strip map of a route to Natchez Mississippi via Brookhaven. We received orders for E Company to secure the railroad marshaling yards in Brookhaven. H Company to secure all river crossings including rail, highway, power and telephone lines in the vicinity of Natchez. Our mission was to prevent sabotage to communication lines.

Three A.M. December eighth the night dispatcher of the Brookhaven police department aroused the Chief of Police and told him; "Chief, y`all better come down heah, they`s a Yankee soldieh boy standin heah sayin he gotta passel of soldiehs on trucks waitin to take the rail road yahds an Ah guess he gone do that." In ten minutes the Chief was there.

We had a cup of coffee, a conversation and the Mayor dropped by, the Mayor called the Superintendent of Schools, more coffee and conversation and the chief "carried" me back to the convoy in his police cruiser followed by my previous mount a two and half ton six by six army truck with a dozen sore assed GI's in the back.

The convoy fired up and the Chief led us to the Hattiesburg High School where the Superintendent of Schools reckoned we needed the premises more than his students besides they would be "honored to have the first holiday in this war." We bedded down in the gymnasium and took over the cafeteria.

By daylight the Brookhaven railroad yards were secured by E Company's first platoon and H Company was in the process of being fed before continuing on to Natchez. Lieutenants Clark and Stover of E Company and Zentz of H Company arrived with a truckload of stragglers from Camp Shelby.

H Company was ready to depart on the final leg of the trip. Lieutenant Zentz joined me and we arrived in Natchez a little before noon, billeting H Company in the local National Guard armory before enlisting the help of the local sheriff to contact his opposite number on the Louisiana side of the Mississippi River and help locate guard posts on the river crossings. I left Zentz to complete the job and returned to Brookhaven.

For the next ten days we were treated to southern hospitality I am sure no other Damnyankee troops had ever before enjoyed. Not even the Oracle at Delphi was quoted more than I over a similar period. We scarcely touched the rations brought with us because of the number of accepted invitations of home cooked meals by all ranks. Ozzy Smith, Sheriff of Simpson County took me quail hunting one afternoon and showed me all his secret hunting areas. The town organized some sort of entertainment for us virtually every night. During this time one serious incident occurred that was like lifting a shroud to reveal a rotting corpse.

One of our sentries heard scraping sounds in an empty boxcar and yelled; "Come on out of there." A figure jumped out of the car and hit the ground running and the sentry yelled; "Halt" three times with no response from the runner he shot hitting him in the leg. The sound of the shot brought the Sergeant of the Guard and other members of the guard on the double. They found a black man and burlap bag with a half bushel of shelled corn the victim had gleaned out of the boxcar. The Sergeant put compresses on the wound, summoned an ambulance to evacuate the victim. I relieved the guard an eighteen-year-old recent replacement now in tears and left him in charge of the Sergeant of the guard.

I went to the hospital where a nurse told me that the victim was in surgery but that the wound was not serious. The next morning after I entered the incident in the company's morning report and sent a message to regiment back at Camp Shelby. I arranged to meet Ozzy Smith at the hospital. There we talked to an elderly black man, that is Ozzy talked to him and I listened, Ozzy; "Uncle, you hurt bad?" Uncle; "No suh, Mistah Ozzy, I be alright in a couple of days." Ozzy; "What you doin in that railroad car? don' you know you aint supposed to be there? Uncle; "Yassa, Mistah Ozzy I know that, that's why I run." Ozzy; "how come you keep runnin when that soldier boy tell you to stop" Uncle; "I guess I jes got rabbit blood, Mista Ozzy." Ozzy laughed and said; "Alright, Uncle, you lay there and get well and maybe I won't put you in jail." On the way out I asked; "Is that all there is to it?" and Ozzy said; "Uh uh, unless you want me to throw him in jail." "You mean that you don't want to talk to my man who shot him?" "Naw, we don't give damn down here who shoots a niggah." End of conversation. Later, it was rumored that the victim died. I don't know nothing came of my report to regiment. After a year in the south I finally saw the difference between Black and White.

On the evening of the sixteenth of December the citizens of Brookhaven held one last dance and reception for us. Betty drove down from Hattiesburg and learned first hand the hardship men in uniform suffered resisting the atmosphere of wartime hero worship.

We returned to Camp Shelby the following day and began the process of fitting into new tables of organization and equipment. Half ton weapons carriers and command cars left for three quarter tons and quarter ton "jeeps". No four wheel steers though they had thrown their last passenger. The division streamlined from square to triangular by dropping the 166th Infantry Regiment and three Brigade Headquarters.

A new battle doctrine that sketched command lines from division to combat teams under the command of infantry regimental commanders and made up of an infantry regiment, an artillery battalion and an engineer company was established. This style of combat organization had been stressed at the Infantry School and we had few Infantry Officers who were not school graduates.

Suddenly and somewhat secretly the 112th Engineers were dispatched to Norfolk, VA where they shipped out for Northern Ireland. It was a somewhat secret because it was an official secret that everyone in the division knew. Their mission was to build a division base camp. They did and the 34th Division eventually occupied the camp. At Camp Shelby the absolute word was that the remainder of the 37th Division would ship out of Brooklyn, NY on the seized French Liner, Normandy to rejoin our engineers. We were en route to Indiantown Gap PA when the Normandy burned at the dock. After the Pentagon said that rumor was a rumor and the 34th not the 37th was slated for Europe all along. There are a lot of 37th Division veterans who remain convinced that the Pentagon applied the CYA procedure and we were cheated out of a chance to tour Europe. The 166th was brought to full strength, before being dropped commanders exercised the age-old army tradition of using the move to cleanse their units of unwanted members.

Captain Al Westrick was one caught up in old vendettas, transferred to the 166th and I inherited command of G Company. That lasted until shortly after the first of the year when I came down with the flu and went to the hospital on the thirteenth of January.

There it progressed into pneumonia. I have two distinct memories of the ordeal. One of Chaplain Connell coming to visit me during the time that I was drifting in and out of consciousness, Awaking and saying; "Not yet, Chappy, not yet" and once while wearing an oxygen mask waking up and seeing Betty sitting by my bedside knitting a sweater and holding my breath, until she stopped knitting and started to get up to call a nurse. I could do that because breathing didn't seem very important to me. Then when she settled back and resumed knitting I repeated the trick, several times.

The finished sweater had one short and one long sleeve and Betty said later that just confirmed her suspicion that I did not have to be conscious to be mean. The hospital sent me back to duty on February tenth barely in time to make the trip to Indiantown Gap Military Reservation.

G company now was commanded by newly promoted Captain Conrad no relation to Private Harold Conrad, Lieutenant Tom Battles' admirer. Once again I was Captain Bill Morr's second in command of E.

Shortly thereafter I developed a hernia from attempting to make an eight mile in two hours speed march carrying full field equipment and returned to the hospital for another six weeks plus recovering from surgery. Doctors treated recovering surgery patients much differently then than now. It was a week before I left my bed and it would have been longer if the doctors had their way. Lieutenant Sue O`Niell USANC returning from checking her patients in the next ward caught me on my seventh night eating ice cream in the ward kitchen. She gave up and joined me.

By the next week I was leaving the hospital on day passes to help Betty explore Pennsylvania Dutch country including some trout fishing. In early April the Hospital granted me a week's recuperation leave before returning me to duty. We spent it in Ohio with our families. When I said good-by to my parents it was the last I ever saw them. Mother died in the following June and Dad in March nineteen-forty-four.

April at Indiantown Gap PA was exceedingly dry and toward the end of the month an ominous blue haze grew to a black cloud as civilian fire crews battled a forest fire on the north slope of Second Mountain along the camp's north boundary. Captain Bill Lorimer had satisfied his curiosity and turned our regiment and the 117th Engineers into a fire brigade all in one motion.

He dropped a handful of extra propellant increments down the tube of one of the eighty-one millimeter mortars before the crew fired the last round during a live firing exercise. He said he wanted to find out how far a mortar shell would go. He found out. It went right over the top of Second Mountain and exploded among the fire crews. They concluded that the war had struck too close to home and left the job to people who were paid to be shot at.

On May sixth we boarded a train and departed for San Francisco. We were pretty sure now that our destination was the Pacific, somewhere. In E company kitchen a pot of chop suey, enough for the company's evening meal, a ladle and a large, very large, hand food grinder missed the supply truck for our train. I was elsewhere doing whatever second in command does elsewhere but ever helpful Betty was close enough to the disaster in the making to be drafted by the mess sergeant to deliver the goods to the troops.

He loaded chop suey, ladle and food grinder in her car she delivered the food to the station but the train was already underway. The last I saw of my wife for the next two years, she was standing beside the open door of a Lincoln convertible waving a large ladle in farewell.

13

HELLO SAN FRANSISCO

The trip from IGMR to Crocker Amazon Park, San Francisco, California, was long, monotonous, uncomfortable but with some high points, non-the-less.

We pulled into Tucumcari, NM. at three A.M. three days and some hours later those awake debarked, stretched our legs and marveled at how close to earth the stars seemed. Later that same day we again got off the train in Albuquerque to stretch and gawk. It was a marvel how far from reality our James Fenimore Cooper Leather Stocking Tale's image of demure young, slim, Indian Maidens had strayed. These ladies from the reservations, offering their handicraft for sale were none of the above as far as one could tell. They were sitting cross legged in a row, along the edge of the platform facing in, draped from the neck to the platform floor in multicolored blankets with a colorful display of turquoise and silver jewelry spread in front of them. Miniature pyramids topped by heads with expressionless faces, completely unimpressed by American soldiers. They conversed with us in monosyllables. "You make `um?" GI for Indian talk. Nod. "How much?" "Two-fifty." "Too much, one fifty?" "No" end of conversation.

Two days later we pulled into San Francisco and got off the train to stretch our legs for the final time. Stretch them we did, for seven long miles, uphill, on pavement with full field equipment to Crocker Amazon Park.

The Park was full of pyramidal tents presumably erected by an advance detail from the division, some one else could have been responsible but we were in a don't ask, don't tell, mode at the time. About 1600 hours an order from Division Headquarters reached unit orderly rooms enunciating the division leave policy of granting passes to one third of the command from retreat (1700 hours) until midnight. Company Commanders responsible for enforcing this policy, were a little closer to the troops than the Division Commander, bowed to the inevitable and issued passes to one third of their command and went to town too, leaving the enforcement of the order to the conscience of their command. The two thirds of troops who were unpassed promptly went to town also.

For the next ten days the night time security of the encampment at Crocker Amazon was left in the hands of those too exhausted or broke from the revelry of the night before to make it back downtown. Duty hours gave no respite; at drill call we assembled and marched up hill in atonement for the night before. We marched four miles to Golden Gate Park to hone our military knowledge.

Mainly we practiced concealment by posting a sentry at the entrance of the training area to warn of approaching spies from higher headquarters. All ranks chose comfortable resting places and remained concealed until recall. While on duty in San Francisco, wherever we went, we marched up hill.

Where ever we went while off duty was downtown. Mainly in private automobiles driven by Native San Franciscans eager to make our last day in civilization as pleasurable as possible and they did. Every morning at reveille some one would start a rumor that tomorrow, for sure, we would load ships and by recall every one was convinced this was our last day. When the last day arrived the prayers that it was were many and fervent.

We loaded the South American Line Cruise Ship, Uruguay pleasantly surprised to discover that we had the 142nd General Hospital for shipmates. Reality set in when Lieutenants and Captains were berthed on the boat deck, Majors and Colonels on the promenade deck and nurses on the sun deck. Enlisted men were relegated to the lower decks. Passes were required for upward mobility except during boat drill.

All this was forgotten the next morning when the convoy got underway and we hit the first ground swell outside the Golden Gate. Attention of the not yet sea sick was directed to enforcing proper shipboard etiquette for the now sick of not barfing into the wind. A task made more difficult by the increasing ranks of the latter and decreasing ranks of the former. A day later those of stronger stomachs began to emerge leaving the bowels of the ship to the Hopefully-soon-but-not-to-be Dead to enjoy a bright new blue world, blue-sky, blue sea, blue viewer.

Soon the survivors of Neptune's welcoming gesture were plotting how to by pass the guarded ladders to the sun deck. Only, I think, Captain Sylvester DelCorso succeeded. He met the future Mrs.DelCorso aboard the Uruguay. It's possible she could have been charged as a co-conspirator. Syl took the Motto posted numerous places on shipboard "Loose Lips Sink Ships" seriously and divulged no secrets.

Shipboard accommodations on this cruise ship were not exactly cruise quality. Cabins for two on the boat deck berthed twelve officers in three stacks of four hammocks each. Not exactly hammocks, rather two by six feet canvas sheets laced to pipe frames separated eighteen inches. Enlisted men had it worse they had to share their bunk with a barracks bag. Their stacks of bunks were in large compartments occupied by hundreds. Boat deck cabins had salt-water showers and toilets serving the occupants. Enlisted latrine and showers were communal affairs serving hundreds. Enlisted mess halls featured stand up tables with garbage cans at each end. Officers were sit downs served by ship's stewards from the ships stores rather than army rations served in the enlisted mess.

Daily routine featured a morning hour of calisthenics and an afternoon boat drill. To be caught, away from quarters, without a life preserver, cost the miscreant a reprimand at least and/or a possible fine. Passengers carried either kapok or cork life preservers, ships crew and army gun crews wore belt type pneumatic types. The cork type were considered slower to become waterlogged than either of the other two. However, unless when jumping into the sea wearing one, the jumper crossed his arms over the preserver and firmly grasped the top of the cork slabs he ran a risk of leaving the device on top of the sea while exploring the depths. Possibly, one of the slabs might lodge under his chin and break his neck when he hit the water in either case rendering the case for a life preserver moot. On the other hand kapoks lost buoyancy from being put to subsidiary usage such as seats and pillows.

Pneumatics' were subject to leakage and most highly desired because no one had any intention of jumping overboard. It did not take long for those unable to hustle a pneumatic to discover the devices Achilles heal. They were a fabric covered rubber tube inflated by carbon dioxide from a plain Seltzer bottle fizz cartridge and were worn uninflated with a doubled back fold secured by a pair of snaps. Inflation drill was for the wearer to reach behind his back with one hand and jerk the fold free, then pull a lanyard on the front of the belt puncturing the fizz bottle seal releasing the gas in a rush.

If the process was reversed the tube would inflate before the snaps released. It became common practice for a Cork or Kapok drillee to reach over and jerk a Pneumatics' lanyard leaving the wearer standing red faced and unable to breath with his middle parts constricted in a contracting eighteen inch perimeter of relentless rubberized fabric.

Otherwise our days and nights were controlled by the ship's loud speaker intruding into our privacy with unfamiliar frequently unintelligible Maritime jargon; "Now hear this, now hear this, this is the Captain speaking—" or "Now hear this, now hear this, Sweepers man your brooms, sweep down clean for and aft." "Now hear this, now hear this, all cooks and mess men report to the galley." The ship did not have a public address system.

It had a loud speaker as in "thunderous" and "often." A good guess would be that the loud speaker was designed to be heard above the din of naval battle in the midst of a thunderstorm. It greeted us at daybreak with, "Now hear this, now hear this, the smoking lamp is lit on all weather decks. And dismissed us at dusk with; "Now hear this, now hear this; the smoking lamp is out on all weather decks." Never once did it say now hear this, always twice.

Morning calisthenics rousted every one out of compartments and on to the decks. Popular GI explanation was, "so medics could clear quarters of bodies of those who died during the night from seasickness." During the day, those who escaped the numerous work details spent their time on deck playing cards, shooting craps, sleeping, B. Essing or plain loafing.

Artillerymen and Tank Destroyers had a real break; they manned the batteries of three-inch naval guns and forty-millimeter antiaircraft guns mounted in "tubs" along the main deck rail. Tubs were just that, circular gun platforms protected by head high armored shields extending outside of the deck rail on port and starboard (sailor talk for left and right) sides of the ship.

Gun crews were under the command of a permanent naval cadre assigned to the Uruguay. The ships officers and crew were merchant marines. Once a week the loudspeaker said, "Now hear this, now hear this, the call to battle stations will sound at 1500 hours. This is a practice alert, repeat, this is a practice alert." Then repeat the message.

At 1500 hours bells sounded, the loud speaker said, "Now hear this, now hear this, all hands man your battle stations, all hands man your battle stations. Passengers to quarters, passengers to quarters." and repeat it several times Gun crews and ships crews would head out to their battle stations, passengers would head in to their quarters, all would meet in the passageways and after sorting themselves out go where they belonged.

In the troop compartments portholes were closed, shuttered and lights turned off. Soon lights would come on and the loud speaker would say; "Now hear this, now hear this, all hands stand down from battle stations." Life then returned to normal. On Saturdays following battle station drill our escorting cruiser launched its scout plane to tow a sleeve target for gunnery practice that was our substitute Saturday Night on the Town.

We crossed the Equator, International Date Line and seventeen days after saying good-by to civilization in San Francisco. We sailed into Auckland harbor on June twelfth with a bang. The bang occurred when one of the gun crews on the Uruguay spotted a paravane being towed by a New Zealand Navy minesweeper and took it under fire on the premise that it was a submarine's periscope and that all submarines were unfriendly. This unexpected gunfire aroused the competitive instinct of the crew on one of our escorting USN destroyers to drop two depth charges and be one up on the Army gun crew.

Passengers (all) on the deck of the Uruguay immediately rushed to the port rail to see what the shooting was all about. Causing some of the more landlubberly to fear for the safety of the ship and prove how combat unready we were.

The following morning the ship tied up at the dock while a New Zealand Army band rendered The Star Spangled Banner and God Save the Queen. In due time we debarked and marched uphill to the Auckland train station. Part way there some one said; "My God, they're playing God Bless America" and it was true.

We rode a train the rest of the way to the 2nd Battalion 145th Infantry's new home at the Pupekohe Race Track. Our host's reception of our presence was genuinely grateful and enthusiastic. No one voiced the English complaint of; "The problem with Yanks is that they are over paid, over dressed, over sexed and over here." Sort of hurt our feelings that reputation hadn't reached this end of the British Empire. It was bolstering to our national pride though to have an occasional New Zealander venture the hope that when this was all over that his country might become part of ours "like we are now part of the Mother Country."

The Australian New Zealand Army Corps (ANZAC) during WWI suffered more casualties than any other British Army Corps. The New Zealand 8th Division currently was being hammered by Rommel's Afrika Corps.

With the Japanese steadily moving south across the Pacific, New Zealanders felt like a cherry at the end of a branch ripe for plucking. Why shouldn't there be dancing in the streets with the arrival of the first American combat unit on New Zealand Shores? We ate it up.

The Pupekohe Men's Club elected all officers of our contingent honorary members. Not only were we doubly honored by being declared gentlemen in official documents we enjoyed a distinct advantage of being able to buy a drink at any time of day or night. Alcoholic beverages were severely rationed in New Zealand. Pubs opened precisely at six P.M. and closed when they ran out of potables, usually an hour or so. The Men's Club had some unknown source of supply they shared with us.

Tom Battles and I cultivated two "Invalided out of North Africa" members of the club, Bandy Crosby and Stan White for the purpose of having a guided tour of Rotorura, rather Lake Rotorura, Bandy and Stan had bragged once too often of the fabulous hunting and fishing in New Zealand's bush back of Rotorura.

We had to see. Friday noon of Fourth of July weekend we loaded Bandy's Austin Bantam. Our gear including a five gallon jerry can of white gas scrounged from our kitchen, two pup tents, four bedding rolls four rifles, two shot guns, two days grub supply and a fly rod all tied down on top of the car. We climbed in and motored a hundred plus miles to Rotorura. There we picked up a small boat and outboard motor Bandy had stashed in a friends garage and crossed the lake to make camp on the opposite side. On the way over Tom trolled a spinner behind the boat and hooked a six pound rainbow. Bandy's comment; "Throw the bugger back he's too small to make a meal for all of us". We did not; he fit our pan just fine.

The following morning Stan and I followed a trail. Stan called it "a stag slot", back through a fern forest into the hills. I had an M1 service rifle I had never fired and a clip of service ammunition with the bullets reversed to expose their lead bases, a technique strictly forbidden by the Geneva Convention for War. Stan carried his favorite iron sighted sporting rifle.

Two hours later we rounded the shoulder of a hill and about four hundred yards across a valley three does, "hinds" Stan corrected me, climbing the slot out of the draw. Stan said: "let's take them". We could scarcely see over the ferns. Our only recourse was to shoot at the hinds offhand. They started running with the first shot, just as the last one was about to disappear around a turn in the slot she went down. Being gentlemen, by proclamation, we turned to each other and said, "Nice shot".

When we reached our quarry we discovered the she had been struck by a single bullet squarely between the ears, two inches higher and it would have been a miss. In all due respect to my considerable marksmanship skills I maintained that was exactly where I aimed, Stan said; "that is where I was aiming too." We field dressed the carcass, severed it behind the last rib and packed it out.

Bandy and Tom were busy dressing a dozen ducks they had killed. We hunted along the lake shore the next morning adding one black swan to our bag. Packed our gear, crossed the lake stashed the boat, loaded the Austin and arrived at the Race Track after midnight. A few nights later to insure our bragging rights we hosted a venison dinner at the 2nd Battalion Officers Mess The Cafeteria at Pupekohe Race Track wands Officer Quarters occupied by the Battalion's Lieutenants. After the first night of battling against the rigid surface of the tables for snatches of sleep a run on air mattresses at local merchants started. After the second night the run extended to Auckland. The third night the last resident to return from Auckland loosened the filler valves on all other's air mattresses and established a precedent. The first train arriving at Pupekohe in the morning from

Auckland was the Milk Train arriving at 0430 hours. By the end of our first week we turned the Milk Train into the last train from Auckland, a fine distinction.

New Zealanders were proud and protective of their bright green turf; in deference of their attitude the Yanks confined training to long conditioning hikes interspersed with calisthenics and lectures thus combining the most boring of shipboard and San Francisco experiences. On the morning of July thirty-first, members of the 2nd. Bn 145th. Inf. rode the Milk train from Pupekohe to Auckland and loaded aboard the USS Coolidge bound for Fiji the fabled Cannibal Isles.

14

VITI LEVU

On September six, the Coolidge, completed her next to last successful mission by delivering the first and second Battalions of the 145th Infantry to Suva Fiji. After returning a shipload of New Zealand troops home, She picked up a load of Americans from the 43rd.Division, destination, New Hebrides. According to New Zealand sources, she missed the Esprito de Santo harbor entrance and ran aground on a coral reef with the loss of most of the 172nd Infantry Regiment. The Navy announced the sinking in December as the ship running into a mine.

Fijians ate their last missionary in 1917. Since then their diet has been friendlier to other Homo sapiens. However, some viewing the changing of their old ways for European style civilization decried the decision as too hasty. Changes like punctuality, cutting sugar cane when it was ready to be cut instead of when the cutters were ready to cut; working for wages when gardens the bush and sea provided food for the taking; clothes as more a matter of style than necessity, were not priorities.

Like other Polynesians, Fijians embraced Christianity with enthusiasm by making room among earlier customs. They embraced Americans with equal non-culinary enthusiasm. Fijians have kinky black hair, are the darkest and tallest of their people. The Fiji Islands claim to be first among Pacific Island groups to be populated by Polynesians and likely had a Melanesian population assimilated in more ways than one by the newcomers. Regardless of points of origin Fijians and GIs enjoyed an instant compatibility.

Fijians lived in burres. A burre not only is home for a Fijian family, it is an ecosystem for a host of others. A variety of insects inhabit its roof and walls, small lizards also live there and off the insects. Rats and mice find haven in the walls. Mongooses include burres on their rounds keeping lizards, rats and mice numbers at acceptable levels. Village chickens, children, an occasional pet pig, cats and dogs wander freely in and out.

Burres are constructed with timber frames covered with grass thatch. Typically, their size is a function of the ridgepole. If the ridgepole is forty feet long then the burre will be twenty by forty more or less. Construction proceeds by setting four corner post and two ridge posts with one or more center posts depending on the need of support for the ridgepole.

Village storytellers claim that in the olden days Tribal Chief's Burre construction was preceded by a raid of an enemy tribe to capture four corner post bearers, who were buried alive as a foundation for the posts, a tradition long abandoned. With posts set horizontal poles are lashed to the posts at short vertical intervals and the ridgepole lashed in place to form a rectangular enclosure. Additional braces and cross rafters are added as required. The framework is thatched with overlapping bundles of Kunai Grass (a tall tropical species of grass) from the bottom up. A doorway is left unthatched mid point of the downwind side, above it a smoke hole.

The interior is finished with a dais on the left end of the burre, as entered. (At least that was its location of all burres I've been in) The center is reserved for a fire pit and the right end for children, chickens, dogs and other lesser occupants. The mat covered dais is the domain of the lord of the manor, his wife, nursing infants and guests. In case of fire no fire escape is needed, occupants depart trough the closest wall. Since burre roofs and walls absorb moisture during the almost daily rains they serve as an evaporative air conditioner during the rest of the day. A distinct advantage over the tin roofed, European and Indian houses common to nonnative villages of Viti Levu.

Fijians belied their cannibal reputation and romantic notion of South Seas Islanders. Villages were extended family habitations with few needs beyond that provided by their immediate surroundings. Gardens grew a variety of vegetables including the staple dalo, (Hawaiian taro) boiled into a thick paste called poi by other Polynesians, yams, a variety of fruits and Kava roots the source of the national drink.

Kava roots dried, pounded into fine flour and steeped in water produced a milky tongue numbing liquid with a flavor resembling dishwater. Rumor among GIs had it that if enough were consumed one's legs became paralyzed. That rumor was easily discounted from the fact that Kava was always consumed seated cross-legged as part of a ceremony. After sitting crossed legged for two or three hours accumulating a bladder full of the foul tasting stuff what American's legs wouldn't be paralyzed? Another stomach turning story circulated was that traditionally Kava was prepared by the village's maidens sitting in a circle around the

Kava bowl chewing the root and expectorating into the bowl then adding water. That one was attributed to "The Brass" to discourage GIs from going native.

Kava was prepared in a huge wooden bowl holding several gallons and presented to the chief presiding over the ceremony by two young maidens. The chief seated crossed legged on the dais with guests and other village men in a semi circle facing the lower end of the burre. Seating was by rank with the honored guest on the chief's right and the ranking villager on the guest's right. The next ranking guest was on the chief's left with the next ranking villager on his Left. This seating pattern continued through the remaining guests and ranking village men. Younger men and village women were seated along the wall of the burre facing the doorway. With everyone seated cross-legged on the floor mats, the ceremony began with the presentation of the Kava bowl.

The two ladies presenting the Kava did so on their knees, then one produced a half coconut shell and dipped a portion of Kava out of the bowl and presented it to the chief. The chief responded by saying "Bula" and slapping his thighs. All present answered; "Bula" and clapped their hands once. The chief drank the cup of Kava without pause and spun the empty cup on the floor mat in front of him. Everyone said "Mothe, Mothe." meaning "Empty", and clapped their hands twice. The chief said "Bula" and the lady served the ranking guest who repeated the chief's performance. The second lady produced a coconut shell and served the guest on the chief's left. Guests and village men were served alternately until all had gone through the ritual of receiving a cup of Kava, "Bulaing, clapping and Motheing" then a second smaller bowl of Kava was brought in for the women who produced their own cups and dipped into the Kava free hand.

The Kava ceremony was introductory to the rest of the evening. Soon after the ladies` bowl of Kava was delivered several guitars would appear among the young men and women and one would start singing and the others would join in. Those without instruments provided rhythm by beating in unison with open hands on the floor mats and the seated women recited in song their ancestors' trip to Viti Levu in the Beginning. The recitation was illustrated in dance as do other Polynesians except the Fijian version is done sitting, solely with the upper torso, arms, hands and facial expressions. Later the Chief would signal an end to the story telling and the beginning of the evening's main attraction, the Tra-la-la.

The tempo of the band picked up, Lyrics were in Fijian but most tunes were unmistakably American. "You Are My Sunshine" was the leader of the Tra-la-la hit parade, "Don't Sit Under the Apple Tree" ranked right up there then there was a local composition entitled "American Airplane" that usually made the program. One of the unmarried women would rise, step up on the dais in front of the honored guest, sway seductively in time with the music, point to the guest with one hand behind the other and hiss between her teeth "Sssss Sssss". The guest, if he followed protocol, would look to each side as though the invitation to dance was meant for someone else then would rise and the pair would step off the dais and circle the fire pit side by side with the man's right arm around the girl's waist and her left around his. the dance step was one, two short steps forward, one back, pause and repeat. As soon as the first pair stepped off the dais the other young women advanced to the dais and selected partners.

When the girl became tired of her partner she led him back to the dais and selected someone else. There was great competition to keep guests dancing. Eventually at the honored guest's plea of fatigue the performance ended with the hauntingly beautiful Fijian National Anthem, "Isa Lei".

Fiji was full of surprises. The stories we had heard from cannibalism still being practiced in the hills, to a South Seas Paradise populated by lazy natives who spent their time on pristine beaches making love, did not fit the facts as we found them. Shortly after E company set up Residence in Nausori a Fijian man came into our compound carrying a stalk of green bananas, unable to make a sale he left and returned with a stalk of ripe fruit and offered them for sale for a shilling Fijian, about sixteen cents American.

The GI bargained said okay, broke off a "hand" of bananas and handed the merchant a silver shilling. While the Fijian expressed his thanks several more GIs thrusting shillings at him and broke off "hands" of bananas. The Fijian was pleasantly surprised, green bananas were more valuable than ripe because they kept longer were tastier when cooked and the going price was a shilling per stalk.

The price of bananas in one transaction inflated twenty fold. We had been in New Zealand just long enough to discover the British monetary system to be scarcely comprehensible. We gave up and assigned American values to the Empire's cash. Pounds became bucks, half crowns half dollars and real confusion reigned with the lesser pieces. Florins were quarters; some times shillings were too then again they might be dimes. sixpence was a dime except when called nickels. Any thing copper was a penny.

Fijians were not the only race foreign to our experience on the island. About two fifths of Viti Levu (Fiji`s main island) population were Hindus, East Indians imported by the British to do what Fijians refused to do, work in the sugar cane fields. Hindus remained an undigested lump in Fiji`s cultural craw.

They maintained their own language, religion and way of life while filling vacant niches in Viti Levu's economic system. They came to the island as indentured cane field workers. At the collapse of the sugar trade they became the islands entrepreneurs, dominating labor and small time trade.

Fijians were unimpressed and declined to compete instead they wrung a concession from the British that Fijian soil remain in Fijian ownership in perpetuity, transferred to foreign use by long term lease and home rule be an exercise of Fijian heredity.

Hindus lived in their own enclaves in the larger towns, spoke their own language, and had separate schools and churches. Physically smaller, with dark complexions, finer features and straight black hair there was no mistaking one race for the other. Indians were not part of the Fijian Defense force or, except for Sikhs, the police force. Sikhs, fierce warrior members of an Indian hill tribe, traditionally had been employed by British colonials as soldiers and police. They were brought to Viti Levu to fill the latter role among the cane field workers. There was no love lost between Fijians and East Indians.

Hindu artisans specializing in filigree and damascene work set up shop on Nausori's sidewalks. They worked barefoot and were a marvel to watch because of their quadapedric dexterity. They used their feet for pedal power to operate jeweler's lathes and bellows that kept charcoal braziers glowing under pots of molten metal.

The arrival of American GIs vastly increased their market and brought a new source of raw material, American silver coins. Dimes in particular were in demand, apparently the silver alloy of dimes better physical properties for their craft. GIs gained advantage in haggling over price if they paid in dimes. We soon learned no one bought any thing from Hindu merchants without haggling.

Riley knew he haggled the price of a saddle horse sans saddle with an Indian horse trader up from the going price to forty dollars, a clear profit for the dealer of two hundred percent. After the deal was consummated the horse turned out to be a one-way horse. The only direction he could be ridden was back toward the dealers horse herd. Finally through a series of trades and additional investment Riley came up with a nag that could be ridden in any direction if one managed to stay aboard. At that point the Division Commander issued an order barring horse ownership to all members of the command. Riley sold his horse back to the same trader for ten dollars and ever after, the mention of horses, horse traders or General Beitler brought unprintable opinions from PFC Riley.

During our stay Fiji was a British Crown Colony and the five percent European population were mainly British Civil Servants who had little in common with G'is, officers were a bit alright if they had eagles or stars on their collars but the rest were bores, don't you know. The going salary for domestics had been a pound a month, less if they lived in. Until the practice was banned GIs were hiring valets for a buck, (one pound) a week, that didn't sit well with the British either.

On a reconnaissance near the mouth of the Rewa river, our battalion's right boundary, I walked into a native village to be greeted by the Chief of the Rewa district who spoke better English than I. In fact he spoke the language of his Alma Mater, Oxford. He said that he had attended school in New Zealand and was an Oxford Fellow. He was well over six feet tall, black, bushy haired and wearing a Sulu, the traditional Fijian scalloped skirt. We had tea and tinned biscuits and would have attended a traditional Meke except for my plea of duty that required me to report to my Battalion Commander that same day. Preparation for a Meke would require at least one more day.

Later on the same mission along the coast we came on a village in which a teen-aged boy had sliced a gaping wound in the ball of his foot that morning while walking on the coral reef in front of the village. Lieutenant Battles, a member of the party was the closest we could come to doctor. His father was a family doctor and had drafted his son as a technician on more than one emergency. Tom borrowed a needle and a piece of fishing line, boiled them, cleansed the wound and sewed it up without benefit of anesthesia. The youngster never flinched.

On another occasion while following a foot trail along a mountain stream the shrill chatter of children's voices could be heard from ahead. Around a turn in the trail the stream cascaded down a sloping lava rock. Part way down the rock sat a Fijian woman with her back to us in the middle of the stream.

We watched silently while she appeared to bend down and fumble around in the water between her legs and drop some thing in a basket. Mystified, we backed up the trail a little way and waited a bit making a lot of noise. When we continued around the bend in the trail the lady, now dressed showed us her basket with several handfuls of fresh water prawns she had gathered by sitting on the rock and blocking the streams flow with her legs and picking the prawns out of crevices in the rock.

Farther down the stream were a dozen or so kids playing in a pool while their mothers dug the soil up around some plants in a clearing. This was one of a nearby village's gardens.

It did not take for members of E Company or any other company of the division to fold into Fijian life. Bula, the Fijian greeting equivalent of Hawaiian Aloha, became a one-word language for anything Fijian. Fijian kids in particular were our natural allies. When off duty, Tommy Battles and I would go into the bush to hunt native (not feral European) pigeons. These birds were both wary and excellent table fare, a welcome change from Army rations that were without fresh meat or fresh anything else.

En route to our hunting field we passed through a native village and were mobbed by kids. The oldest stepped forward and noting our hunting gear, point out that he was an experienced hunter who was in intimate contact with all prey species of the local bush and would be honored to guide us to our quarry. At least that was our interpretation of his Pidgin English presentation. With negotiations concluded we continued our quest led by a self appointed teen aged guide, followed by a bevy of assorted retrievers and critics. Our entourage was entirely male, the older girls having fled giggling into the village Burres, the younger driven off by the boys. This was a man thing, girls not welcome, end of conversation.

Soon, the guide pointed out a tree filled with resting, fruit eating bats, these were flying foxes. After an eloquent sales talk in Pidgin English, over Tom and my reservations, we stealthily drew within range and killed several of the animals.

Our entourage pounced on the fallen and departed for the village without explanation Later on our return through the village with a half dozen or so pidgins we were descended upon by our former allies who made it clear that we were welcome, expected, to stay and share the bats now roasting over the fire. The invitation was declined on the basis of duty, a concept not quite within their grasp. In our future hunting expeditions we shot pigeons first, flying foxes second or not at all.

15

OLE BLOOD AND GUTS

The 2nd. Bn. 145th. Inf. arrived in Suva, the capital, and main city of Fiji and were trucked to Nausori at the site of an airport, occupied by the New Zealand Air force and a nearly defunct sugar mill. E Company was billeted in several sugar company houses adjacent to the mill Head quarters and G company in several more of the same nearer the cane fields. Companies F, H and 2nd Bn. Medical detachment jointly occupied a former Presbyterian Mission school just across the Rewa River from Nausori.

Our mission was to provide security for the airstrip and ammunition dump, defend a coastal sector stretching from the Rewa River north to the Wainmbuka River, while conducting Jungle Warfare training in our spare time. We succeeded in achieving these objectives because the Japanese let us alone, they never penetrated south beyond the Ellice Islands.

Jungle Warfare was a new U.S. Army concept backed only by Spanish-American War and Marine experience in Central America. Fragmentary reports of British futile attempts to stop or slow the Japanese thrust in Southeast Asia did little except to inflate our view of Japanese capabilities. Our enemies became our teachers and they were remarkably uncommunicative. To top all this confusion the regiment's command changed from Colonel Luke Wolford who was a well-known fatherly figure respected by all ranks to Colonel Temple G. Holland.

Colonel Holland, a West Point graduate, ring knocker in GI parlance, last stateside assignment had been Division Operations Officer for General Patton. There were many rumors explaining the Colonels abandonment of the Generals coat tails. No one bothered to find out Colonel Holland's view; we all were busy avoiding Colonel Holland's scrutiny. He was an imposing figure, tall and with an impeccable military bearing. He came to the 145th. Infantry with a self imposed mission of converting a sloppy, un-military, politically corrupt, soft bunch of uncooperative National Guardsmen and draftees into a cohesive military machine of mindless clones. For the next year we learned from him, reluctantly, some good some not so good He also learned in that year. He learned about fear but not how to cope with it. A year later he returned to CONUS with visions of fame, glory and high rank buried on the bloody battle ground of New Georgia, a battle in a minor campaign of a secondary theater of war. He was not mourned. Nine years later in another war, still with the rank of Colonel, he again brushed shoulders with the 37th Division at Camp Polk, Louisiana.

Nothing much changed for a time after the Colonel's arrival until he called a senior officer's meeting to announce the issuance of a new regimental "Official Song". The Beer Barrel Polka had identified the 145th Infantry since before induction and in our area was high on most Fijian kids` hit list. The new song was the Colonel's composition with a title, now forgotten, expressing patriotic resolve and dedication to duty. The band learned the song and everyone in the regiment was ordered to learn the lyrics. Fortunately we were never tested.

Next was an announcement of a new set of regimental Standard Operating Procedures. S.O.P.'s, precisely what the title implies are used extensively to avoid the need to re-explain routine matters. All military units use them and while Holland's concept invoked sound military principles they over reached to the point of nullifying American soldiers secret weapon, improvisation.

Under the Colonel's direction we developed set solutions for every conceivable situation tactical or otherwise. The regimental S.O.P. dictated that we both attack and defend with the First Battalion on the right the Second on the left and Third in reserve. Each Battalion's formation had the first letter company on the right (A, E, I), the second (B, F, K) on the left and the third (C, G, L) in reserve. Platoons and squads likewise were deployed in set formations. Supporting weapons had similar prescribed formations and missions. The rational behind this system was to avoid the need for decisions and avoid confusion on the battlefield. Coping with confusion is what battles are all about and units have leaders to make a decision that is how battles are won. We learned that later.

The Colonel also was greatly concerned over these soft civilian soldiers; he was about to take into combat, particularly about their reactions to the sights, sounds and smells of the battlefield so he devised a unique exercise to prepare his command for the "Horrors of War" that earned him the nickname of "Ole Blood and Guts."

He assembled the regiment a battalion at a time and delivered a lecture to the troops about the savagery of infantry combat, the terrifying vision of having comrades blown to bits and being covered with their gore. He ended the lecture by having a tub of slaughter house offal covered with a blanket wheeled out in front of the crowd and saying: "Get used to it; this is what it looks, smells and feels like to wipe the blood and guts of your comrades off your face." With that he would roll up his sleeves, whip the blanket off the tub and plunge his hands in the offal, hold up a piece for all to see, drop it and step back bloody arms folded across his chest. Then he turned to the Battalion Commander and said "Your turn". Every officer and man was supposed to go through this gross ritual of handling slaughterhouse offal.

At first the reaction was a bit grim but it was not long before the hunters, farm and small town boys in the outfit familiar with butchering meat animals and disposing of offal turned the exercise into a gross practical joke at the expense of queasy reactions of the city slickers.

Not long thereafter my assignment was shifted to leader of H Company's Antitank Platoon and my residence to that of the former Superintendent of the now defunct Presbyterian Mission across the Rewa River from Nausori. Chez Colee, named for the senior occupant, Captain Carl Coleman C.O. of F Company housed three Captains and eight assorted Lieutenants and an occasional visiting chaplain who seldom lingered.

As a late comer my bunk was on the once screened verandah now more of a tattered metal lace porch. Here at Chez Colee safely out of the view of the enlisted members of the units stationed at the mission, pandemonium reigned.

In deference to the rank conscience formality of the Regimental Mess, we developed our own set of rules for Chez Colee Mess. Captain Coleman sat at the head of the table, Captain Lorimer at the foot and Captain Friedman, the Battalion Surgeon where ever he could find a seat except when he reached the table first then he sat where ever he pleased usually at the head, based on his claim of superiority based on intelligence, superior education, superior religion and superior physiognomy over his uncircumcised gentile mess mates.

Instead of saying grace, dinner started with an insulting toast, response by toasted and vote on which was most insulting. The common ruling was neither statement qualified due to its truthful content.

Requests for food had to be specific as to portion, container and method of delivery. Unless requested otherwise food was passed "through channels" i.e.; longest route, bread came "airmail". Food arrived S.A.P. (Soon As Possible) only when duly requested. Requests for food were ignored unless prefaced by the daily password, if all else failed try "piss on Friedman". Hazing at College Fraternity houses is a one-time ritual At Chez Colee it was a way of life. Outrageous? Perhaps, but it sure broke the monotony. It was easy to rationalize Chaplain's infrequent visits to our mess, though.

H Company's antitank platoon had the mission of denying entry into the Battalion defenses through Mbau Bay. Mbau is phonetic spelling for Fijian Ba to avoid confusion with the village Ba some ninety miles to the north, a single dirt track led to Mbau from Nausori negotiable by jeep. The Battalion's tactical scheme included a delaying action whereby after initially engaging the Japanese as they entered the shallow bay in small boats, to pull out our four thirty-seven millimeter guns and occupy successive positions inland. A single route wasn't enough so PFC George Thompson, my jeep driver and I started to find an alternative route through abandoned cane fields.

The fields were on the coastal plains and had been abandoned because of salt-water incursion during a hurricane sometime in the past. Water had breached the dikes protecting the fields and over the road bed of a narrow gauge railway that had hauled sugar cane to the mill in Nausori. Secure in our ignorance Thompson and I left town on the rail bed, glad to note that both rails and ties had been removed leaving a passable but bumpy road. Progress was slow. We soon left the high ground near the mill and entered the fields laid out in rectangles and separated by dikes. That created a problem; the direction to Mbau ran at a forty five degree angle from the field boundaries. To reach our destination we had to drive down a vertical dike to an intersection and turn down the horizontal. After about four zigs and three zags we ran into a wash out. Thompson climbed out of the jeep and walked down to the bottom of the wash. His last step took him up to his ankle in mud. So he came back and we jockeyed the jeep through a one eighty turn and went back to the last zig and turned down that one. Very soon we were at another wash, so we repeated the process, more mud at the bottom, same thing at the next and the next. Finally we found a wash that appeared to have a firm foundation; it even had vegetation growing on the surface. Thompson got out of the jeep and walked out on the surface of it and yelled back; "It's like a rock." I followed him and walked all the way across the wash. The soil on the far side seemed moist and shaky so I said; "It looks soft to me on the far side." He said; "No Lieutenant, I can make it." Then I made a big mistake, I said: "Okay, try it, but keep it in low four and take it easy." Thompson climbed back into the jeep, shifted down and floored the accelerator. The jeep hit the bottom of the wash doing about fifteen miles an hour and kept right on down through the top crust of the bottom. The engine stalled with the front end buried up to the windshield and water trickling over the door.

The vulnerability to the loss of government property to one lieutenant's paycheck loomed large. Possibility of salvation arrived in the form of a young Indian entrepreneur who approached and said: "Ah, Sahib Lieutenant, perhaps I can help you out of your difficulty." I turned Indian, American Indian, by asking: "How?" "Sahib", he said I have a pair of bulls, very powerful, those bulls. For ten pounds they will pull your truck out of the mud." "Too much" proving that I had learned how to bargain with Good Samaritans' ulterior motives. We struck a bargain at the usual fifty percent of the asking price and I opened my wallet took out a five pound note as though my gullibility level was somewhere between my heart and head, put the note back in the wallet, the wallet in my pocket and said: "My friend I know that your bulls are very strong and will pull my vehicle out of the mud. Because you have said so and you are an honorable man, so I will pay you when the bulls have completed their task."

My friend departed. Thompson and I sat and watched the water trickle over the jeep door. We did not say much to each other. We maintained a very professional Officer—Enlisted man relationship. I did not know what was going in Thompson's mind; I was busy reviewing possible defenses in my upcoming court martial for destruction of government property. About the time that my best conclusion reached the hope for a Jap attack so I could claim the jeep as a battle loss, salvation arrived and my hopes sunk further. The "Powerful Bulls" were a yoke of scrawny oxen neither of which would weigh more than six hundred pounds.

Our savior hooked the yoke chain to the jeep's pintle and addressed his bulls in Hindu; they eased their necks into the yoke, leaned against it, went to their knees with their full weight and absolutely nothing happened so they laid down and stayed there in spite of all efforts to get them to their feet. The bulls thus displaying superior wisdom to the consortium of humans who had gotten them into this mess.

Our Young Entrepreneur said: "Lieutenant, Sahib, My cousin has a pair of bulls, more powerful than these, I will bring him and his bulls and we will pull you out for ten pounds." "No, I replied, "You are an honorable man who said your oxen would pull my jeep out of the mud for five pounds, they have not done so but I, too, am an honorable man who will pay you and your cousin five pounds, six shillings to pull my jeep out of the mud." We settled at six pounds. He left and soon returned with his cousin and another pair of oxen, same size.

They hooked the second pair to the yoke of the first and the original pair refused to get to their feet. After much shouting and flailing of the down oxen the drivers held a conference and unhooked the first pair, they got to their feet as soon as they were unhooked, replaced them with the second pair then hooked the original pair as the lead team.

By this time we had a sizable biracial audience, fortunately, not multiracial including GIs. With a dozen or so Hindu boys adding their strength, to where ever they could get a purchase on the jeep, our contractors put their bulls to work. While the audience cheered the bulls leaned into the yoke went to their knees then all four laid down and stayed there until they were unhooked. My friend came to me and before he could begin I said; "Your bulls are very strong but could not pull my jeep out of the mud and you both are honorable men who would not ask pay for a task you did not perform and I, too, am an honorable man who will not insult your honor by paying for a contract not kept, but here is a sixpence as a token of appreciation for your offer of help." I was proud of myself for thinking up that speech while the oxen were demonstrating their dumb wisdom.

When the first rescue attempt failed I sent an unhappy PFC Thompson back on foot to the Nausori-Suva highway to catch a ride to the 145th motor pool at Samambula for help. He returned shortly after the four oxen failure with the 145th`s eight ton wrecker backing down the railroad bed behind him.

The attempt to winch the jeep out was no more successful than the bulls. The wrecker backed further down the dike until the end of the boom aligned over the jeeps pintle and hooked up so the pull on the jeep would be vertical and started the winch. The front wheels of the wrecker lifted off the ground. Finally after diving stakes into the ground, lashing the front end of the wrecker to them and draping the hood with all the native volunteers it would hold the jeep swung free. Thompson rode with the wrecker crew to Samambula where he spent the next two days cleaning up the jeep and I walked back to Chez Colee and only admitted to my part in the fiasco as information dribbled in a little at a time.

16

SETIPANI

The Japs could have the cane fields when and if they came we would find another route to Mbau Bay. There was a foot path from Nausori winding through a range of knife edged ridges that we had explored earlier and gave up on but with the cane field route beyond our capabilities the Antitank Platoon shouldered axes and shovels to widen the path to a jeep trail.

The first day it took two hours to reach the first obstacle and by mid afternoon the best estimate to reduce that obstacle to a jeep trail was a minimum of one full day, two with travel time, the war would be over and we still would be playing in the dirt. Captain Lorimer was susceptible to the suggestion that we convert the project to an on site job, in fact he was susceptible to any suggestion that would keep me and the Antitank platoon out of sight of the Battalion Commander who had yet to mention cane field railroad beds. We packed up and moved out of Chez Colee for Fiji's hills in search of Mbau Bay's beaches.

The next day midmorning Corporal Wiseman said: "We could get this job done a Hell of a lot sooner if we had some dynamite." Mid afternoon he said: "I know where there is enough dynamite to blow this island into the middle of next week." "Where?" He had me hooked. "In the Ammo dump." he paused. "Belongs to the New Zealanders but I know the Sergeant in charge and he said he has to have a bloody officer's signature, he just can't hand it over to any bloke, don't chyew know."

Wiseman's imitation Kiwi was less intriguing than his answer to my suspicious: "Why?" "Ah, Lieutenant, back in Wisconsin on the farm we used dynamite all the time to blow out tree stumps and stuff." Mollified but still suspicious I asked: "how would you use dynamite to move this job along?"

I had a distinct memory of my father blowing an apple tree stump out of the ground leaving both of us shaken by the experience. The first charge just displaced some dirt. The second, much, too much larger lifted the stump about twenty feet in the air and sent an ax minus handle sailing over our safe haven some hundred yards from the stump. My father was a lot more cautious than Corporal Wiseman.

Wiseman showed me where he would place charges and gave good answers to my questions, so I asked: "Does that bloody Officer have to be a New Zealander?" "He didn't say so," was the reply, "just your name and rank." Some how, I couldn't shake the feeling that Corporal Wiseman brought out the worst in me. We drew up a hand written requisition and Wiseman left by jeep for the ammunition dump on the far side of Nausori. He was back in an hour with: "The bastard said he would not take a bloody chit that was not on the bloody proper form, so I snuck one off his desk when he wasn't looking." That queasy feeling didn't go away but I made out a requisition for dynamite, fuses and caps anyhow and we were in the blasting business.

While the pick and shovel gang cleaned up the results of Wiseman's first blast a delegation of about a half dozen Fijian men came down the trail from Mbau direction. Their leader inquired politely about our project and told me that they were from a village near the bay headland some two miles from where the Nausori trail came out of the hills.

They accepted an invitation to sit and smoke cigarettes. We sat cross legged and made polite conversation about the Japanese and what terrible people they were and how we Americans were here in Fiji to protect the Fijian people and pretty soon we would go north to drive the Japanese back to their home island. All this was met with polite giggles and agreement. Their spokesman said his name was Setipani and was the village chief therefore his last name was Nackawanga (my spelling) same as the villages. His father and his father's father had been the village chiefs in their times. Finally we got around to the trail, what we Americans were doing to make it wider and why didn't we ask them to help since it was on their land. A nice point, which put things in prospective for a bunch of Americans too stupid to act like the guests that we were.

Just then, the cry; "Fire in the hole!" came back from the work site." We stood and watched while a muffled thump signaled the cascade of more dirt and rocks onto the trail from another charge of dynamite. Setipani said something in Fijian to his companions and they joined the work crew clearing up the debris from the blast. He grinned and said; "They will help your men and I will help you, Boss."

As long as we remained in that sector Steve, his choice for an Americanized name, was my close advisor. In his village Setipani reigned, on our project the Americanized version of Steve prevailed.

The next morning besides four men accompanying Steve were a dozen plus Fijian kids, boys ranging in age from sub to mid teens. We had a serious discussion about child labor and the precedence of education over labor and agreed that this was an American project American rules would apply whether or not they made any Fijian sense. Steve held a short conversation with his contingent and all except two or three of the older boys departed. A favorable compromise recognizing that; if those boys were not out of school they should be and working in a multinational force would be an educational advantage.

Setipani honored us with a Meke, the Fijian welcoming ceremony that includes the recitation in song and dance of their people's history and consumption of much Kava. In the days following the ceremony Steve interpreted the dance, relating the details of the seas crossed and battles fought including the last Great War between the Mbau people led by Thakambau and the Rewa people.

The surname of Thakambau continues today among that of Fiji's political leaders. He also told me that a large grass covered mound on Mbau Island was a resting place of bones from the defeated Rewa people who were sacrificed and eaten by the Mbauans. Later on Mbau in answer to questions about the mound, which was about twenty feet high, twice that in diameter, grass covered and carefully kept I was told that this was a sacred place, taboo and not to be mentioned. Being a visitor outnumbered by residents we quickly changed subjects.

In another week the Nausori-Mbau Freeway was completed and our Fijian crew paid off in cigarettes, candy and chewing gum for the younger workers, pocketknives, safety razors and US Army insignia for the older. Steve received a Zippo lighter, a can of lighter fluid and a package of flints. As well as a set of first sergeants stripes in deference to his rank as village chief. When we finished digging in weapons emplacements and test fired the weapons we put Steve on one of the machine guns and had him fire the first burst.

He left the emplacement with a noticeable swagger and to the cheers of his villagers and said to me; "Boss I did that very well, I am a very good gunner. I too, will go north and fight the Japanese by your side." One burst does not a machine gunner make and there were no vacancies in the Army of the United States for Fijian Nationals.

Lacking guts to turn him down bluntly, I said; "To have you by my side when we go north to fight the Japanese would be a great honor. Together we would kill many of those Japs who deserve to die but I am only a Lieutenant and must ask my Captain who must speak to the Colonel who will talk to the General about it. Until an answer to that question is given, let you and I put the matter aside and keep on being good friends." Over time he became reconciled to staying in Nackawanga as Village Chief but never convinced that he wouldn't have been a Hell of a Jap killer. He was probably right.

On completion of our super highway the H Company Platoon with the exception of Corporal Wiseman, returned to Chez Colee for much needed clean up and respite from our own cooking. Wiseman volunteered to stay behind and keep the remaining dynamite out of the hands of inquisitive Fijian kids who had been daily observers of our engineering efforts, I should have guessed. The following morning, on the way to the trails end with a couple of men to relieve Wiseman, we topped the last ridge and there in the midst of the panorama of Mbau Bay, scarcely a mile from shore was a flotilla of outrigger canoes. Field glasses revealed that the Fijian kids who had been so attentive of our road building efforts and a few more manned them. Corporal Wiseman led the parade in a canoe.

My worst fears were realized as Wiseman stood up and threw a large package trailing a wisp of smoke over board. There was nothing to do but sit, watch and wait as the canoes scattered and then surrounded Wiseman's drop point. Nothing happened, the canoes edged closer, still nothing. Wiseman stood up in his flagship and waved every one back then headed his crew toward the drop point with all the rest of the canoes edging ever closer.

I began rehearsing my opening statement to the International Board of Inquiry that would be appointed to look into this disaster about to happen when the sea erupted directly under Wiseman's craft dumping its passenger and crew into the midst of a huge boil. By the time we reached the Bay Shore Wiseman and crew were on their way to shore in a ruptured canoe. I asked: "Wiseman, what in Blue Bound Hell were you trying to do, drowned these kids?" He answered: "Hunh?" In a couple of hours, though I got through to him when his hearing cleared a little.

One Saturday morning Steve and his half grown son took me fishing. We left the beach in front of the village in an outrigger canoe carved out of a tree trunk. Steve sat up front, his son in the stern and me in the middle. The boy provided paddle power, Steve direction, relegating me to inspiration, only.

We, rather Little Steve, paddled the craft two or three miles out to sea (gauged by stolen glances over my shoulder) to where a break in the reef let the ocean swells through. Under Steve's direction we fished with hand lines baited with what looked like clam meat and smelled worse. After an hour or so of watching various reef fish inspect our bait and listening to Steve's prediction of what their next move would be, all incorrect, and moving locations several times. Steve said; "We go home now." Little Steve applied the paddle and we headed back across the lagoon not toward Nackawanga but toward a fish trap in front of the neighboring village.

Fijians built fish traps in shallow water at the edge of the beach at low tide. Slender poles are pushed into the lagoon bottom in the form of a V with the open part of the V toward shore. The small end of the V opened into a circular enclosure of poles. The construction was tied together with vines. The wings of the trap might extend several hundred yards so that the catch basin of the trap would be in five or six feet of water at low tide and the last pole of each wing would be on dry land.

Normal tides ran about six feet so at high tide the whole affair was awash with six feet of water. Several species of fish made a living scouring the mud flats at high tide. A variety marine life lived in the tidal pools. By baiting the fish trap with cooking refuse to attract crabs and other crustaceans the cruising fish were enticed inside the wings of the trap at high tide. As the tide receded the fish were guided into the catch basin until at low tide they were trapped and easy prey for the trap owners.

The tide was out when we reached the trap and the catch basin was loaded with fish of all shapes and sizes, mainly in the two to six pound range. Steve and Little Steve went over the side of the fish trap like pirates swarming over the side of a Treasure Galleon, leaving me to cope with the flow of fish they were tossing out of the trap into the dugout. Their technique was to grab a fish with both hands, bite through its spine just back of the eyes and toss it into the canoe. After a few minutes of furious action they climbed out of the trap to join me and the two dozen or so quivering fish in the canoe which now was nearly awash. Steve said something to Little Steve in Fijian. Little Steve laid his paddle down, climbed out and pushed us to the Nackawanga landing, some times wading but often swimming. I wanted to help but Steve said: "No, Boss, my boy is very strong; he will push the boat to shore."

Concerned over territorial rights over fish traps I asked: "Steve, does that fish trap belong to your village?" Oh, no," he replied, "Next village." "Then didn't we steal these fish?" "Oh, yes," was his answer with finality, "but that's alright, tomorrow is Sunday. I go to church and make it right with Jesus."

Shortly thereafter, the Antitank Platoon's sector was changed. We went elsewhere to dig more holes in Viti Levu. I never saw my friend Setipani (Steve) Nackawanga again, nor did I ever again accept Corporal Wiseman's advice.

17

WEST MEETS EAST

On December 10, 1942 the squadron of P40 aircraft manned by members of the New Zealand Air force stationed at the Nausori Airdrome received orders to move to Esprito Santo in the New Hebrides. Upon departure, just to set a standard of skill and pure guts for us Yanks left behind, formed up and flew one plane at a time under the Rewa River Bridge at Nausori. They had about fifty feet of vertical space to clear less than twice that horizontally under the bridges center span, every aircraft made it.

On June eighth, nineteen forty-three while on an LCI in The Slot off Guadalcanal I watched these same aircraft as part of a stack of well over a hundred Allied fighter planes engage a Japanese armada of one hundred twenty planes.

Assignment of junior 145th Infantry Officers continued in a state of flux and I found myself transferred to A Company in Suva just a day before some members of the first platoon were ejected from the Grand Pacific Hotel by a patrol from the 37th MP Company. The entire A company platoon returned and ejected the MP Patrol who called in reinforcements. The donnybrook escalated until virtually all of both companies. It was finally stopped by the intervention of all the officers of both companies. Casualties were equally distributed and neither fatal or duty voiding. The MP Company won a Pyrrhic victory by causing A Company to be banished from Suva's environs but being required to have a Division duty officer with each patrol and having The Grand Pacific placed off limits.

This move brought us in close contact with a Fijian Commando. The Fijian Defense Force was the designation for the Fijian Army. To further the confusion Commando designated a unit of no fixed size or organization. This one was roughly the equivalent of a light Infantry Battalion, they were about six hundred men organized in squads, platoons and companies. The platoons were led by New Zealand "Leftenants" spelled Lieutenants, companies by New Zealand Captains and the commando by a Major. Non Commissioned Officers were Fijians as were all the privates. Indians were barred from membership. A Company shared a training area with the Commando and both units were training in small unit tactics and took rest breaks at the same time. The first joint break turned into an international incident of near epic proportions.

A Company had a sizable corps of addicted tobacco chewers. It was inevitable, at the first break the Fijians were over the Americans like a pack of friendly puppies. It was more inevitable that the Americans would share "chaws" with the Fijians, still more inevitable, at the break's end only Americans would return to duty. Fortunately Fijians are fast learners and quick forgivers and that problem did not repeat it's self.

My stay with the First Battalion was short lived. Colonel Holland was filling out his staff and I moved into a vacancy there as a Liaison Officer whose primary function was to represent his commander's interest with an adjacent unit. There being no adjacent units my duties were many and varied, like Regimental Duty Officer Christmas and New Years Eve and Control Officer for one more of the Colonel's Battle Field hardening exercises.

This one was physical rather than mental. A three day forced march by a battalion at a time, over native trails, up the Waimanu River valley to its headwaters, continuing through a pass in a mountain ridge to the headwaters of the Navua River and back down to the coast. The march covered some sixty-five miles and reached over five thousand feet in elevation. The march was made over the same route and trail by each of the regiments three battalions. The excuse for this exercise was spawned by the official report of the difficulties encountered by the Allied forces crossing the Owen-Stanley Mountains in New Guinea.

My assignment was to accompany the battalion to make sure no stragglers were left behind. Respite from the task was that I rode the final ten miles to the departure point and another ten miles on the last vehicle departing the casualty pick up station. Between rides I watched each battalion enter the cross country phase of the exercise, fell in at the rear of the column and completed the hike.

The exercise was planned for three days per battalion but stretched to four including a day to evacuate those injured in the process. By the time the last man passed over the trail it was nearly impassable. I know I was the last man but I had a great view of Viti Levu from the top.

My tour of the regiment didn't stop at headquarters, sectors were being changed, units shifted and Officers transferred. I became CO of M Company pending return of Captain Walton who was on TDY as an instructor at the 37th Division's Officer Candidate School. The third battalion 145th Infantry was commanded by LTC "Ding" Freer an old friend from pre-induction days and his Operations Officer Bill Moor was my former CO. This transfer seemed like a return home. Another plus was that we were located near Nandi on the dry side of the island. Viti Levu is a two-sided island.

The upwind side has daily showers during the dry season, two during the wet. The dry side has the same number but of shorter duration with much smaller and widely separated drops. A monsoon shower on the wet side is like standing under a fire hose on the dry side it is more like standing under a leaky umbrella. Clouds roll in off the sea strike the precipitous mountains of the island and drop most of their moisture on the eastern slopes.

Sector responsibility rested with the 129th infantry whose commander delegated more authority to his battalion commanders than did Colonel Holland creating a more comfortable atmosphere. A supply ship with a supply of potables had recently docked at Nandi and Colonel Fredrick, the regimental commander divide the regiments share into two portions, one for enlisted personnel and the other for Officers. He had a burre built by Fijians on the opposite bank from regimental headquarters of a surging tributary of the Nandi River. The Fijian builders used a single log as a footbridge. The log remained in place pending construction of an American style bridge after the construction was completed. On the night of the club opening, the Colonel stayed late and failed to negotiate the river crossing on his return. His staff pulled him out of the water with only his pride injured. He vowed that the log would remain in place until he completed a round trip to the club with dry clothes. When we left Nandi for Guadalcanal there was no bridge across the stream. Colonel Fredrick was a man of his word.

A few days after Captain Walton's return to command M Company, L Company's commander shattered his pelvis in a jeep accident and I inherited his command at 0300 hours on a Monday morning. At reveille, besides Captain Mostyn's driver who had been accounted for in the jeep Accident, three noncoms were absent. By drill call two were present for duty only Corporal Joe Butler remained AWOL.

Interrogation of Butler's companions revealed that the trio had been in Suva on pass and missed the truck returning pass holders to Nandi. So they hired an Indian (Hindu) Taxi Driver to return them to Nandi for five pounds apiece. Nearly back to their destination the taxi jolted to stop and the driver announced that the vehicle was out of petrol, but he a most honorable man, could procure more petrol for another five pounds apiece.

Corporal Butler, himself an Indian (Chippewa) from Wisconsin, grew tired of his companion's haggling with the East Indian and proved that West could meet East by dragging the driver out of the taxi and beating him then returning to the vehicle and driving the other two to camp. Still steamed over the failed fraud, Butler drove back to the scene and found the Hindu on the road headed back to Suva. Seeing his own taxi bearing down on him with his nemesis at the wheel the owner took refuge in a grove of small mimosa trees with Butler in hot pursuit. The car stalled, the Chippewa threw the keys at the departing Hindu and caught a ride back to Nandi on a US Army supply truck, arriving at L Company headquarters at about 0830 hours.

As a survivor of one recent international incident with A company I had no interest in participating in another with L company and without hope for escape I involved my old friend Colonel Freer, With the first Sergeant present, the Company clerk transcribing a record of the proceedings I resolved the situation by the authority granted by army regulations for company commanders to impose disciplinary punishment. All three were reduced in rank and confined to quarters for thirty days. The Colonel endorsed the record.

A few days later an Officer from the Provost Marshals office arrived to investigate the incident, he left with a copy of the transcript of the proceedings and a bad attitude without accomplishing his mission of bringing the miscreants to international justice, I already had and he couldn't touch them.

18

GUADALCANAL

On April 1, 1943 the 3rd Battalion 145th Infantry left Lautoka Harbor, Fiji bound for Guadalcanal on the transport George Clymer. I won six hundred dollars, quite unintentionally, playing poker. My objective had been to lose and borrow a few dollars each from a lot of different people so they would have a vested interest in keeping me afloat in case the ship sunk. It worked out about the same though, the Clymer stayed upright and I survived to send the gains home where Betty invested the bulk of my good fortune in a fur coat to which she was allergic.

The Clymer dropped anchor about a mile off Guadalcanal`s Lunga Beach at about 0800 hours on April 6 1943. By night fall we were unloaded with all equipment and bivouacked just inland from the beach. In the tropics night falls with a thud. The sun touches the horizon minutes later it is dark, day ceases and night starts. It is like turning out the lights in a movie theater after the matinee ends and before the coming attractions flash on the screen advertising the main feature.

We had been warned that Air Raids were a nightly occurrence and had dug foxholes well before nightfall but still were surprised when sirens up and down the beach wailed condition red; "air attack imminent" holes deepened but nothing happened. Then a finger of light probed the night sky north toward Cape Esperance then went out. Out over the Slot towards Tulagi several flairs blossomed in the sky followed by strings of tracers and flashes of exploding shells. Thunderous sound of gunfire rolling across the sea engulfed us.

Hey this is pretty good our first night here and the Japs are making a run on the Navy's battle group anchored on the other side of the Slot and we have orchestra seats. Faintly back of us the drone of un-synchronized aircraft engines grew louder filled in the pauses of the cacophony from across the slot. Searchlights come on and probed the sky.

One picked up a bright spot like a tiny moth, high above caught in a flashlight beam and Hell broke loose as ninety millimeter guns opened up around us, shell burst dotted the sky and shell fragments whistled to earth. The air battle was over us. A new pulsating, whistling sound never heard before joined the Devil's chorus growing ever louder ending in a tearing shriek as an exploding bomb rendered its casing into death seeking fragments. The first bomb hit the beach in front of us and the rest of the stick burst one after another on out toward the ships we left earlier.

Without warning the gunfire ceased and the sound of different aircraft could be heard. The searchlights went out soon high in the sky a string of tracers, red asterisks punctuating an incomplete sentence moved out to a red glow turning into a dripping cauldron of flame falling toward the sea. We had experienced our first air raid, terrifying beautiful and emotional draining. Foxholes got a lot deeper.

The next morning the Third Battalion moved to a new home away from home. A bivouac area just off the north end of Fighter Strip Two. Most days planes took off north, that kept every one on their toes since there was always some doubt whether or not fighter aircraft fully loaded with fuel and ordnance would be airborne before clearing this end of the runway. Not to mention if the exterior bomb shackles would survive the vibration from the trip down the coral runway.

Fortunately they all made it while we were there. L Company's mess sergeant, Bud Wayman found the silver lining. Seabees were hard at work lengthening the runway with bulldozers, knocking down Lever Bros. coconut palms at twenty-five dollars a tree (rumored) cost to the US government, a supply of palm cabbages, and the foundation for "Millionaire's Salad" was at hand. We dined richly.

It wasn't long before KPs from other companies, ax in hand, were following bulldozers poised to sever palm tree terminal buds. Meanwhile, threat of near bomb misses of the strip during anticipated Japanese air raids made foxhole improvement THE favored recreation.

Amid all this on the second day of our occupation George walked into camp, he walked because someone had trimmed his flight feathers on one wing severely limiting air mobility. George was the name bestowed on a Sulphur Crested Cockatoo obviously an escaped mascot. He stayed with us about a week before resuming his search for an ideal sponsor. It was rumored throughout L Company that he would have taken up permanent residence except for Mess Sergeant Wayman's attempt to teach George to quack as the first step to a duck diner.

Guadacanal was declared secure less than a week before our arrival and was in the process of being converted from combat zone to a base of operations. It had a healthy population of what Bill Mauldin on the other side of the world and war, dubbed "Garritroopers", "they're too far forward to wear ties and too far back to get shot." The Island was littered with debris generated by months of battle. These latecomers from rear echelon units ranged far and wide in search of souvenirs and personal transportation. It behooved truck drivers to remove rotors from vehicle distributors as well as keys. Otherwise they found themselves afoot and in debt to Uncle Sam for someone else's transportation.

Ship's crews became particularly adept at converting Army and Marine Corps jeeps to private use by applying a coat of battleship gray paint and bogus Navy ID numbers. One Navy Crewman recently from Akron Ohio in search of home town buddies in L company pulled his "midnight requisitioned" jeep off the road and walked a few steps toward L Company's bivouac before being knocked flat on his face by an exploding Japanese mine he had inadvertently parked over. Japanese had tricks of there own to discourage minefield clearance, delayed fuses.

We had two stays on Guadacanal, from April 6 until July 3 1943 and from September 7 to November 19 1943; air raids were more frequent during the first, more often at night but occasionally a daytime affair. Japanese tactics were shaped by sophisticated allied air defenses built around Coast watchers. The Solomon Islands, a trust territory of the British Empire, was administered by Australia.

When Japan began its march across the Pacific Island, British Missionaries and District Officers closed their stations to move back into the interiors with natives who remained loyal to the Crown, contrary to Japanese calculations otherwise. Equipped with radios, these Aussies formed a network of "coast watchers" who kept the Allies informed of Japanese troop movement. Our Intelligence People knew when every aircraft took off from a Japanese airfield, its probable destination, type of aircraft and likely bomb load. A Jap plane's combat destination, leaving Munda airfield on New Georgia had to be either Guadalcanal or shipping in the Slot. Their limited range ruled out more distant targets. By the time they reached Green Islands our people could estimate their time of arrival within minutes.

Their most likely targets in the "slot" between Guadalcanal and the smaller island of Florida were ships unloading supplies and troops on Guadalcanal's beaches. Next most likely the Navy's squadron lying off Tulagi, a deep harbor facing Guadalcanal on Florida Island. The first night time air raid we witnessed was a classic example of their primary tactic. Mid afternoon as the Jap flight left Munda, the Guadalcanal air defense command issued a warning, "Condition Yellow, Air attack likely," later confirmed by a message from the coast watcher on

Green Island. Then moved to a Condition Red when the picket line destroyers' radar showed the hostile blip on their screens.

Shortly before reaching the target area one Jap plane broke off and circled behind Florida to come over Tulagi at high elevation and drop flares illuminating the Navy's battle group. Bluffing a low level attack by torpedo planes and dive-bombers. The Navy ships took him under fire as he broke off and headed back to Munda. In the mean time the attack group, on the deck swung in behind Cape Esperance and gained altitude to come in over Mount Austin for a bombing run on the shipping off Lunga beach. The American defenses had been with them all the way as their battle plan unfolded. When the Japs passed Green Island Northrup night fighters, aircraft equipped with radar, launched and moved to altitudes beyond the reach of the approaching bombers, American radar picked the Japs up as they gained altitude to emerge from behind Mount Austin. Searchlights probed the sky and illuminated the attackers. 90MM AA guns sent up a flak barrage and ceased fire as the Japs began their bomb run. A night fighter trailing the bombers from above at the cessation of the flak dove and hit two of the attackers. The remainder jettisoned their bombs and headed home. Conceding the Yanks a two to nothing win in this deadly game.

While at Fighter Strip Two, L Company's more or less permanent home a work detail taking a break, practiced knife throwing (a favorite pastime) at a shattered coconut tree stub. One contestant was unfortunate enough to hit the mark, a sort of raised burl, dead on. His knife point penetrated the burl that turned out to be no burl at all but the nose of a Jap 20MM shell resting just beneath the surface of the tree trunk. The shell exploded wounding four of the five contestants, none seriously. Because of the letter of the regulations they were awarded Purple Hearts and counted as L Company's first casualties from Enemy Action. They never ceased hearing from their Buddies: "Tell me how you were wounded in the war, Papa?" It was not so funny when a member of F Company also earned a purple heart defusing a Japanese 20MM round. He failed to survive the explosion.

Regiment built an outdoor movie theater toward the sea from our cantonment area with coconut log seats and the screen toward the sea. The theater played to capacity crowds until one night a Jap sub sneaked into the slot, surfaced and fired a round from its deck gun through the screen. The shell exploded fifty yards beyond the last seat, the sub escaped and the theater emptied in record time. One man fell and broke his leg he didn't receive a purple heart, it was ruled that he was injured escaping, not by enemy action. That wasn't the only broken leg suffered by a member of the 145th Infantry on Guadalcanal.

Another GI found a Jap "knee" mortar and a round of ammunition and fired it breaking a leg. This piece of ordnance fires a two-inch diameter shell and is unique among mortars in that it has an integral concave base plate fixed to the base of the tube with an eight inch stem. The whole contraption is about two feet long. Looks something like a steel tulip. Unlike the 60 MM mortar, smallest of the U.S. family of mortars this one is fired by a trigger and is a one-man weapon rather than crew served. Conventional non-veteran GI wisdom had it that the weapon's curved base plate was placed on the firer's knee, loaded and discharged by pulling the trigger. Not so, he who does so breaks his leg. "Ni" pronounced knee, in Japanese translates to English two, this is a two inch mortar that is fired by placing the base plate on the ground and putting a foot on top of the base plate to prevent it from skidding when fired. Ni, stupid, like in counting cadence; "ICHI, NI, SANS, SHU", Hup, Tup, Trip, Hoor.

After we put our tent city in order with brush cleared away from the tents and the area sprayed with DDT to eliminate mosquitoes; showers and latrines were screened, pools of standing water drained air raid shelters over headed with timbers and sand bags, we moved up on Mount Austin to police the battlefield, recovering tons of supplies and equipment abandoned or lost during the fighting. The first night L Company bivouacked on a nose sloping gently toward the sea giving us a ringside seat for the "Washing Machine Charley" show. W. M. Charley was GI's pet name for Jap aircraft because of their un-synchronized engine's sound. Supply Sergeant Fuvio Germano dug himself a particularly deep and comfortable foxhole duly noted by several less caution minded members of company headquarters who had gone through the motions relying on knowledge that Mount Austin was no longer of much interest to the Japanese.

Night fell and on cue we heard the wail of sirens below us and we watched the show begin. The searchlights wavered across the sky. Searchlights lit up a plane and out of the first salvo from the 90MMs there was an air burst directly over us. Without exception, every one dove for a foxhole, most for Fuvio's. He claimed afterward that he was the fifth man in and at least six inches above ground level.

On our return from Mount Austin we began intensive training for the New Georgia exercise, daytime air raids slacked off but nightly harassing raids continued with fewer planes but more often, sometimes three or four a night. Shipping was a popular target but airstrips claimed more attention.

The Morrow, Pottieger and Lash tent air raid emergency routine became; bed at nightfall, crawl out from under mosquito bars at siren, don shirts, pants, hats, (mosquitoes, you know) and boots, stroll over to shelter when ready, watch and enjoy show, enter shelter when AA fire approaches overhead, wait for all clear, except for Ap. Ap was 1st. Lt Alfred P. Pottieger an independent thinker and L company ExO. He waited for Lt Lash and me to get ready to leave, then one of us would shake him awake and leave with Ap behind us dressing and grumbling over inconsiderate Orientals.

One night Lash and I did our thing and left without bothering with Ap. Search lights went on, off, on again picking up the Jap plane and the 90s spoke. We went into the shelter and shortly; very shortly thereafter Ap joined us wearing one boot and his mosquito bar like a bride's veil, upset that his bosom buddies would abandon him in the face of the enemy. We didn't see any enemy, just one little plane way up in the sky flying by.

On the 16th of June we were practicing assault landings on Kukum Beach from LCI's (Landing Craft Infantry). Each craft had passenger space for an infantry company, some two hundred men and combat equipment carried on their backs. Armament was two pairs of 20MM guns mounted one pair fore, one aft. They also mounted two extendable gangplanks, one on each side of the bow. When the craft grounded on the beach they were run out from the troop compartment to shore, troops poured over the gangplanks onto land in a rush. The lightened LCI backed off and the infantry went on their way to do what Infantry always does, shoot and dig holes.

By ten hundred hours we had made one run at the beach, landed, reloaded and were back out in the slot ready for another try when the ship's radio signaled a condition yellow. Munda coast watchers had just counted a hundred thirty Jap aircraft in the air headed south for Guadalcanal.

I told the skipper to put us ashore; we wanted the comfort of dry land and the security of gritty dirt surrounding us in foxholes. He said no, he wanted the security of the open sea and maneuver room. I considered introducing my forty-five into the argument but gave it up because of a lack of ammunition. We cruised the slot off Cape Esperance, sort of hiding behind Savo Island trying to look inconspicuous. When the signal moved to condition red sailors secured the troop compartment that is sailor talk for locking troops below decks; another reason why soldiers are inclined to not trust sailors very much. Until one has been there, there is no way to describe the feeling of being locked in an iron room with the lights out knowing that you are separated from water, deep water by just inches of flimsy steel. I was lucky; I was on the bridge and the skipper refused to open the troop compartment so I could join my men. I made friends with the JG commanding the LCI and remained on the bridge until all clear sounded an hour and a half later.

The Flyboys had ample opportunity to arrange the Ballroom before this Dance began. They set up a reception line off Florida and stacked it with P39s on the bottom, P40s, Navy Wildcats, Navy Hellcats, Navy Corsairs and P38s on each succeeding step up according to their altitude ceiling. Catalina flying boats rendezvoused off Tulagi to pick up the fallen.

From our vantage point the air battle began with what appeared to be a swarm of gnats rapidly approaching from the north. Some turned to specks of flame and disappeared into the sea. As the swarm neared individual planes became recognizable as ours or theirs and a deadly ballet filled the sky with dogfights. The LCI crew cheered wildly as Jap planes were shot down. American planes were hit and parachutes blossomed.

We saw pilots machine gunned in their parachutes and the gunners shot down in turn. Geysers of water spouted among the ships. Angry black mushrooms with stems of red marked flak burst in such volume to seem that no plane could escape but escape they did. Allied planes broke off and returned to Guadalcanal airstrips refueled and returned to the fight. A flight of New Zealand P40s of Rewa River Bridge fame flew over our LCI and was taken under fire in spite of their circular red, white and blue markings and their wheel and flap down posture, the international signal of harmless intent. Our crew was poor marksmen and the tracers passed harmlessly behind the planes tails.

They refueled at Henderson and rejoined the fray wisely avoiding us. A P39 Bell Air Cobra in hot pursuit fired the death burst as a Jap fighter hit the sea and followed him into the same watery grave.

The fight swirled across the slot and back north out of sight. All clear sounded, hatches opened and shaken L Company was put ashore at Kukum as American planes returned. Coast watchers counted three Jap planes landing on Munda. American losses were reported as seventeen aircraft one destroyer and one cargo ship.

19

ANCHORS AWEIGH

Official History has it: "On the 25th of June 1943 orders were issued that the First Marine Raider Regiment (less two battalions) with the 3rd Battalion 145th Infantry and the 3rd Battalion 148th infantry attached will land at Rice Anchorage, New Georgia Island, secure Enogai Inlet block the Bairoko-Munda Trail and later occupy Bairoko." That more or less happened but not in the way planned.

The objective was to take Munda Airport on New Georgia as the next step in the Navy's plan to roll back Japanese forces in the South Pacific. The plan was to use the Armies 43rd Division with help from the Marine Corps` 1st Raider Regiment, backed by the 37th in reserve and the 25th on stand by. Details were not simple; The Raiders would secure small islands south of Munda as artillery bases for the 155 MM Battalions of both divisions and some Marine heavy Artillery units.

With the Artillery Islands secured Raiders would withdraw, regroup and secure Bairoko Harbor to keep the Japanese from reinforcing Munda from their garrison on Kolumbangara Island fourteen miles north of Bairoko. Then with Munda isolated and under fire from allied artillery the 43rd Division would receive their baptism of fire with an assault landing and capture Munda.

Had the Navy run their plan past the Infantry School it would not have passed. Army Division artillery Battalions were equipped with Howitzers that lacked range to cover the full depth of the target from the offshore Islands. The Marine 155 MM gun units with the range to cover the target were assigned to the most distant islands where they too were out of range. The Raiders were assigned two essential tasks. The Infantry Battalions were an add on not included in the original plan. They had only about a week's practice of assault landings and that off LCIs. LCIs have little resemblance to landing barges. The practice landings were preliminary, walk through, day light exercises without field equipment.

Plans called for a 0300 hours landing with full field equipment plus three day's field rations and one unit of fire. If the 25th of June order said: "(less two battalions) with the 3rd Battalion 145th and 3rd Battalion 148th attached" the word never reached the Raiders or the 145th or 148th Battalions. Murphy's Law stood solidly in the way.

On the 25th when the marines were to start their disengagement the Japs didn't want to let them go, they had two Raider battalions pinned down. Command said: "Keep trying, we'll think of something." On 2nd of July they said; "We got it, we'll give the Raiders a couple of battalions from the reserve division. One of their regiments is on the New Hebrides anyhow, if we reinforce the Marine regimental headquarters and battalion it will look good on paper." No one consulted with those who were to execute the plan. The Command's rationale that Infantry Battalions are like ships to be shifted willy-nilly in a combat formation flies in the face of common sense. There is no rule in the conduct of Warfare that Command use common sense, never was.

On July 2nd L Company was spread over thirty miles. The third Platoon was some where up the Matanikau River looking for Jap deserters. Under duress G Company made L a gift of their third platoon. Asked if they had volunteered, they all said yes but it seemed obvious that the volunteering followed an old army tradition: "Men, your country needs one rifle platoon to volunteer for a dangerous mission from which many of yew will not return, G Company Third Platoon one pace, fo-waad, HUP, thank yew Third Platoon, yewer comrades owe yew a debt that will long be remembered. At least until payday when yew aren't here to pay yewer debts, so, pay up now." Not really they were much too good of an outfit for that, but it crossed my mind.

They joined us the following morning, with all personal equipment, in time to draw Marine Corps camouflage uniforms. There was great mutual relief and greater confusion from man to man uniform switches when Lieutenant Chet Phillips and his platoon reached camp shortly before noon on the 2nd.

Colonel Harry Liversedge and his staff met with the officers of his new battalions mid morning to outline battle plans and stress some ground rules based on their previous experience. The battle plan was to intercept enemy traffic between Bairoko Harbor and Munda airport, capture Bairoko and prevent reinforcement of the Munda garrison from Kolombangara. Japs concentrated on killing American leaders; therefore remove all insignia of rank, address officers by nicknames substitute carbines for pistols, do not move at night any one caught out of his foxhole is a Jap. Nothing new, what was new was that the force was going to make the run in APDs, Navy talk not to be taken literally for Armed Personnel Destroyers. APDs were WWI destroyers with torpedo tubes and rear engine removed. The cargo space gained became a troop compartment, berthing approximately 300 men. As the meeting broke up, M Company's Captain "Aitchy" Walton said in an aside out of the subject's earshot: "Damn, I've seen bigger Marines and I have seen uglier Marines, but I have never seen a bigger, uglier Marine." He had a right to his opinion, marines called the Colonel "Harry the Horse."

Between noon July 2nd and 10:00 hours nothing much happened except the troops packed up, marched to Kukum beach, loaded in LCPs (Navy talk for Landing Craft Personnel, Higgin`s Boats to GIs), ferried out to and boarded APDs. That is besides having their morale raised by visits from former and future regimental commanders, several chaplains and the 145th Regimental Band who serenaded and made us homesick. Adding one days C rations (six cans), two full canteens of water, one unit of fire (enough ammunition including grenades, 30 caliber for riflemen, automatic riflemen, machine gunners and mortar shells to sustain an infantry unit in combat for one day) to already loaded packs.

On average each man was carrying over eighty pounds of equipment and supplies. More ammunition, supplies and two more day's rations were deck loaded. The last man had barely cleared the landing net at 1330 hours when the 22-ship flotilla headed south at flank speed, 25 knots. The situation was getting seriouser and seriouser all the time.

A little later Colonel Liversedge held a commander's meeting on his Flagship and issued orders for the landing those who expected a formal five-paragraph field order were surprised. The order went something like this: "Gentlemen, at approximately 0130 tomorrow we will land at Rice Anchorage on the northern coast of New Georgia. We expect the landing to be unopposed. We will be met by Native Guides led by Flight Officer Corrigan of the Royal Australian Air Force a Coast Watcher. Corrigan's Guides will signal by flashlights for troops to disembark as individual ships reach their station. As ship's LCPs are loaded they will form up and follow the guide through the channel in the reefs to shore, disembark troops and return to ship for second loads.

Troops will move inland to high ground and form a perimeter defense linking with units on their flanks without regard for organization. Troop Commanders will assume command of units in their vicinity. Ships will engage Enemy targets already assigned on arrival on station, as soon as all troops are ashore I will release you from your mission. At first light Commanders will regain control of their units and report to their commander. Gentlemen my past experience in similar landings tells me that it would be futile to issue an order any more complex than this." It took time to sink in but sink in it did. This Colonel expected all ranks from private to colonels to exercise America's secret weapon the use of common sense and initiative. Commanders returned to their ships. The ships resumed flank speed and went to condition red, locking all troops below decks.

Riding out an hour-and-a-half air raid off Savo locked below decks on an LCI was a relaxed delightful thrill filled pleasure cruise compared to this run. The WWI diesels that powered the APDs were noisy and stinky when new, Twenty years later they were deafening and pukey. The bulkhead between engine room and troop compartment was high noise conducting steel.

Conversation was impossible. Some men sobbed and others screamed with the same result, no one heard them. Company commanders gathering platoon leaders in a tight group and shouting the instructions face to face relayed the Colonel's order to the troops. Platoon leaders repeated the process to their squad leaders who in turn relayed the information to their squads in groups of three or four men.

Ventilators were elbowed standpipes rising from the deck facing forward spouting outside air into the troop compartment. Outside air was hot and friction flowing down the pipe didn't cool it any. Light was by four faint red two by four inch lenses one over each exit hatch.

The ship had a vicious double roll. That is; with the mast and keel aligned vertically the ship rolled starboard as far as it would go, rolled back port as far as it could go and returned to vertical. In moderately heavy seas APDs put their rails under. Fortunately seas were calm enough to make the roll just sickening. When the ships came on station, off Rice Anchorage, if the hatches had not been unbolted immediately, the men would have torn them out of their moorings and crumpled them like empty beer cans by hand.

The convoy moved on station only slightly behind schedule and there was a moment of relative quiet as engines shut down and troop compartments opened. A steady down pour of tropical rain met the first boatloads of troops moving to landing stations at the rail. The first salvo from the combined guns of the twenty plus ships of the task force momentarily froze a realistic scene of gray ships etched like gravestones on a black sea. The roar of the first salvo rolled into a drumbeat of concussions as the ships continued the fire on their own. Muzzle flashes gave glimpses of a bizarre picture as native guides in canoes signaled troops to load LCPs. Men went overside and down the landing nets gauging their drop as the barges rose on the swells toward the rail.

Two men from M company on the Waters missed and fell between the ship and landing craft and disappeared into the sea before their boat mates could grab them. One a medical corpsman unbuckled his pack and came back up to climb the landing net and survived the other an 81 MM mortar crew member weighted down with two mortar shells was lost.

Native guides led their convoys of landing craft through the reefs and sandbars landing sites with pinpricks of light through masked flashlight lenses. On shore another guide with a dim flashlight led the debarking troops to assembly areas, only they didn't. The heavily loaded troops could not match the speed of the agile natives and soon were floundering through the morass on their own.

By now the Japanese were answering our wakeup call and tracers were criss-crossing the sky Jap guns at Enogai tried to bring the landing site on the south bank of the Pundakona River under fire but their shells fell well back on the opposite bank. Some of the landing craft ran aground on sand bars or submerged logs and dropped loading ramps prematurely and their passengers struggled ashore through shoulder deep water.

A Jap Submarine joined the battle and sunk the APD Strong. Other ships were hit but sustained light damage. Shortly before dawn the American ships closed shop and went home. The troops did not, they moved inland, joined whatever unit they found, established a perimeter defense and waited for daylight.

At daybreak L 145 was intact and accounted for, attached were one platoon each from I 145, K 145, and D First Raider Battalion. Units sorted themselves out and rejoined their proper command on their own with surprising expediency. Twenty-four hours after leaving Guadalcanal the Northern landing force was ashore on New Georgia and ready to move.

20

ENOGAI

The Solomon Islands are a double chain of volcanic and coral islands thrust out of the sea. They lie east of Australia, south of Asia, some 2500 miles southeast of Yokohama Japan and 3200 miles west of Honolulu.

At the northwest top of the chain lies the largest island Bougainville, stretching southeast in order are, Choisul, Santa Isabella and Malaita.

South some one hundred miles lies a parallel chain of islands; some smaller and clustered with atolls includes the Shortlands, Treasury, Vella Lavella, Kolombangara, New Georgia, Rendova, Vangini, Green, Florida and Guadalcanal.

New Georgia except for several dormant volcano cones forming the central highlands is a portion of ocean floor rising out of the Coral Sea. It has all the convolutions of a coral reef. The island is just south of the Equator, green, tropically hot and humid. Humid translates into ten inches of rain a month, more during the monsoon season.

It is populated by typical South Pacific Melanesians and administered by Australia. July is at the height of the Monsoon season making wet an understatement and forcing streams out of their banks.

A giant lizard similar to Komodo Dragons is the source of the name of Dragon's Peninsula given a portion of the islands east coast. It also has a population of bushy tailed opossum that had a disturbing habit of urinating frequently and in great volume from their perch high in the treetops. Not all the moisture that fell on GIs was rain.

Fourteen miles northwest across Kula Gulf is Kolombangara the upper portion of a volcanic cone that trails a wisp of steam from the top. At the base lies Vila the Japs main base supporting Munda Airport.

Bairoko, a shallow harbor on New Georgia`s north coast opposite Vila and in line with Munda was the way station for off loading supplies from barges onto the backs of Jap soldiers for a twenty-five mile carry to Munda. The Japs would have used New Georgia's Melanesian Natives except they were working for us.

Besides the physical obstacles of terrain and Jap opposition several other factors complicated the Northern Landing Forces mission. Command's prospective that Army and Marine units were similar to Navy ships and could be shifted in battle formation exploiting fleet battle array without regard to command structure did not compute.

Marine Raiders were highly motivated volunteers, trained to conduct sea-supported raids of short duration with an element of surprise. There had high morale and were superb fighters. None were better at their task.

However, in an organizational sense they were light infantry without integral supporting weapons, supply or communication structure to sustain combat over extended periods.

Army battalions, equally trained, motivated and as deadly fighters were organized to be part of a combined arms team to sustain combat for whatever time it takes to destroy their enemy.

The Northern Landing Force relied on New Georgia natives under the leadership of Australian Flight Officer Corrigan to move supplies from Rice Anchorage to two separate forward bases from which combat operations were conducted. Given the fact that the round trip time to either of the bases was two days and the bearer's individual carrying capacity was forty pounds re-supply was woefully inadequate.

There had been no opportunity to train together, develop teamwork and establish a division of roles exploiting each other's strengths. Even with these shortcomings the Northern Landing force succeeded in choking off the Japanese efforts to re-supply and reinforce their Troops defending Munda. However, the force was not able to prevent the evacuation of Munda as planned.

The Army Map Service constructed terrain maps from air photos annotated from sketchy Australian local charts and maps. A common error ran through all the sheets. New Georgia's coral ridges with thin soil supported low vegetation, stream valleys and flood plains grew a towering rain forest, and tidal flats were covered with an even growth of mangroves. It is quite possible that to photo interpreters unfamiliar with tropical terrain, valleys became ridges, ridges valleys and mangrove flats coastal meadows. It took a while to interpret the interpreter's interpretations.

Intelligence placed the Jap garrison on Dragon's Peninsula at 500 Special Naval Landing Force troops (so called Japanese Imperial Marines). They were correct the day before our landing. A contingent of 3,000 Jap Army troops, reinforcements for Munda landed at Bairoko hours before the Northern Landing Force put ashore at Rice Anchorage some fifteen miles north.

Other obstacles developed. The ability of Corrigan's natives to keep the force re-supplied became moot when the Japanese were able to block re-supply of the base at Rice Anchorage from the sea. The three days ration had dwindled to two per man by the time the troops moved out from Rice Anchorage.

Replacement ammunition for that expended in taking Triri and Enogai had not been replaced. The ammunition remaining that was in the hands of the troops including salvage from casualties redistributed so that each rifleman had twelve rounds. Machine gun and mortar ammunition was depleted before an air-drop from Guadalcanal on July tenth raised hopes of survival. At that time men were hoarding there last D bar against tomorrows' hunger and talking of saving one last round for themselves.

Jap corpses were regularly searched for rations they might have been carrying. Sago Palm cabbages, terminal buds that is, were eagerly sought as dietary supplement. This practice continued after re-supplying was successful. Rice and canned beef Japs sometimes carried were a welcome change from American C, K and D rations.

The supplies air dropped were salvaged from a liberty ship sunk in the June sixteenth raid on Guadalcanal and only partially usable.

The Battle Plan was to march overland and take Enogai destroying a Japanese outpost at Triri on the way. At Triri the 3rd Bn 148th Inf. would follow the south fork of the trail to establish a roadblock on the Munda/Bairoko trail as it left the harbor.

1st Raider Bn with 145th's K and L Companies in reserve would seize Enogai, establish a base of operations and prepare for a coordinated attack on Bairoko. The 3rd. Bn 145th Inf. minus K and L companies, with the navy small boat detachment would hold Rice Anchorage.

The 3rd Bn 145th Infantry held Rice Anchorage but sporadic shelling and frequent nighttime visits from Washing Machine Charley, interrupted sleeping but little else. The Raiders cleaned out Triri outpost and the 3rd Bn 148 Inf left for the Munda/Biaroko Trail Intercept.

During the first twenty-four hours out of Guadalcanal we covered 600 miles, on the second twenty-four, three. Three miles through waist deep mud for the last man in the column and that included one night's sleep or what counted for sleep in a swamp.

K and L Companies 145th Inf. closed the perimeter defense at Triri in time to take a Jap company sized counter attack, K company, plus two that is, Captains Fouse K Company, Morrow L Company and Major Ferguson the raider's operation Officer were about seventy five yards in front of the K/L limiting point (the point on the ground where the two units joined) coordinating final protective lines of fire for the two companies light machine gun sections.

A very normal procedure except the three were standing up in full view of anyone who happened to be interested in what they were doing, which is not normal for highly trained smart Infantry officers. Not by Fort Benning`s nor Marine Corps` book.

The lead man of the Jap unit was interested, he opened fire with a burst from his Nambu light machine-gun shattering Fouse`s left elbow and Ferguson's right hip. Standing between the other two I was unscathed except for a badly bruised ego.

A brisk firefight erupted with the Jap`s point element, I was into my third clip of ammo when I realized that there was no return fire. The Japs had turned their attention to K Company, with a Banzai charge that fell short by seventy-five yards.

Alerted by the short fire fight and premature Banzai attack K Company countered with blistering fire into the confused Japs who withdrew with their wounded leaving some two dozen bodies in front of K Company, all Japanese. My withdrawal followed half carrying, half dragging Ferguson with me and accompanied by Fouse under his own power.

Ferguson, Fouse and Morrow were not the only Americans out of position. Staff Sergeant Glen Murphy of K Company with a severe case of diarrhea had sought solicitude from his affliction at the base of a banyan tree some thirty-five yards ahead of his platoon when the firefight broke out.

His account of return to safety and propriety while engaging the enemy, one handed, clutching his pants in the other and by sworn testimony of his K Company Cohorts, carrying a wad of toilet paper in his teeth, became a classic specially when performed with a Greek Chorus of K Company Critics.

The Raiders took Enogai in the face of heavy resistance. The 3rd Bn 148th Infantry took the high ground overlooking the Munda/Bairoko trail after a grueling fifteen mile march and hard fight. Casualties were evacuated over jungle trails to Enogai by Corrigan's natives.

On the evening of the seventh of July two PBY`s, flying boats, landed at Enogai to evacuate casualties. Before they finished loading W.M. Charley from near by Vila joined the party and the flying boats unwilling and unable to abandon their mission sort of skittered around on the surface of the lagoon as their waist gunners kept Charley engaged.

All available riflemen and automatic riflemen not otherwise occupied also took Charley under fire and in the face of this unexpected unfriendly reception he dropped his two bombs hitting nothing and went home to Vila. The PBY`s completed loading casualties and returned to Guadalcanal without further incident.

Two naval battles and nightly skirmishes between the New Georgia motor Torpedo Boat Squadron commanded by Lt. Commander Robert B. Kelly and the armored barge trains running from Vila to Bairoko were fought in Kula Gulf before the Northern Landing force was re supplied from the sea.

Kelly had commanded the PT Boat that evacuated General MacArthur from the Philippines Lieutenant John F Kennedy and PT 109 were part of Kelly`s command.

The results of the first of the two naval engagements was the loss of the American cruiser, Helena and Japanese destroyers Niizuki and Nagatsuki and in the second the American destroyer Gwin and the disablement of the cruisers Honolulu, St. Louis and our old friend, New Zealand`s cruiser Leander who had escorted us into Auckland Harbor.

The Japanese lost the cruiser Jintsu and four destroyers. These battles took place out in Kula Gulf at night and the troops on Dragons Peninsula could only hear the rolling thunder of naval guns and watch the sky light up from muzzle blast and exploding shells not knowing who was winning or who might be next to absorb the fury of battle.

We could watch the nightly skirmishes between PTs and barges used to re supply Bairoko and Munda and watch them we did. The choreography for these skirmishes remained much the same. About the time the rim of the falling sun touched the horizon the drone of an approaching PT boat could be heard and soon we could see a rooster tail of spume following a gray dot up Kula Gulf toward Bairoko at flank speed.

After passing Enogai, Vila`s shore batteries would take him under fire, soon followed by the six inch guns on Bairoko's headland. Invariably the shell burst fell in or behind the rooster tail kicked up by the boat some fifty yards ahead of the spume. It seemed as if either the Jap guns were unable to traverse fast enough to track The PTs cruising at upwards of sixty knots or the gunners were confusing the wake kicked up by the boat with the boat itself, perhaps a little of each. The result was always the same; no PTs were lost.

When the boat reached a point where Jap shore batteries were firing directly toward each other the boat would make a hard left turn into Bairoko Harbor and the batteries would cease-fire as if on cue.

The boat would disappear from our view and we would hear the chatter of fifty caliber machine guns and the slower paced deeper toned belch of forty-millimeter guns. The Pt would reappear retracing its course down the Gulf with the shore batteries once again firing at his rooster tail. Later we learned that the PT usually ran into a Jap barge and engaged him that accounted for the machine gun fire we would hear but not feel the frustration PTers suffered. Their fifty caliber machine guns were no match for the Jap forties and the barges with shallow draft ran over the PT main armament, torpedoes.

On July 10 an airdrop gave some relief. Unfortunately some of the rations dropped were spoiled and some of the ammunition was corroded.

For the next ten days L Company remained attached to the 1st Raider Battalion occupying a portion of the perimeter and extensively patrolling the area between the two perimeters, that of the First Marine Raider Regiment and that of the Eighth Special Landing Force, Japanese Imperial Navy.

During this time an L company patrol led by the company commander ran head on into a Japanese patrol also led by a captain on the Enogai/Bairoko trail. The collision cost the Japanese their Captain and four others and the Americans none. Jim Lucas eloquently describes the incident in his book Combat Correspondent.

Lt. Col. Ding Freer, CO 3rd Bn. 145th Infantry had a moment of notoriety he could have lived without, or a thrill beyond repetition. While in the process of moving his Command Post to Triri from Rice Anchorage by Higgins boat a pair of Jap planes made a strafing pass at the boat. The coxswain took refuge in the nearest inlet where they remained hidden until all danger passed.

It was nearly nightfall when after a quick look at his chart, the coxswain ventured forth and continued the journey. They entered what they thought was Triri Inlet and passed a large barge loaded with Japanese soldiers all facing forward intent on their destination. Freer said to the coxswain, "My God, son, those are Japs. We're in the wrong place." "Your right, Sir" replied the coxswain and promptly set course in the opposite direction toward Kolombangara.

Ding and his men crouched in the bottom of the boat scarcely daring to breathe and remained there until well out in the gulf and the coxswain cut their speed back and made a wide turn back down the gulf and Triri. Lt. Col. Ding Freer was the first American Commander to enter Bairoko Harbor.

L Company's command post at Enogai was at the base of a coral ridge just short of the company's perimeter positions. For reasons known only to the Japanese a sixteen-foot section of six foot diameter steel pipe had been hauled ashore and left there. With the dint of much hard labor and improvised pries the headquarters section maneuvered the pipe into place against and parallel to the ridge. Blocked one end with coral rocks and closed off the other except for a narrow entrance with the same material.

The pipe became a community air raid shelter that is except for Pfc Mayberry. Of course it took practice to learn to sleep in the pipe but that was better than shivering feeling exposed through W.M.Charley`s half dozen or so nightly visits.

Mayberry had a different theory. He was convinced that sharing a foxhole with another doubled the chances of that foxhole being hit, thus, logically sharing an air raid shelter with a half dozen others increased the odds of the shelter being hit seven fold.

Every morning he started scraping out a foxhole in a new location. No mean task in the thin flinty coral plagued soil. It occupied all his spare time and was never completed to his satisfaction. Before the beginning drone of W.M. Charley`s unsynchronized engines the rest of the Headquarters would settle into there selected softest spot of the steel mattress.

Before the echo of Charley`s first bomb blast faded Mayberry would be with us his theory overwhelmed by the naked feeling of an uncovered foxhole.

On the 18th The Fourth Marine Raider Battalion had extricated itself from the "Artillery Islands" mission and rejoined their parent regiment. Marines reinforced by one more battalion and the roadblock reinforced by I Company 145th Infantry. Liversedge was ready to take Bairoko.

Preliminary to the attack scheduled for the 20th he requested and was granted an air strike on Bairoko scheduled for the following morning. During the night via radio word was received canceling the strike. At first light L Company was directed to send a patrol to Bairoko, by ten we were on high ground just short of the harbor. The rescheduled air strike arrived on the canceled schedule.

Dive-bombers worked over the harbor defenses. The first Torpedo-bomber laid a stick of bombs conveniently close. On the principle that lightening never strikes the same place twice and Navy bombers do not approach celestial accuracy we dived into the still smoking craters and quivered through the next twenty minutes as our allies in the air worked over the ridge we were on.

Our assumption was correct no two bombs hit the same place. The planes reported back to their ship or where ever they came from and we reported back to regiment, indignant over our humiliation and the bombers annihilation of a barren ridge. Tomorrow's show went on any way.

21

BAIROKO FALLS

On July twentieth Colonel Liversedge initiated his plan to take Bairoko. He finally had troops on hand and in place to accomplish the task in spite of the attrition of two weeks of combating New Georgia`s hostile environment. The four intact battalions under his command had sufficient supplies to sustain combat for several days.

An air strike by torpedo and dive-bombers on Bairoko preceded the attack by the two raider battalions from Enogai and the 3rd. Bn 148th Infantry from Triri.

L Company 145th Infantry was again attached to the 1st. Marine Raider Battalion as the battalion reserve. L 145th and companies O and P of the 4th Raider Battalion initially manned the perimeter defenses of Enogai.

By midday all three battalions were bogged down in face of determined Jap defenses. The Marines in particular were being pounded by Jap 90 MM mortar fire and without any means of counter battery fire were forced to dig in on the high ground overlooking the harbor. Later in the afternoon L Company moved out of Enogai carrying extra water and reinforced the Marines. With the 3rd Battalion 148th Infantry bogged down in face of heavy resistance and the Marines pinned down and being hammered with mortar fire Liversedge ordered a withdrawal. L Company attacked through the 1st Raider Battalion and gained the next ridge against scattered sporadic small arms fire and dug in. The Marines withdrew to Enogai with their casualties. The 3rd Bn 148th Infantry withdrew to Triri.

At midnight word came forward that both main elements had successfully disengaged and were within defensive perimeters. Before daybreak P Company of the 4th Marine Raider Battalion pulled back and shortly after L Company followed with out further incident.

On the other side of New Georgia the 43rd Division secured Rendova, a sizable island just off Munda airport against light resistance and stockpiled supplies and ammunition for the main effort to take Munda airport. On July 2nd the

172nd and 169th Combat teams from the 43rd division landed unopposed on Zanana Beach, some five miles east of Munda, on the 9th they launched an attack on Munda and two days later bogged down against stiffening resistance but that was not all.

As a prelude to the battle for New Georgia there had been a growing flow of war stories over the rumor network to the troops preparing for the invasion. The stories had a solid base in fact. Besides demonization of the enemy common to warfare, atrocities were endemic to Japanese tactics. Prisoners were tortured to force confessions; wounded prisoners were routinely killed to avoid transporting them. Their code of conduct required individual soldiers to commit suicide rather than surrender. They waged psychological warfare with all manner of tricks and devices. Japs used their artillery sparingly and mainly only when Americans used theirs. Creating the impression that American guns were shelling their own troops and They demonstrated extensively at night to locate American positions.

The stories credited all Japanese with the ability to speak flawless English often with a Harvard accent. By the time these stories percolated back through casualties and other GIs returning from the battle zone and to the troops in training they gave the Japs almost a superhuman persona.

Somewhere along the chain of command it was decreed that since Japs moved freely at night Americans would not thus Americans could shoot anyone or thing moving at night and kill Japs only. Whatever merit this tactic had close in was lost long range because it gave the night to the Japs and ability to harass and terrorize GIs huddled in their foxholes. The last experience Americans had with jungle warfare was by the Marines in Central America against poorly armed and led guerrillas.

The Japs were not and while the reputations they gained in the Philippines and Maylasia were overblown American doctrine tended to counter the reputation rather than sound principles and enemy capabilities. It took a while to sort things out.

When the 43rd Divisions attack bogged down in the face of the Japs well organized defenses of a series of convoluted coral ridges perpendicular to the shoreline. Their left flank was anchored on the beach and their right opens some two miles inland in dense jungle. Casualties mounting and the Japs drove a wedge between the two Combat teams giving them free reign of the divisions support installations.

The Japs cemented their reputation for atrocities by raiding and bayoneting thirty-four American wounded in an aid station. They waylaid supply convoys and demoralized the attackers with night raids. On the eleventh the two under strength (two battalions each) infantry regiments from the 37th Division reinforced the 43rd whose casualties now numbered in the thousands many of whom were labeled victims of "battle fatigue", a euphemism for psychotic.

Eventually the remainder of the 37th Division were committed plus the 25th Division, veterans of Guadalcanal. For the next seven weeks The Americans doggedly dug the Jap defenders out of their holes and fought vicious battles defending supply lines.

Japs were not the only enemy. Sometimes they were easier to cope with than the other, mud. Supply routes crossed swamps and streams kept full to overflowing by rain. Trails bordered on impassable and were kept open to traffic by constant effort of engineers who had to remain alert to defend themselves at a moments notice. Finally on the twenty fifth of August elements of the 25th division linked up with the 3rd Battalion 145th Infantry in Bairoko. Who had walked in unopposed the day before. On Munda the mop up continued well into September 1943 when the last of the 145th Infantry returned to Guadalcanal.

From the twentieth of July until the twenty fourth of August Dragons Peninsula seemed the scene of an uneasy truce. Both sides held their prepared positions and patrolled the jungle in between. The Japanese Navy limited their operations to evacuating troops out of Kolobangara leaving Kula gulf American country. The Americans on Dragons Peninsula were supplied with new clothes, rations and ammunition. After all a month between sock changes was a bit long.

The first rations received were a new "J", for jungle, ration that came in a ten man pack made up of canned meats, dried fruits, vegetables and crackers. The ration could be cooked or consumed cold by groups of ten men or spread over a longer time by smaller groups. The real star of this pack was a tin of red skin peanuts mixed with raisins.

It was not long before an issue of B rations was received, the standard U.S. Army Field Ration made up of canned goods and staples in the bulk. Cooks and kitchens were still on Guadalcanal so these too were distributed to squads and platoons. Fistfights over canned fruit broke out between men who daily risked their lives for their buddies.

While there were no kitchens or cooks present it was surprising at the number of gourmet cooks hidden in the ranks and the ease that ammo boxes, tin cans, 55 gallon drums, sheet metal and other salvage can be converted to usable cooking gear by American ingenuity. The effective cruising range of our diesel driven barges shrank drastically as the fuel appeared to evaporate at an unprecedented rate or so it was said.

W.M. Charley continued to rearrange sleep patterns and Pfc Mayberry continued to pock mark L Company's C P area with unused foxholes but a new hazard was added. As the battle for Munda on the opposite side of the island progressed Jap night time air raids increased and the Americans moved up some 90 MM Antiaircraft batteries.

When the Jap raiders broke off their attack they usually departed via Dragons Peninsula and the American guns continued engage them as long as they remained in range. At extreme range many 90 MM shells armed with proximity fuses missed their target, fell in the American perimeter or close and exploded.

In the middle of one raid PFC Thibadeaux of L Company on a hunch abandoned his foxhole and took refuge in a crevice in the coral rock and survived a near miss. The next morning it became apparent that his foxhole had been demolished, his belongings scattered and impaled on a splintered branch twenty feet above the ground was half a twenty-dollar bill he had been saving as in case money.

Patrols continued to make contact but the Japs seemed less aggressive and contact was more common closer and closer to Jap positions. Typical patrol combat would be a meeting engagement between two patrols quickly turning into a fire fight lasting only a matter of minutes before the Japs would pull out with their wounded leaving their dead behind. American policy did not permit abandoning casualties. The only exception was if there was no other choice. During this time the box score of casualties was overwhelming in favor of our patrols.

On the twenty-third of August Colonel Liversedge again ordered an attack of Bairoko for the following morning. This time the newly arrived 1st. Battalion of the 27th Infantry attacked from the vicinity of the roadblock and the 3rd Battalion 145th Infantry from Enogai.

I Company reached the Japs defenses about 1000 hours and found them empty. The Japs had abandoned Bairoko the preceding night.

The following day General "Lightening Joe" Collins led an advance party from the 25th Division into Bairoko. His aid was Captain Bud Russell and the point company commander was Captain Pat Patterson, my old Fort Benning classmates. They brought the word that Captain Johnny Norris, the third member of our Fort Benning car pool had been hit, but were uncertain of his condition.

The 3rd Battalion 145th infantry remained in Bairoko until August twenty-eighth then moved back to Enogai and cleared Dragon's peninsula on September second rejoining their regiment on the Munda side of the island. Two things remain in mind about half way through the voyage by Higgins boat from Enogai to Lambeti Plantation a flight of Navy Corsairs passed over us and "Tail End Charley" peeled off and strafed us, didn't hit us though and only made one pass. Maybe he noticed the American Flag painted on deck of the boat or his flight commander told him to close ranks. He couldn't have seen any of us we made ourselves small and hid under the boat's gunnels.

The other is that on our hike from the beach to our bivouac area Captain Steve Garay, an old friend from Camp Shelby days greeted me and walked with me for a way and said me, "Cliff, I'm sure glad to see you and I want to apologize." "For what?" I asked, totally trusting. He replied: "For all the nice things I said about you when I heard that you were dead." All was well I was home.

22

I KILLED THE SON OF A BITCH

Our stay at Munda was short lived and limited to catching up on food and sleep although the Japs hadn't given up the idea of keeping us alert by air raids. For a while we shared the skies with them, our planes by day theirs by night. By the time our battalion left Sea Bees had repaired the Munda landing strip sufficiently to house American Air units and our night fighters made Jap after dark excursions into our air space a hazard to their health.

One afternoon a sizable contingent of bathers from the 145th were moved back from the beach while a Marine demolition crew planted quarter pound charges of TNT in the sand and camera crews set up. Marine Shore Patrol cordoned off the area. with cameras grinding several LCIs pulled on the beach to disgorge Marines in full battle gear who charged across the beach amid the exploding charges. Bathers turned spectators engaged in long range caustic coaching. Several months later on Bougainville during a lull in the fighting a Fox Movie tone News short showed the exercise under the head of: "U.S. marines Take the Island of New Georgia in the South Pacific."

On September 7, 1943 the 145th Inf Regiment embarked on LCIs and returned to Guadalcanal without incident arriving the next afternoon at Lunga Point. The 145th Infantry Band greeted us playing "the Beer Barrel Polka. Mainly the troops were glad to be reunited with their kitchens and the opportunity to loot the galleys of the merchant ships as they unloaded of fresh victuals in their new role of stevedores. The Divisions command structure changed during this interim. Most important to the 145th Infantry was the transfer of Colonel Temple G. Holland to command the 169th Infantry of the 43rd Division. Majors Carl Coleman and Luther Miller were especially relieved to be rid of the duty of burying the Colonel every night and digging him up again in the morning, well, in a way.

The Majors Miller and Coleman were the regiments Intelligence (S-2) and Operations (S-3) officers respectively, Coley was a Distinguished Marksman in his own right who engaged in an occasional sniping foray when he could escape the Colonel's close supervision. They were the main operators of the Regiments Operations Center. The Center was a dugout on the reverse slope of one of the many coral ridges just back of the battle zone. Dug deeper in the ridge and connected to Op Center was the Colonel's Cave. There he spent the nights in close consultation with his bottle of "Peroony", grain alcohol cut half and half with reconstituted grapefruit juice. At nightfall it was the S-2 and S-3`s duty to block the entrance to the Colonel's Cave with sand bags and spread their sleeping bags on the Op Center floor. In the morning they removed the sand bags. The Regiment's Op Center moved many times. Jap infiltrators did not molest the Colonel during the two-month battle for Munda Airport.

The Regiment's Executive officer, LTC Colonel Cecil B Whitcomb who had served with the regiment as a private in WW I took command and dropped the LT from his designation of rank. When the game of musical chairs played with Officer's assignments was over LTC Russell Ramsey commanded the 3rd Bn 145th Inf. Major Bill Morr was the Exec. Eventually I inherited the S-3 job.

Stateside replacements filled enlisted ranks and openings in the Officer's cadre. At that point it became obvious the Pentagon considered the South Pacific a backwash of the War or the managers of the replacement system were unusually inept. L Company received a Replacement who was 52 years old and had served in WWI and a 19 year old who had been born with webbed fingers on both hands. There was nothing wrong with their motives, both had lied a little here and there to get over seas and assigned to a combat unit but one had to use the tip of his webbed thumb to pull the trigger on an M1 and the other passed out from the heat almost daily. They both would have stayed and taken their chances if they could instead they had a round trip cruise to the tropics at government expense.

When we returned to Guadalcanal we were rewarded by assignment to the ship unloading detail on Lunga beach. Except for company details, the company was divided into two groups. One worked a ten-hour shift on shipboard loading Ducks, amphibious 2 1/2 ton trucks, driven by members of a Quartermaster unit. The other on shore unloading the ducks in supply dumps, that left fourteen hours a day for recreation, mainly air raid drills, eating and shift changes. The bright spot was that on board ship there was time between ducks to explore the ship and explore they did specially ships stores that yielded all sorts of goodies like fresh eggs, meat, fruit and vegetables.

The ships were mainly victory ships manned by civilian seamen rumored to be paid double while in the combat zone and triple facing enemy action; loosely defined as the presence of enemy ships or aircraft within striking distance. In view of this obvious injustice GIs took advantage of the situation by developing a thriving market in war souvenirs, mainly GI manufactured.

Sergeant Bill Neiswanger reaped a small fortune off Japanese good luck flags manufactured from American parachute flares. The parachute portion of the device saved from the New Georgia Operation were decorated with a rising sun of red ink and Japanese writing copied from salvaged equipment and boxes. They were sold with a gory story of Bill's capture or killing of the former owner. His price was in American booze, much, much more valuable than greenbacks. Bill's commercial empire came tumbling down when he sold one to a newly arrived Chaplain who took the flag to one of the Division's interpreters and learned that the Japanese good luck message copied from a packing crate read Argentine Beef.

One evening after condition red sounded Lt Lash among others was at the end of the company air raid shelter with "Greasy Maleski", the KP pusher, all KP pushers are called Greasy for obvious reasons, when the night fighter dropped its external gas tank over us. Big bombs falling sound like a distant freight train, an empty gas tank sounds like a huge freight train bearing down on you from above. Lt Lash and Greasy entered the shelter from opposite ends. Both head down and at full speed to collided in the middle of the shelter and send Lash to the hospital with a broken nose. No Purple Heart.

Life for Company Commanders and Executive Officers of units assigned stevedore duties was a bore. Platoons worked twelve-hour shifts either on board a ship being unloaded or on shore in a supply dump unloading Ducks. Without troops to administer there is a limit as to how much administering one can do. So Ap Pottieger and I scrounged a pair of aircraft external fuel tanks and built a raft. Our original plans called for a catamaran but we were unable to come up with a suitable mast. We settled for a paddle-propelled raft instead. That would have achieved our goal of catching a mess of reef fish except we never discovered bait they would take. However it was a great fish watching station. We also watched one of the drivers of an amphibious truck ferrying supplies from ship to beach accept a second cargo net of stores and have his craft sink out from under him.

One air raid we participated in had an unusual twist. Charley hit a fuel dump adjacent to our camp. So the company spent the rest of the night fighting fire. The dump contained 55 gallon drums of aviation fuel. The drums were scattered in groups of perhaps fifty drums under a camouflage net. Each group separated from the next by about seventy five yards a distance deemed by an unknown expert to be sufficient to prevent fire spreading from one island of drums to the next. The expert deemed wrong. The islands were separated just far enough to insure fire spreading from island to island. After the first fire spread to the second group of drums we isolated the fire; by rolling the drums surrounding the burning island back another fifty yards or so and beating out the grass fire that moved out from the main fire. By dawn the fire burned out and succumbed to an early morning rain shower. I sent word to the Beach master that due to circumstances beyond our control L Company would report to work late, a day late.

Before breakfast was over a Jeep loaded with a QM Colonel pulled into camp and the Colonel demanded to know who was in charge. The thought crossed my mind to turn command of L Company over to Ap but decided against it and reported to our visitor who wanted to know, "Who authorized those gas drums to be moved." While pondering an appropriate answer a second Colonel bearing jeep pulled in this one bearing Colonel Cecil Whitcomb, CO 145th Infantry. For the next half hour I was privy to a high level discussion that ended with a suggestion of where a certain QM Colonel could put his gas dump. I had the good sense to keep my mouth shut.

After being brought to strength, re-equipped, retrained on how to get on and off ships via cargo nets the Third Bn 145th Infantry sailed to join the rest of the 37th Division on Bougainville.

From a personal point of view this voyage was an epic experience. A few days before loading, as the Battalion's newly assigned Operation Officer I received orders designating me Loading Quartermaster, for the U.S. army troops embarking on the transport Adams. I was directed to report to the Beach Master at 0800 hours the following morning. The Beach Master turned out to be an affable Colonel of the Army Transportation Corps who explained that I was to organize the supplies and equipment accompanying the troops sailing on the Adams for loading and debarking on Bougainville's beaches.

That queasy feeling began to gnaw at my stomach. It got worse when he introduced me to the not so affable Lieutenant Commander, Executive Officer of the Adams, who informed me that he was in charge of loading the ship. Who then informed me that the basic principle of seamanship was to load the heaviest items in the deepest part of the ship. That created a quandary. Soldiers must be prepared to fight when they reach land therefore their weapons and ammunition must be the first of the cargo off loaded and they are heavy. I explained this to the Exec. Who countered that it was the ship that had to get the soldiers there in the first place and that he would make sure she was loaded in a seaworthy manner so she could weather storms and survive enemy attacks. Since he had interjected sex into the conversation I was about to answer in kind but thought better of it and returned to Battalion Headquarters and explained our dilemma to Colonel Ramsey who corrected me. It was my dilemma not his, ammunition and weapons would come off that ship with the troops. Since he put it that way I could only agree.

Embarkation day morning began a battle of wills. I sent barge loads of equipment out to the Adams and the ship's Exec. sent it back ashore. I made cosmetic changes in the load and sometimes the Exec. sent it back and some time he did not. Finally, with troops aboard and sailing time minutes away I rode the last barge out to the ship. By the time we arrived along side the ship had weighed anchor and was underway. The barge's Bosun was reassuring, he said:" Don't worry, Sir, the Captain has only left me behind once before." We came along side before the ship reached full speed caught a trailing davits line, made all lines fast and signaled a crewmember on the boat deck to haul away. He did and the Bosun and I rode the boat up to its station.

Being incompletely nautical literate I stepped over the rail of the barge before it was secured in its berth. The boat gave a lurch upward and slammed my head into the underside of the edge of the deck above knocking me to my knees. I was wearing a soft hat and knew immediately that my head had suffered more than the ships rail. I could feel blood filling my cap.

I finished climbing aboard the ship and headed for my stateroom shared among others with our Battalion Surgeon, Captain Lew Cannazzaro. I opened the door not wanting to risk my reputation as a wise ass, said: "Hey Lew, thread your needle." and took off my hat. A red veil covered my face and Captain H. E. Walton combat veteran CO of M Company.promptly fainted. I had to wait, seeing red while our esteemed surgeon threw water on the supine Captain before he put seven stitches in my scalp, after all I was still standing.

The next day out a young replacement Lieutenant assigned to I company was seated in front of a deck loaded barge writing a letter home when the ramp retainer gave way and the ramp fell forward crushing him, a quieting tragedy. A tragedy in that he died with out a chance to do what he came to do more Death was a fact of life we lived with but without purpose it lost its meaning.

The third day out Bougainville emerged on the horizon and the Battalion landed on Torokina Point, Empress Augusta Bay amid a welter of supplies and flotsam of war.

Before the battalion could sort out its gear and clear the landing zone sirens sounded and a lone Jap plane made a low level strafing run the length of the beach. Men dove for cover, made sand fly digging in and some emptied their weapons at the invader mostly after he had passed. One in particular pursued him at a dead run emptying his .45 caliber pistol at a rapidly receding target.

About two hundred yards down the beach a burst from a pair of 40 MM guns caught the plane and he veered out to plunge into the sea trailing flames and black smoke. His pistol-bearing pursuer stopped in mid stride jumping up and down shouting: "I got him! I got him! I killed the Son-of-a-Bitch!" Nobody disputed him, every one is entitled to his moment of glory.

23

BACK IN THE ARMY

Unlike previous landings in the Solomon's the one at Empress Augusta Bay was to secure and defend a perimeter enclosing an air base rather than to seize an entire island. Bougainville, the largest of the Solomon Islands is about one hundred twenty five miles long by sixty wide, located some four hundred miles east of New Guinea and a hundred and fifty miles south of New Britain.

The Japanese had nine airfields on New Britan. Rabaul, the major base was intended to support the invasion of Australia by the way of New Guinea. MacArthur's forces had stopped the Japanese advance at the head of Huon Gulf and were battling for Lae.

The neutralization of Rabaul was vital to MacArthur's success. Empress Augusta Bay on the west coast of Bougainville isolated by the towering Crown Prince and Empress mountain ranges from the three other Jap bases on the island was vulnerable. On November 1 1996 the 3rd Marine Division landed at Torokina point and the battle for Bougainville was joined.

A week later the first elements of the 37th Division landed, on the thirteenth the 145th Infantry regiment. The following week the final elements of the Division arrived.

The Marines had cleared the landing zone and driven the defenders south of the Torokina River where they dug in and stubbornly resisted forcing the Marines to the all too familiar task of digging them out of hidden defenses in difficult terrain.

On the 37th Divisions side of the perimeter resistance was scattered and less well organized. Combat was bloody short-lived fire fights between small units.

The 3rd Battalion 145th Infantry was attached to the 129th Infantry of the Division and pushed out to the perimeter's final defense line. The 1st battalion reinforced elements of the Marines on the southern arc of the perimeter and played a vital role in the vicious battle to establish the right side of the Empress Augusta Bay defensive line.

On December fifteenth the U.S. Army, Americal Division relieved the 3rd Marine Division and Command passed from the 1st Marine Amphibious Corps to U.S. Army XIV Corps. After twenty months we were back in the Army.

Jap air attacks along the Numa-Numa trail, a well-defined footpath that served as Bougainville's main trans island super highway, impeded moving out to the final line. These strafing runs at first occurred during daylight hours and only when our units were careless and let themselves be caught in open stretches on the trail.

Later as air defense units came ashore air defenses stiffened and the Japs reverted to nighttime sorties against stores off loaded on the beach. Airstrip construction, headquarters and support units shared the Jap's attention. The effect of these raids was negligible. Few casualties and little damage were inflicted to our forces.

They were not negligible to those who were casualties or even the near misses. Lieutenant Petersle was one of the latter. Pete had joined our staff shortly before we left Guadalcanal. Alan Markman our S-2 and I had sort of taken Pete under our wing for various reasons.

The first day after leaving the beach the Battalion had made good progress and bivouacked astride the trail some half dozen or so miles off the beach.

The three of us dug a comfortable hole in the sandy soil, Pete had done most of the digging, he needed the experience Markman and I were excellent supervisors with lots of experience.

A little before dark Alan and I were in the hole making our nests comfortable. Pete was off on an errand when a bomb exploded back down the column. The chatter of machine guns sounded above the unsynchronized drone of a Jap plane.

Alan and I cowered against end of the hole toward the sound. The plane passed and immediately Pete dove into the hole, jerked a poncho over his head and yelled: "Jesus". In the morning the Sergeant major wanted to know why that new Lieutenant was chasing a Nip plane down the trail last night.

Shortly after we reached our destination on the perimeter's junction with the Numa-Numa trail we were rudely awakened one morning by a battery of the 136th FA Bn from positions fifty yards behind our bivouac registering their 155 MM howitzers on the trail's Laruma river crossing.

Later that day a patrol of Fijian Commandos passed through our wire to scout Jap positions in the passes of the Crown Prince range. The first thing they did after passing through the barbed wire was to take off their boots and cache them beside the trail. They returned three days later after a successful fire fight with a Jap outpost killing all except one prisoner. The prisoner was all smiles to see

Americans. He had been firmly convinced that he was saved to be the main course at the Fijians victory feast.

Fijians continued to patrol the far approaches to Empress Augusta Bay Perimeter with great success. They suffered their first casualty, one of their New Zealand Officers, after killing over three hundred Nips.

The initial battle for The Empress Augusta beachhead barely touched our Battalion. While the Marines on right flank of the perimeter fought a series of bloody battles through swamps and sharp ridges and had to be reinforced by our regiments 1st Battalion, the third Battalion moved some ten miles out the Numa-Numa trail to near the apex of the perimeter without contact set up defensive positions and established a line of combat outposts another two miles further out. We patrolled extensively without a major incident except for a tragedy involving a native party who walked into the Numa-Numa outpost.

The lead native "boy" spotted the outpost and moved off the trail, a fatal mistake. An alert sentry noted the stealthy approach of a shadowy figure through the dense jungle growth assumed the outpost was about to be attacked shot and killed the native. This was the only shot fired in anger by a member of our Battalion during the initial phase of the battle for Bougainville.

In the middle of December responsibility for the defense of the Empress Augusta Bay perimeter passed to the U.S. armies XIV corps and the Americal division relieved the Marines in the eastern sector. The 3rd Battalion 145th Infantry rejoined its parent regiment and moved to a new sector later known as Cannon Ridge.

The Division's 117th Engineer Battalion obtained a saw mill from the Marines. There might be other terms more accurately describing the transaction but obtained suffices. It was obvious that no paperwork covered the exchange. In all likelihood the Marines who brought the equipment to Bougainville in the first place were glad to be relieved of packing and loading it on shipboard having never used it.

With the saw mill came a flow of rough-cut lumber to rescue troops from their omnipresent companion, mud. For a while the ring of hammers driving nails to construct duck boards, floor mess tents and revetted dugouts drowned out the clatter of bulldozers building airstrips. Slowly we pulled ourselves out of the mud.

With this Battalion area we inherited a unique natural resource, Lake Kathleen. The lake was really a wide and deep spot in the Piva River. Perhaps a mile long and a quarter mile wide, Lake Kathleen was filled with delicious, two to three pound, white fleshed, fresh water fish.

The Battalion had assigned to it the ultimate fisherman in the person of Lieutenant Norman Mantey Liaison Officer from the 135th Field Artillery Battalion. Norm formerly of Venice Ohio on Lake Erie's Sandusky Bay was an old friend from pre-induction days. He also was well versed in the effect of explosives on fish.

He established one of his Battalion's base points on a point in lake Kathleen just off the outlet into the Piva River. Whenever the Artillery Battalion checked the registration of its howitzers we would have a patrol of expert swimmers standing by to retrieve stunned fish floating down the Piva River. Fortunately for the fish, the skulking presence of increasingly aggressive Jap patrols put a stop to Mantey`s Fresh Fish Supply Service before the demand overwhelmed the supply.

Lake Kathleen was not the only source of fresh food on Bougainville. An Australian refrigerator ship loaded with frozen mutton cast anchor off Torokina point and a near Jap bomb miss on the first night persuaded the captain of the wisdom of unloading his cargo and returning to port in all due haste.

The commands Quartermaster without refrigerated storage and a shipload of thawing sheep carcasses on hand commandeered all available transportation and made a forced issue of fresh lamb(?). Solving his problem and creating hundreds more for the island's mess sergeants. Promptly dubbed "gray hounds" by GIs these carcasses hung in every fly proof structure at mess sergeants` command.

Americans are not big mutton consumers. Lamb chops for breakfast passed, roast mutton for lunch not quite, mutton stew for dinner not. The odor of mutton tallow brought rebellion the next morning. Mess sergeants across the perimeter laid out neat cemeteries and interred their remaining gray hounds.

Archaeologist at some time in the future will boggle their minds over the skeletal remains of headless sheep cadavers neatly laid out in graveyards amidst the artifacts of desperate battle.

For the next two and a half months a surreal atmosphere descended on our Battalion. The sector we occupied was tucked behind the barrier of Lake Kathleen on the left and a nearly vertical ridge leading to a precipitous hill rising seven hundred feet above sea level on the right.

Days were spent building fighting positions and laying barbed wire behind the protection of long ranging patrols without disruption from the Japs. This was about as exciting as building fence back on the farm. Increasing signs of Jap interest in our activities though kept us at the task.

The battalion twice in quick succession survived a near disaster brought on by boredom. General Beightler the Division Commanding General, taking advantage of Jap inactivity inspected the state of our defenses by walking the perimeter.

He looked in the fighting positions, questioned occupants, surveyed fields of fire and belts of barbed wire.

The Piva River flowed through I company's defenses. The defenses were first laid out by the expediency of felling one of the jungle's taller trees across the river for a bridge. Later a substantial footbridge complete with handrail was constructed down stream around a bend in the river. The sergeant showing the general through his squad's fighting positions followed by General Beightler started to cross the river on the log.

In my mind's eye I could visualize the general's descent into the river and him standing waist deep in water with the sergeant blandly asking: "How deep is the water, General? The General replying: "Ass deep, Sergeant, ass deep." With tremendous foresight I yelled. "This way, General, here's the trail to the bridge." The General heeded my call. Disaster was diverted.

Further along in the L Company sector, the General looked into one of the dugouts and backed out red faced and shaken. Visible in the dim light of the cave-like structure, on one of the bunks lay a naked blond woman. This turned out to be a masterpiece carved by Sergeant Bill Neiswanger from a log of pure white soft wood he had discovered among the timbers cut for fighting position roofing. Bill was disappointed in the lack of appreciation of his artistic talent. General Beightler never visited the 3rd Bn 145th Inf sector again, at least not during my stay with the Battalion.

On Christmas eve a wild pig, or a herd of wild pigs, set off an alarm mounted in the wire in front of the 148th Infantry sector and started a one sided fire fight with all projectiles fired outward that proceeded around the perimeter unit by unit. Not to be outdone, at 0001 hours New Years 1944 Lt. Col. Robert Chamberlin had his 135th FA Bn fire one round for effect as a salute to his old buddy from Cleveland Ohio COL Cecil Whitcomb, they were toasting each other at the time.

24

HILL 700

Chamberlain's salute to Whitcomb might have been the 145th Infantry's most epic event of 1944 if later that year Japs hadn't decided to drive the Americans off Bougainville. Shortly after New Year intelligence reports from natives, radio intercepts and patrols indicated that the Japs were on the move and their objective was Empress Augusta Bay. By February radio intercepts confirmed that they were about to make one final do or die effort utilizing every available man to accomplish this end.

Their game plan was to take hill 700, the dominant terrain feature with a suicidal assault concentrating their forces to give them a ten to one advantage over the defenders who just happened to be the 145th Infantry's Second Battalion. Once this goal was reached, they would widen the gap and pour their remaining troops through the breech and destroy all rear area installations before turning their attention to the remaining Americans on the perimeter.

Hill 700, occupied by the Second Battalion, was a crag jutting out of the first of the foothills leading from Bougainville's coastal plain to the islands spine, the Crown Prince Range. On the west slope of hill 700 Cannon Ridge occupied by the 3rd Battalion sloped away from a sheer rock face. The 164th Infantry of the Americal Division occupied a similar but less steep ridge on the west slope. A jeep trail ran along the base of Cannon ridge and ascended the hill to cross over at the bottom of the rock face; from there it followed a saddle to the reverse slope of hill 700.

In preparation for the defense of the perimeter common wisdom rated the sector occupied by the 164th Infantry as the most vulnerable to attack followed by Cannon Ridge held by the 3rd Battalion 145th Infantry. A radio intercept of Jap plans voided that assumption. Hill 700 was their initial objective.

Hill 700 while the dominant terrain feature was assumed too precipitous for serious consideration by anyone in his right mind. The Japanese had never staked a claim to sanity.

During the two and a half months of relative tranquility preceding the Jap attack the most vulnerable units worked diligently to lessen their vulnerability. The result was a formidable defense built around fighting positions with interlocking fields of fire. Hill 700 had an Achilles heel, its steep rock faces on the forward slope provided cover for massing troops in defilade positions virtually beneath and out of reach of the defenders. There was little room to organize a defense except on the military crest of Hill 700. The Japanese were willing to take a thousand casualties to put a hundred men on their objective and they did just that only in the end to lose those hundred men plus thousands more.

Bill Morr and I had a dugout constructed whose roof became the floor of our Pyramidal tent. We took advantage of slight drops in the night time temperature to rest secure from mosquitoes beneath mosquito bars luxuriating on air mattresses brought all the way from New Zealand. Bill had already departed for the mess hall when at 0630 hours on March 8 1944 the first Jap shell fell in our command post compound.

Minutes later, dressing on the fly, I emerged from the tent and fell flat on my face as the ground moved sideways accompanied by a rumbling roar. The trunk of a huge mahogany tree some thirty feet away exploded in thousands of shards and its upper reaches toppled to earth leaving ten feet of splintered trunk standing.

My first thought was that the tree had been hit by a Jap shell but as I picked up my clothes and a splinter from the tree trunk for proof. It struck me that Someone up there had just shaken us awake to get on with the job at hand of killing Japs.

When I reached the operations dugout dirt was still trickling from between the overhead timbers and the morning crew was certain that we had sustained a hit from a Jap artillery shell three times larger than any known before. Forty-eight hours later when Bill and I returned to quarters the dugout was in good condition but our penthouse was a shambles from Jap shelling. We moved underground.

The Jap shelling continued throughout the day from cave positions dug into the face of Blue Ridge to our front, all visible to our artillery observation posts. Our artillery poured hundreds of rounds of counter battery fire on the Jap positions with no noticeable slackening of the Jap bombardment. Their tactic was simple and effective; they wheeled their guns to the cave mouths and fired one or two quick rounds at a selected target before pulling the guns back into the cave.

American counter battery fire blanketed the cave mouth with little effect. The Jap gun was safe back in the cave. Difficulty was that American Howitzers looped their shells in high parabolas to the target. The targets were dug in on the face of a knife ridge and for a hit to be effective it had to enter the mouth of a cave, American shells were falling nearly perpendicular to the axis of the Jap gun positions and even hits on a cave mouth were ineffective.

Our all-purpose Artillery Liaison Officer, Norm Mantey, again came to the rescue. He paid a visit to the headquarters of the 251ist AAA Bn. who had moved their 90MM guns to positions on the Reserve Line of Resistance and convinced their CO to lend us one of their guns with crew to take the Jap positions on Blue Ridge under fire. The 90MM gun threw a fourteen-pound shell at a velocity of nearly 3000 feet per second and was capable of putting high explosive shells well back in the caves. Shortly after dark a tractor towing a gun and carrying a crew pulled into position behind the ridge. By daylight our pioneer platoon and the gun crew had the 90MM winched into a sand bagged direct fire position and the unnamed ridge leading to hill 700 went down in history as "Cannon Ridge".

For the next three days the gun crew from the 251st dueled one on one with every Jap Artillery piece on Blue Ridge that dared to poke its snout into the open and won every duel. On the third afternoon an L Company patrol returned under fire to Cannon ridge. A short round from the concentration intended for the following Japs hit the 90MM emplacement killing two and wounding eight including members of the gun crew and the L Company patrol.

Besides incoming artillery rounds the 2nd Bn 145th Infantry was receiving small arms fire by nightfall and our artillery was pounding the approaches to Hill 700.

By dawn the following morning Japs held four pillboxes on the summit of the hill. For the next three days the battle raged with the Japs unable to do more than stubbornly hold the summit of the hill in the face of counter attacks by the 1st Bn. 145th Infantry and the 2nd Bn. 148th Infantry supported by 37th Division Special troops. There was no route to counter attack except up the reverse slope of the hill and then by only a half dozen men at a time literally crawling on their bellies. The Japs on the forward slope continued to reinforce their position by crawling over their own dead.

While the Japs held four pillboxes on the summit of Hill 700 our positions on both of their flanks had been reinforced during the day. They could only dig in and hold their ground. During the night the 2nd Bn 148th Infantry moved into position at the base of the hill in preparation for "reducing the salient." Very formal, high level talk for GI basic: "Dig the Bastards Out", and dig them out they did, almost one by one.

Artillery and mortars pounded the base of the Japs penetration to keep the Japs in their supporting bunkers built during the past days of fighting. Shells dropped within fifty yards of our fighting positions. Exploding shell hurled Jap bodies or parts of bodies in the air. This triangular area, of no more than ten acres had its base resting on the top of a sheer cliff rising a hundred feet or so from the valley floor and sloped upward with its apex on the summit of hill 700. Twelve hundred Japs living and dead occupied Hill 700 that morning. It held the same number at nightfall, all dead.

The men, members of our sister regiment, 148th Infantry, who began the digging process from the top down, crawled up the reverse slope of the hill two at a time until the gained the cover of a rock shielding them from Jap fire, they blew out the Jap positions one at a time with bazookas and demolitions but it wasn't without a price.

On March 11 1944 the final counter attack by the 148th Infantry killed the last Jap on Hill 700, none were captured. 1200 bodies later were buried in mass graves bulldozed on two small benches in front of positions occupied by E and G companies 145th Infantry.

Stanley A Frankel documents this battle in great detail, as well as all others the 37th Division participated in during WWII, in the Infantry Journal Press` "The 37th Infantry Division In World War II."

On the night of the 12th the Japs grouped their survivors from Hill 700 in a small draw leading into Cannon ridge for a final Banzai attack. The draw was too steep to permit artillery fire reaching its occupants. AAA searchlights focused on the low clouds reflected light, illuminating the scene so direct fire from rifles, automatic rifles, machine guns, anti tank guns loaded with canister, from both L and G company sectors were brought to bear on the target. In the morning 170 Jap bodies were counted, there were no American casualties.

The attack on Hill 700 may have been the Jap`s main effort but it was none the less determined than their secondary attack in the 129th Infantry sector. The 129th had dug in a classic defense in depth with fighting positions using interlocking fields of fire on relatively level, albeit jungle terrain.

During the early stages of the Hill 700 fight the 129th were engaged in fierce patrol actions as the Japs probed their positions while those on Hill 700 were decimated. The Japs weren't through yet. They gathered remnants of their defeated units and reorganized them for one more attempt to drive through the Empress Augusta Perimeter.

Their final effort gained toeholds in the 129th defenses but were always driven out with heavy losses by counter attacks led for the first time in the history of jungle warfare by tanks. By the end of March Japs were no longer a threat to the American base on Bougainville.

They had lost over 7000 confirmed dead with 5000 of these stacked in front of American fighting positions, the remainder counted later in assembly areas. The 37th Division paid a price of 246 killed and nearly 1400 wounded. Of the grim statistics of this battle one stands alone to attest the ferocity of the struggle and the sheer courage of the Americans. The 37th division captured 44 Japanese, the Japanese captured no Americans. Surrender was never an option for our troops. Labels give statistics little meaning until a name is put to each number

25

GAS ATTACK

Shortly after New Years 1944 I learned that my father was terminally ill with cancer and his life expectancy was a matter of months at the best. Mother had passed away while I was en route to New Zealand in 1942. Dad's wish was to see me once again before he died. It didn't work out that way, I put in for an emergency leave backed by a wire from the local Red Cross chapter. The request was endorsed through division but stalled somewhere beyond. My father died on the sixth of March and I received word on the eleventh, my birthday.

Shortly after midnight on the twelfth Colonel Whitcomb called me from regimental headquarters to tell me personally that I was now in command of G Company. G along with E Company had born the brunt of the Jap attack and had lost two company commanders in the past four days. The last Lt. Pat McLaughlin under protest had been carried off the hill earlier that evening.

At 0300 hours on the 12th a 3rd Bn jeep dropped me off at the beginning of "the No Drive Zone" some 200 yards short of the G company Command Post I moved out smartly on the remainder of the journey.

First Sergeant Earl Faulhaber met me at the entrance to G Companies headquarters bunker. The same Earl Faulhaber who as a newly enlisted private had beat the pre-induction "shots" system in the Norwalk armory. My relationship with G Company had come full cycle from recruit to company commander in combat.

The rest of the night was routine, artillery and mortar fire continued to hammer the Jap positions and each of their return rounds was met by a dozen more from our counter battery guns. Occasional small arms fire on our bunkers received an immediate response from our close support artillery and mortars. Later that afternoon the 148th eliminated the last Jap position on Hill 700. However they did not eliminate the last Jap machine gun firing on Hill 700. Proof of that came the next morning while returning to the company command post from a visit to our forward bunkers. Half dozen strides past the point of no return on the exposed portion of the trail beneath the face of the rock, a burst of machine gun fire kicked up dust behind me. I covered the next fifty yards to safety breaking all records. My pace was much too fast for a malnourished Jap to traverse his gun for his fire to catch up with me. Sergeant Faulhaber and Lieutenant Wynn Rasch were cheering me on from behind cover.

As the focus of the battle for the Empress Augusta Bay perimeter shifted away from Hill 700 a great story (rumor?) from the 129th Infantry emerged. From November until February the effort of the units manning the perimeter had been first building an impregnable defense, second creating safe and comfortable living conditions. The 37th Division's engineer battalion having acquired a saw-mill went into the lumber business in a big way.

As the demand for bunker timber dropped off production of construction material increased. Tents were floored, kitchen and mess tables constructed. Straddle trench latrines disappeared in favor of sit down Chick Sales complete with mosquito proof screen doors and windows. In fact in the 129th Infantry area an impromptu competition sprung up among units for the most ornate Loo. Entries to the competition were described in superlatives.

When the Jap attack swung from Hill 700 to the 129th sector it was quite logical for Jap soldiers, whose only experience with indoor plumbing had been a "benjo" resembling a slit trench cut in a solid floor with painted footprints appropriately located to insure accuracy. To assume that these edifices were command posts, communication centers, officer quarters or some equally tactically important structure.

Initial Jap artillery and mortar fire hit one of these facilities scattering the contents of the pit and drum of quick lime causing a noxious odor to drift across the battlefield triggering a gas alert on both sides. For a while gas-masked participants on both sides continued the battle. Latrines lost their popularity as hiding places.

The Japs withdrew from the approaches to G Company's sector but their memory lingered on in the stench of decaying bodies left behind where they fell.

As the Japanese tide ebbed G Company had one more life to sacrifice, Lieutenant Steve Fejes walked into an ambush while leading a patrol toward Blue Ridge. We recovered his body the following day without incident. Lieutenant Fejes had been awarded a Distinguished Service Cross for bravery under fire in New Georgia and was one of several who were cited for gallantry in action during the battle for Hill 700.

Lieutenant Pat McLaughlin and Staff Sergeant John Kunkel were awarded Distinguished Service Crosses for their heroism. Their bunker was outflanked by the Japs shortly after midnight on the eleventh. Leaving this untenable position they continued the fight for the rest of the night moving from position to position in exposed connecting trenches preventing the enemy from ever gaining the crest of Hill 700, 185 Jap bodies were counted in front of their platoon's position the following morning. It was ironic that the Battalion Commander shortly after I assumed command of G Company suggested that I investigate McLaughlin's abandonment of his position as a violation of a standing battalion order that no bunker be abandoned in the face of the enemy. My recommendation for Mclaughlin and Kunkel`s awards pointed out their decision to fight from the trenches saved the 2nd Bn CP. from being over run. Perhaps it was only coincidental that the efficiency report received from this Battalion Commander was not one of my better. At that point in life I did not give a damn I was waiting transportation to the states.

A few nights after the last shot was fired the command bunker of G Company's 2nd Platoon was nearly demolished by an unusual invasion. Lieutenant Red Russell, the Platoon leader manned the company sound power phone net while Sergeant Harry Lodge kept contact with the Platoon's other positions on the other sound power net.

Sound power phones were a wartime innovation. They generated enough electricity from the sound of a voice talking into the receiver to carry an electrical impulse over the wire to other phones with out the aid of a storage battery or other source of "juice". They had one drawback, they didn't ring or other wise signal that someone was on line. Users had to keep the receiver to ear. To operate a net the control station had to check to make sure other stations were on line before sending a message.

At the moment I had the control phone in the company net talking to Sergeant Orrin Doane of the weapons platoon when my conversation was interrupted by a scream followed by the thud of blows being struck, oaths and other sounds of mortal combat.

I checked both company outposts, answer all quiet. First platoon responded all quiet, second no answer, third and fourth all quiet. Just as we were about to send a squad from the third platoon over to the second to find out what the uproar was all about Russell came on and said; "Oh man, let me catch my breath."

At that point I was relieved to know that Russell was alive and certain that a lone Jap intent on killing one more American for the Emperor had crept into Russell`s bunker, now the question was Lodge OK and was the Jap dead or captured. Russell said; "Never want to go through that again." Me; "You all right?

What about Lodge?" Russell: We're fine, but this place is a mess but we got him Harry cut the S.O.B.`s head off with his bayonet and he was a big one."

The story began to develop. Russell half asleep on his bunk, back propped against the wall manned the company phone net. Lodge manned the platoon phone while keeping watch through one of the firing slits. The two platoon runners were asleep. A candle shielded from the firing slits broke the gloom of the bunker. According to Russell; sensing a slight movement out of the corner of his eye, he turned and found himself face to face with a snake slithering out from behind the bunker's revetment.

He reacted as any normal snake fearing city boy would. He threw the phone at the snake and screamed. Maybe he screamed first anyhow the phone hit the candle turning the bunker into a pit of darkness. Lodge and the two runners put their backs to the wall and felt for weapons. Lodge grabbed a bayonet; one of the runners grabbed a flashlight and snapped it on to discover the other with a hand grenade and about to pull the pin. Russell was tearing at the revetment trying to free a piece to use as a club. The snake was disappearing back behind the revetment. The ensuing melee wrecked the interior of the bunker before the snake was cornered and decapitated. It was a shame; too, the snake was just an ordinary rock python exploring the bunker in search of rats.

He was just coping with environmental changes brought on by GIs. They brought food into bunkers enticed coconut rats down out of the palm trees into the bunkers in search for food. Snakes followed them for the same reason. After all rats are snake food. How did the snake know he would encounter four non-environmental maniacs who hated snakes?

With the Japs gone the biggest problem in G Company's command post was keeping tree leaves from collecting on our tents. Rain forest trees do not shed their leaves in the fall, they shed them whenever the notion strikes them constantly, a few at a time. Leaves gather on tents, moisture collects under the leaves spawning mildew that rots canvas causing leaks.

Keeping leaves off tents wasn't that much of a problem all it took was to have a GI armed with a stick patrol the area and knock leaves off as they fell. The problem was that the road leading to the rest of the 2nd Battalion area curved around a ridge overlooking G Company's Command Post and every time Colonel Cecil B. Whitcomb, The 145th. Infantry Regimental Commander visited the 2nd Battalion area, which was often, he passed G company's Command Post. He would lean out of his jeep and yell: "SERGEANT FAULHABER," he knew Sergeant Faulhaber well, "GET THAT GODDAMN LEAF OFF THAT TENT." Sergeant Faulhaber would dash out of the orderly tent, salute smartly at the rear of the departing jeep and yell: "YES, SIR, YOU OLD SON-OF-A-BITCH." Secure in the knowledge that his voice could not heard over the noise of the Colonel's jeep, the Colonel knew that, too.

I waited through April and most of May for word that transportation was standing by for my long journey home, finally Regiment called and said: "Report to Torokina Point Beach Master your ship sails in two hours." I made it in less time than that. I reported to the ships captain he said: "Ah`ve been waitin` for a Captain to take back to Gaudacanal for two days and you`ah a Lieutenant". I explained to him that Army Captains wear two silver bars and out rank Navy and Coast Guard Captains who wear a silver bird on theirs since the Army is the senior service.

He was a freshly commissioned Coast Guard Ensign wearing a single gold bar on his collar and in command of an eighty foot clinker built dispatch boat with a crew of six. He also was a recent graduate of Bowdon College, born and raised on the Maine coast; who talked "down east" with dry wit. It took us four delightful days of cruising through the Coral Sea dodging rain squalls to reach our destination. We would have taken five but the USS West Point was due to leave on the 31st of May, the next day. We had given up the idea of finding a deserted island and founding our own independent nation.

26

HOME AT LAST

The USS West Point, a newly commissioned Army Transportation Corps Troop Transport cruised at twenty-five knots, faster in emergencies, cutting the time between Guadalcanal and San Francisco down to two weeks.

After an authorized delay in route the time for reporting to Camp Butner in North Carolina for reassignment approached Betty and I drove to Ravenna Ohio for a short visit with our mentors from Camp Shelby days, Ben and Gladys Kilper. Their daughter, Benita, was now six and quite proper young lady. She remembered us well, particularly Betty who she was a frequent visitor.

When the 37th Division departed for overseas two years earlier the Kilpers assumed the de-facto role of Guardian Angels over the war widows and orphans left behind by Ben's Boys. Their doors were always open as were their arms and hearts to any wife who needed a shoulder to cry on. Gladys organized regular social gatherings for her brood and was a driving force in the 37th Division's Wives club. Ben offered expert opinion on all military news and overwhelmed dark thoughts with optimism. He took movies of all social gatherings and shipped them with his comments to 145th Infantry Regimental Headquarters to bolster his Boys morale. I brought him up to date with what I knew of his Boys to bolster his morale.

We reported in at Butner near Durham NC on schedule and found a room from the post's registry and over the next couple of days processed. Army talk for answering all the silly questions answered at the last place where you stopped. Gi`s have a pithier version but GIs abound in pithier versions. Then waited for orders for about ten days, had lunch with Betty`s cousin Dr. James Young, Professor of Romance Languages, Duke University and several lunches as well as nearly all breakfasts and diners with a young Army doctor and his wife who also were waiting orders and living across the hall from us. We had a car, they didn't, we still don't know whether or not they survived after we left. In due course orders for the Infantry Replacement Training Center in Fort McClellan Alabama arrived with a reporting date in three days. We made it but not by much.

27

IRTC

Fort McClellan, Alabama named after a Civil War Union General, perhaps best known for designing the saddle used by the U.S. cavalry; ironically was home to the East Coasts premier Infantry Replacement Training Center. The center received draftees from induction stations, assigned them to basic training companies where they received eight weeks of individual instruction on becoming a GI, the acronym for government issue. Units overseas received everything they required either through issue from the government or by "scrounging" (appropriation from other sources.) Soldiers were definitely Government Issue.

After basic came advanced individual training, followed by either entry into one of the specialists' schools at various other posts, for a selected few who had shown leadership qualities the next step was into Officer Candidate School for the rest the overseas pipeline where they emerged assigned to Infantry Divisions. There they received additional small unit tactical training before being assimilated into combat units that was the way it was supposed to happen, Germans or Japs willing. Sometimes things worked out as planned.

By the fall of 1944 a number of Officers and Enlisted Men were returning from overseas combat units for various reasons. The intent of War Department policy was; these combat experienced personnel would use their hard earned battlefield knowledge and skills to train replacements. This was another one of those curbstones along the proverbial super highway to Hell.

At Fort McClellan the system "Homesteaders" were considered to be too skilled in their assignments to be replaced. They knew the system, they knew the policy, they knew protocol and they knew that people in the combat zone got shot at, sometimes hit and even killed.

People returning from over seas knew the latter part but they didn't know the IRTC territory. They were stuck with the most onerous jobs so in time they would figure out a way to get out of the IRTC. The catch was that the main escape route leads overseas.

The rationale to protect homesteading rights and give lip service to War Department policy said if draftees were kept in contact during non training hours with combat wise veterans and trained by expert professional trainers during training hours combat wisdom would rub off on them while they were being indoctrinated with militarily correct skills.

Veteran officers were assigned as unit commanders who marched their trainees to and from classes accompanied them into the field, filled out evaluation reports and were responsible for all other administrative matters as well. Enlisted personnel's duties followed a similar pattern; they were drill sergeants, first sergeants and other administrative posts. Trainees stayed as far away from veterans as possible.

There were exceptions; those no longer fit for combat roles filled the homesteader replacement pool. Captains Bill Lorimer and Carl Hinemiller qualified Lorimer because of severe allergies and Hinemiller because of combat fatigue. Carl, who had been evacuated from New Georgia, gained a position on the Demolitions Committee and had the misfortune of exploding a quarter pound of TNT in his hand losing three fingers and one eye. He became notorious among trainees as "that Crazy Captain" who caught a Jap grenade in his bare hands.

Captain Dave Marshall former CO of Company I 145th Infantry was now CO of Company D, 289th Replacement Training Regiment, that is until I arrived and replaced him. Dave had a bad case of reoccurring Malaria and divided his time between the hospital and convalescence leave.

The regimental commander, his name long since forgotten, was rumored to have a lower promotion number on the permanent list than General Eisenhower. He was still a Lieutenant Colonel while most of his classmates had long since gained star rank. He had not experienced combat and had little use for those that had.

Fort McClellan IRTC Company Commanders were not a happy lot. They spent much spare time pouring over school catalogs and other assignment vacancy publications. Bill Lorimer was my secret escape hatch. Now a Major, he headed Personnel's Officer Assignment section and gave me the first shot at every opening for infantry captains that crossed his desk. I applied for all of them; I was still being accepted for hardship posts when the war ended.

Dave Marshall, his wife, Ruth and eighteen-month-old daughter Dee Dee rented half a house in Oxford, Alabama. The tenant in the other half was moving out on the first of the month and Dave's landlady was happy to rent us a room until then. The tenant moved out on schedule and we moved in.

Our half of the duplex consisted of a bedroom, kitchen, living room and bath, when the Marshalls weren't using it. The mansion was uninsulated frame with a tin roof mounted on piling with a roofed porch across the front. The floor was broad-board-knotty-pine with missing knots here and there, quite unique except for that locale and age. *It* gave a great view and audio of the almost nightly tomcat fights. That is until an elderly, mendicant, stinking, mostly English pointer took up residence on the front porch glider, being dog lovers we were unable to deny him this Spartan comfort and in fact added board to his appropriated room and dubbed him Rover He paid his keep by greeting residents and visitors alike and maintaining the peace amid the piling. Only once did he fall from favor by taking eighteen month old Dee-Dee bird hunting. Fortunately the frantic female posse headed by Ruth and Betty caught up with the adventurers just before they entered the brushy vacant lot across the road. Neither Rover nor Dee-Dee could understand what all the uproar was about.

Another interesting aspect of our habitation was that we were not alone; numerous other Alabama residents shared our digs, none by our invitation. Mice were the most persistent. They were held at bay by a half dozen snap traps baited with peanut butter and placed near the most likely entries. There were times that the morning trap line haul was six mouse cadavers matched by the evening toll. They were disposed of by being dropped down among the denizens of the pilings through a knot hole in the yellow pine floor labeled "Morrow's mouse morgue". No matter the number of bodies resting in the morgue in the evening they were gone in the morning Our landlady invited Betty to accompany her on an overnight visit to her sister who lived in rural Georgia. Betty had a car and the landlady did not. They arrived at their destination mid afternoon. The sister delighted with the opportunity to visit went all out to make her guests comfortable and as evening approached put a kettle of water on the stove and when the water neared boiling went out into the door yard caught several young chickens, wrung their necks, plucked, gutted, dismembered and had them frying before they were hardly through with their death throes.

Betty was a small town girl and while not entirely unfamiliar with farming was not up to the full process of converting living animals to table fare particularly when served rare.

After dinner the party visited a neighbor residing deeper in the piney woods, so deep that he transported the fruit of his labor to market in Mason jars. The next morning Betty and her landlady returned to Oxford the object of the expedition now quite clear and Betty driving very carefully alert for the possible sound of splintering glass in the trunk or the wail of pursuing revenuer sirens. The result produced an odd tasting but palatable martini.

Meanwhile on Fort McClellan's training fields, D Company was in the advanced individual training phase conducted deep in the boonies. Having recently undergone a couple of advanced practical exercises in these skills at the invitation of the Japanese Imperial Army this was not something I could develop deep enthusiasm for. My function was strictly administrative. What I saw being taught frequently made me shudder. My notoriety was firmly established among trainees of that cycle the second day of the first two-week sojourn in the field.

At the first ten-minute rest break after lunch, I selected a comfortable spot in the shade of a pine tree to rest my back against the trunk after scanning the area for snakes. I had just settled when I heard the buzz of a rattlesnake followed by a scream and a trainee starting to sit down under a tree about fifty feet to my right front took off at a dead run. I knew instinctively that he had been hit by a snake and most likely in the buttocks. Where there was no chance to use a tourniquet to slow the spread of the venom. Running would only make a serious problem worse. I took off and tackled him as he passed in front of me and was busy tearing off his pants when he finally got through to me that he hadn't been bitten. The thing that saved my reputation was that the snake waited for us. Killed and decapitated the cane break rattler measured six feet, by guess.

The end of September brought an affirmative reply to the applications for transfer. It was for the initial class in an Air/Ground Liaison School at Key Field, Mississippi. Bill Lorimer cut orders for me and sneaked them past my regimental commander without disclosing that I initiated the application. Thus I escaped the Fort McClellan IRTC.

28

POST GRADUATE COURSE

The U.S. Army Air Force established the first Air/Ground Liaison School at Key Field near Meridian, Mississippi. The criterion for attendance was the rank of Captain or Major in one of the ground combat arms with combat experience and preferably decorated. Combat experienced so he could relate to the emotional stress of those who flew into enemy territory also explain the mission and tactics of the units fighting the ground war. Ground Liaison Officers were vital links between ground units and pilots flying ground support missions. They were part of a Field Army staff assigned an Air Group. Their mission was to weld the combat capabilities of two different elements into a unified force with a single objective.

The system had been developed by the British Army after early and disastrous experiences in North Africa with casualties from "friendly fire." Well intentioned but poorly informed fighter/bomber pilots in some cases had inflicted casualties to British ground units exceeding those suffered by German forces. Hardly cricket, you know besides it hurt like Hell to have your own Infantry and tanks knocked out by your planes or enemy. Such activity inclined to increase the proclivity of ground units to shoot down aircraft first and identify markings later. Americans had the same experience but the British had been first with remedy that became standard for the Allied Armies.

The system was not overly complicated and based on communications between Air and Ground units particularly at the point where aircraft were engaging enemy ground units. Air units were equipped with different radios and other communication equipment than ground units for many reasons. The battlefield appears different from the air than it does from the ground and is viewed differently by its occupants.

The psychology of the two sets of warriors is different, each believes in the superiority of his mission and each is convinced of the higher degree of danger and hardship of his service. There is a big difference in rank structure and relationship between commissioned and enlisted ranks. Officers in Air units run the machines, enlisted men serve in support roles. Officers in Ground units direct enlisted men who run the machines.

Air combat particularly between fighter air craft is a meeting engagement usually entered and over in a matter of minutes. Bombing runs may extend to hours of pounding from flak and interceptors. Ground combat runs a gamut of a fire fight between small groups lasting minutes or a sustained battle that last days, weeks or even months without relief. A ground unit's metaphor is that Air GIs sleep between sheets while Ground GIs sleep where ever they can. There is a profound difference of perception as who plays the dominate role, who faces the greatest danger or suffers the most. Since the argument is one of perception, it remains moot.

The mechanics of the communications link were easily solved. The human element was a little more difficult and was the foremost reason for a school and the reason students were selected who had experienced combat up close and personal not to define the differences between the two but the similarities.

The Commandant of the school was an American Army Air Force Colonel; the major players of the Academics staff were three British Army officers, Leftenant Colonel Mike Ferense, Major Bobby Miller and Captain Cliff Fields, later promoted to major. All three were North Africa veterans and had served in combat and as Liaison Officers with British Air Force units. They brought a great deal of insight into the problems with a British slant. Ferense was "of the Peerage" and afforded deference subtly beyond the privileges of rank. Miller was from Liverpool and spoke "Liverpudian" while Fields was from London and occasionally lapsed into Cockney. American faculty members covered the technical aspects of the system and were typical American Service School Instructors with whom the students had considerable experience. The Britishers were a new breed for the dozen and half American students.

With British domination of tactical curriculum the school was definitely off beat. Students learned early on to take class titles with a grain of salt. The instructors did, their lectures were informative and interesting but by the end of them students were hard put to match the subject with the published topic in the schedule. Then too, they were big on the idea that a qualified representative of one command to another should never be without an answer.

It was their common practice to call on a student thusly: "Captain Graves, as a qualified Artillery bloke please explain to us why Japanese artillerymen always ride backwards on their caissons and do take your time, at least three minutes." Poor Jocko Graves, he had been with the US 8th Division in North Africa and knew Artillery tactics and techniques but had never seen a Japanese soldier in his life. Now he was stuck with spending the inflicted next three minutes providing a plausible answer to a question that he knew nothing about and cared less.

A good response might have been, Captain Graves: "Thank you Major Miller for asking me to speak on the subject of Japanese Artillery gun crew's transportation modes. There are many questions concerning Artillery customs throughout the world including those of His Majesty's Royal Cannoneer Corps that I would be hard pressed to answer. However it so happens that just recently I picked up Colonel Hatsu Maku Nuru's eighteenth century epic poem 'Hiwatso Ipso Facto' about the rigors of a life time service in the Mikado's Personal Artillery Regiment." With that launch into a fanciful recital of the fictitious Japanese Colonel's adventures including Japanese sounding gibberish quotes from his nonexistent epic poem followed by English translations until three minutes had passed then say: "Major, please accept my apologies for being unable to more fully answer you question within the imposed time limits. Perhaps at some future time we can explore this fascinating subject further."

Soon we learned that as long as one could talk through the time limit in a reasonable manner it didn't matter if the answer made any sense at all. These sessions grew more hilarious every day. It's hard to say what this had to do with winning the War but it made us stay alert, think fast and keep words flowing while thinking on our feet.

The best part of the school was that Betty and I were able to find lodging in a private home along with Captain Tom Curtain and his wife Bernie. Major Carl and wife Helen Gilbert had lodgings nearby. We were regulars at Weidman's Restaurant, a Meridian establishment with a national reputation of not closing its doors since some time in the eighteen hundreds. We were so regular that the management reserved a table and a particular waiter, "Hienkel", for us without request. Nearly ten years later Heinkle was still there, a little grayer claiming he remembered us but not very convincingly.

The Curtains were from the Bronx and the Gilberts from Philadelphia. Nothing remarkable about that except that Tom was in the process of teaching Bernie (aka Murph) to drive and Murph had problems with driving terminology, technique and tactics, Tom's problems were gender related hampered by temper, tact and tantrums.

Every evening the Curtains would leave the house as the very model of matrimonial bliss for Murph's driving lesson and return with one white lipped and red faced the other in tears and humming the popular song "You Always Hurt the One You Love". Dinner conversation was politely strained breakfast was back to normal. After about two weeks of frustration Murph announced that she would take driving lessons while Tom was overseas and the strains of You Always Hurt the One You Love no longer echoed through our halls, only the memory lingered.

The classroom at Key Field was not all fun and games. There was a great deal of solid information to be absorbed during the time spent there and not much time was wasted. However, during off duty hours particularly Saturday nights the Officers Club was well patronized and Britishers were the social lions and ate up the attention they received.

Toward the end of November we began a tour of Air Force Schools starting with the Strategic Bomber School at Key Field where we were observers on several training missions. From there we were flown to fields in Oklahoma and Texas to observe tactical bombing, tactical reconnaissance and fighter-bomber training. By the time we returned just before Christmas we had logged more flying hours than most members of the U.S. Army Air Force, really not a surprising fact, since more Air Force members had not flown than those who had.

Our British friends were back in Old Blighty replaced by a trio of newcomers who were teaching the second class of Air/Ground Liaison Officers how to cope with the English language as spoken by lineal descendants of its originators several hundred generations later. A dozen of the first class had orders to report to Fort George Meade Maryland on January 8 1945 for reassignment to the European Theater of Operations.

The group arrived on schedule to begin processing for over seas shipment with the expectation of clearing post within forty-eight hours. Transport space would determine which east coast port would be our next stop. So we all went to Baltimore that evening and stood a bleary eyed reveille the next morning. At reveille the word was; "Not today, tomorrow for sure." That night we went to Washington D.C. After a week of "Not today, tomorrow for sure" in which a steady stream of Second Lieutenants, Infantry passed through our replacement company the word became "Call in tomorrow and we'll let you know".

Units chewed up by the Battle of the bulge were getting replacements for their losses. Second Lieutenants Infantry led the parade. On the twentieth Betty arrived at her cousin's in Silver Springs MD and the next day we joined Tom and Bernie Curtain at Fort Meade's Officer's club. For the next two weeks we spent five days at the Officers Club and a night at her cousins. We were not haunted by the strains of "You Always Hurt the One You Love: Tom left his car in New York.

Among other occupants of Fort Meade were several hundred of Hitler's finest, Storm Truppen from the Afrika Corps, who had been captured during the North African Campaign. They were housed in tents inside a well-guarded barbed wire enclosure not far from post headquarters.

Somewhere up the American chain of command the open handed Natzi salute had been deemed as inappropriate and an order issued prohibiting American Officers acknowledgment of same. The order spawned a game among the Natzi P.O.W.s. of tricking an unsuspecting American Officers passing the P.O.W. compound into answering a stiff armed salute and a shouted "Sig Heil!"

Civilian employees were in short supply because of wartime manpower shortages. Many POWs were under parole to work in various menial jobs on post replacing civilians. On one occasion, a particular obnoxious American Lieutenant Colonel, (American Lieutenant Colonels can be as obnoxious as the best any other country has to offer), complained bitterly about the quality of the brake adjustment a German mechanic performed on the Colonel's car at the post-exchange garage. When he drove out of the garage after having the brakes readjusted and applied the brakes before entering traffic he coasted out into the street and was creamed by a full Colonel. The German mechanic had drained the hydraulic system on the victim's car and standing at rigid attention, right arm thrust skyward in the banned salute, paying silent tribute to a blow struck against the tyranny of all Army's over bearing and obnoxious Lieutenant Colonels.

Tom Curtain fell victim in a different way to one of our captured enemies. Tom, Bernie, Betty and I were having dinner correctly served by an immaculate, blond, Aryan captive in the Officers Club Dining Room. Tom asked for a second pat of butter and received the following reply in flawless English; "Sir, one pat only is allowed, does the Captain not know there is a war on?" Red faced, Tom abandoned his quest for additional butter.

Shortly after the first of February there was room for our contingent on the Queen Elizabeth, Betty went home and the first school trained contingent new contingent of A/GLOs shipped out for England.

29

Q E

The Queen Elizabeth was virtually a floating city accommodating fifteen thousand passengers. We boarded at about three one morning in early February of 1945. Before nightfall of the fifth day we were anchored in Scotland's Firth of Clyde having traveled some thirty-five hundred nautical miles across the North Atlantic Ocean not counting miles up and down on Atlantic swells, a new record. As a matter of fact every crossing set a new record if not for speed of crossing, for the total number of troops transported on one ship.

It was not a pleasant experience. This was a hot bunk ship, carrying twice as many soldiers in her troop compartments as bunks. Officers fared better they had their own bunk even if there might be twelve bunks in a cabin designed for two. Enlisted men with all their worldly possessions in barracks bags had a bunk for an uninterrupted twelve hours a day. The other twelve hours a different enlisted man held possession. One hung his barracks bag on one end of the bunk the other on the other end. Fifteen thousand men at a time endured a five-day crossing.

When a man began his off bunk shift he reported first to the mess hall for chow as he went off shift he reported last to the mess hall for chow, in the intervening ten hours he performed some ship board duty, mainly clean up, by the time the Queen passed the Statue of Liberty she had suffered her first casualties to mal de mer. The epidemic continued until the last passenger left at his destination. Barf buckets located at strategic locations failed to keep the decks from becoming slippery with vomit. Mainly the off bunk shift swabbed decks or other housekeeping tasks.

In normal seas the ship was exceedingly stable. There is nothing normal about the North Atlantic in winter. The ship's bridge was eighty feet above her plimsoll line, the line on a ship's hull that separates the part of the fully loaded ship that is below water from that above water.

When underway, spray regularly washed over the bridge's windscreen. As the Queen Elizabeth ran on to an oncoming swell the bow dug into the sea and sent spray flying over the fore structure and began a shuddering rise as the swell ran under the ship past its point of equilibrium then fell with a thud to dig into the next swell as the preceding swell lifted the stern. With the rise and fall was a constant roll that in the worst of storms put the lee rail under onrushing seas. There was nothing remarkable about this motion, it is common to all ships weathering heavy weather what was remarkable was the magnitude and time of the bow's rise and the ships roll. What would be truly remarkable is if one veteran of a hot bunk winter crossing of the North Atlantic on the Queen Elizabeth would come forward and state that he enjoyed good health during the experience, not even pathological liars would tempt the dare.

By now the German Wolf packs of submarines that during the early days of the war had roamed the Atlantic at will were confined to their pens in the Baltic by the lack of fuel and Allied sea and air patrols over the North Atlantic. Only occasionally did an undersea raider venture out to open sea and none had the speed to intercept the Queen Elizabeth. No other passenger ship and few warships in service at that time could keep up with her. With the remnants of the Luftwaffe confined to the continent. The lack of precise knowledge of the big ships course and schedule left German subs vulnerable and surface ships at the mercy of the British Navy if they attempted to lay in wait off the Firth of Clyde Within hours of our arrival lighters were ferrying troops to shore. Trains bound for channel ports were loaded. Troops were pouring into the European Theater of Operations replacement Pipeline. Our route took us to Dover, across the channel by ship, Calais and a numbered replacement depot near Charleroi, Belgium. There for the first time I encountered innocent victims of War, children refugees. As we exited the chow line with mess kits loaded we ran a gauntlet of ragged waifs holding pans, tin cans, whatever could serve as a food container thrust toward the emerging GIs saying; "A piece of bread, M'ssuer, I am very hungry."

For newcomers the first trip through the gauntlet was a jolting experience that ended with an empty mess kit. Eventually truth prevailed, it became apparent that that the most woe begone mendicants were holding their place in the begging line by exchanging full plates for empty and a price.

At Liege we processed and waited, after a few days we moved by truck to Verdun, France, where the scars of WWI remained. Here we processed and waited before moving by truck to the Replacement Depot at Nancy, France where we processed and waited. Finally on the fourteenth of March we reported to Seventh

Army Headquarters G3 Air Section where the chief of section, a colonel whose name has long been forgotten said; "Where in Hell have you people been I sent in a requisition for your types six weeks ago." Having taken the lectures on diplomacy delivered by our British friends in Meridian Mississippi seriously, no one said;" Touring France, sir."

That afternoon Perry Graves and I reported to Fighter/Bomber Groups at separate air fields a few miles out of Luneville, Tom Curtain reported to a Tactical Reconnaissance Squadron and the rest of our group were sent on to Twelfth Army Group Headquarters. Perry and I met frequently when we were called to Army Headquarters to receive briefings as orders for new operations were issued. We didn't see Tom until after the war ended and never did see the rest of our class. We completed a month long tour de France without bicycles or seeing Paris.

30

BACK TO WORK

Captain Rob Carter, my new assignment boss greeted me with; "I'm really glad to see you, here are briefing notes for today. There is one more flight scheduled in a half hour and three still out. I haven't had a day off in a month and been up since three this morning; I'm going to hit the sack." Our operations sergeant was posting the bomb line on the operations map as I entered the briefing room. The immortal words of wisdom from Her Royal Majesties' Leftenant Colonel Mike Ferense came to mind; "If you don't want to face a bloody board of inquiry with your bloody trousers around your ankles enter your bloody briefing with the last bloody bomb line report posted." Glad to be spared the indignity by the grace of another efficient noncom, I had barely time to go over Carter's notes and meet the other members of the group briefing team before the pilots of the day's last mission filed in.

The mission was a routine armed reconnaissance in which the planes would fly a prescribed route over enemy territory and engage any German troops or transport the pilots observed. If during the course of their recon no targets of opportunity were spotted they would unload their ordnance on a designated railroad marshaling yard. The briefing went well. I made doubly sure that all knew the location of the bloody bomb line, both going and coming. By the time the last pilot left the room pilots from a returning mission were filing into the briefing room and a debriefing was underway before I finished writing my debriefing report the next returning flight was entering the debriefing room and the final mission was landing. Somehow all the debriefings were done and my reports turned over to our radio crew for transmission to Army without my standing in front of a bloody board of inquiry with my bloody trousers about my bloody ankles thank you Leftenant Colonel Mike Ferense. Carter met me in the Officer's club where we had a couple of drinks and chow. Rob went back to the bar and I hit the sack, tomorrow I started my second day at three hundred hours.

This routine continued for several days before Captain Carter Magnanimously agreed to an alternating system. He had received orders to return to Army Headquarters for reassignment. The bearer of the order was 1st Lt Lloyd Martin late of the US 45th Division temporarily assigned while recuperating from wounds.

The second day was no less hectic than my previous day's introduction to the air war had been. The bits and pieces from the Air/Ground Liaison School begin to fall in place. Our liaison section of two officers and a like number of enlisted technicians plugged into the operations of the Air Group Headquarters and passed information vital to the joint operations of both ground and air units.

Information passed in both directions. The mechanics of the system was a cycle within a cycle that began when the Army Commander issued an order covering the next operation. This order contained the plan to bring the allied forces under the command of General Patch; Commanding General of Seventh Army to the next phase line established by General Eisenhower and usually covered a period of a week to ten days. The chief of each Air/Ground Liaison section attended these briefings and returned to his Air Group to coordinate ground support missions assigned to the group. The Commanding Officer and key members of his staff attended a similar briefing by the Air Division Commanding General. As a follow up, teletype transmitted a daily combat order. This message carried the specifics of the responsibility for assigned mission of both ground and air units. This was the realm in which the Air/Ground Liaison system lived.

Our section was divided into two teams of a liaison officer and an operations noncom, one Master Sergeant David Johnson. The junior noncom, Staff Sergeant Tony Lazzeri was also our jeep driver. The teams alternated responsibilities every other day. The team on duty started their day two hours before the first flight took to the air by picking up the day's combat orders from the communications room. This information had been transmitted in code by teletype from Army Headquarters and was decoded by machine before being printed. It included an update of the current battle and operations planned for that day. The message had a security life of five hours. Five hours after operations began the Germans would know what our troops were doing to them, obviously at that point the information was no longer a secret.

The operations sergeant posted the large operations map in the briefing room with the information contained in the ops order including location of both our own forces and known enemy positions, most importantly, the Bomb Line. The BL was an arbitrary line established by Army HQ beyond the furthest advance by our troops (usually a thousand yards). Ground units could not advance beyond this line without clearance from their operational command and air units could not attack targets on the friendly side of the line without clearance from the same command and then only under the precise direction of forward air controllers. In the meantime the GLO poured over the Ops order and incorporated ground support information into his briefing notes.

This information included the objectives of the day's ground operation, known and suspected enemy locations including anti-air artillery (flak) concentrations, adjacent friendly units and colors of the day. Ground units carried colored cloth panels to mark their positions. These panels were displayed in a different sequence each day. Thus, one day the panels might be displayed red, green, and yellow from front to back, the next day in a different order of colors.

The ground support mission assigned to the flight being briefed was next, followed by the code name of the controller, his map location, radio frequency, expected time of arrival of the flight and time on station with the forward air controller. This latter information involving an air controller was omitted if not pertinent.

Briefings were conducted by a team with the object of providing the pilots who would perform the mission with all information needed to accomplish their job and return safely without boggling their minds with superfluous details. Pilots needed to know what German air defenses they might encounter including new equipment and tactics. The air group's Intelligence Officer provided that information, he also provided them with escape information in case they might be shot down. The Weather Officer provided forecasts of cloud cover and visibility at the base, over the target and along route to and from the target. The Operations Officer filled in the details of mission; take off time, flight route, altitude, and time over target, approach, and other units in the air, ordnance and similar items. If the mission was in support of ground operations the Ground Liaison Officer was responsible for providing the pilots with all pertinent information for successful execution. Finally the mission leader provided his command, whether it was a six aircraft flight or a group operation involving sixty, his direction as to how they would accomplish their mission.

As soon as a flight left the briefing room the briefing team turned its attention to preparation for the next flight, which might or might not be assigned the same mission. In any case the Operations map had to be updated to reflect the current location of friendly and enemy forces. This information constantly changed and was reflected by a flow of Teletype messages. Every change in troop location triggered a change in the bomb line. In turn the constant updating of information required each briefing to be a new effort.

Our pilots flew P47s, Republic Thunderbolts, better known among pilots as "Bucket of Bolts" or "The Jug". The aircraft by the Pilots bragging version; "Weighed in at seven tons, five tons of it engine." and mounted eight fifty caliber machine guns on the forward edge of its wing. By the war's end it carried the reputation of being the premier fighter/bomber in the air. Depending on bomb load and other factors, the aircraft sustained flight for three to six hours. Missions varied from close support (most common) where in, a flight of four to eight planes would report to a forward controller at a given location and remain on station for a period of time and hit a target at the direction of the forward controller. If no target became available the flight might fly a prescribed road network looking for targets before dumping its ordnance on a bridge, suspected communication center or similar installation. Some missions were armed reconnaissance flights well forward of the bomb line, searching for targets of opportunity, without contact with a forward controller. Occasionally fighter sweeps looking for German aircraft or bomber escort missions were flown.

Within a period of two or three hours from departure the first planes would be back on the ground with pilots ready to be debriefed so their observations could be fed into the stream of intelligence currently being evaluated. In the interest of brevity messages were written in a short hand jargon unique to the Air/Ground Liaison system. Tanks became ARVE, trucks MET, horse and wagon HDT, motorcycle MC, bicycle BC, troops in the open TROP. Verbs were reduced; destroyed to des, damaged to dam and much more. A full report of a mission might fit on a three by five sheet from a standard army message pad. This information was sent directly to Army G3 Air by radio. Each liaison section had exclusive support of an Army short-wave radio station operated by a twelve-man crew around the clock. Message priority was to Army as long as combat reports remained to be filed. Maximum effort days kept the duty crew in motion from three hundred hours until twenty-two hundred hours, even with the off duty crew coming in to brief flights until the last flight was in the air. Then there were days that we were weathered in and didn't do diddly.

Air controllers were important members of the team. In the main they were pilots equipped with Air Force radios detailed to this duty on a temporary basis. Their job was to contact their compatriots overhead by radio as flights entered their jurisdiction, identify targets and visually direct the attacking planes to targets selected by ground commanders.

Pilots did not seek this duty, while it gave relief from air combat; it offered no respite from combat. They traveled with the advancing ground units; usually with artillery forward observer party or leading armored units. The experience was a great leveler for young pilots who had flown just enough successful combat missions to believe that they were the only ones fighting a war. They discovered that they were not winning it single handedly.

After a week or so of sleeping on the ground, ducking incoming artillery and occasionally dodging sniper fire they were glad to get back to flying airplanes and coming home to hot chow and a warm sack.

This air group was a veteran outfit that had fought its way across North Africa, up the Italian peninsula and helped breach Hitler's Fortress Europe through Southern France. Some of their staff and command personnel as well as a number of their ground crews were still in place. However, pilots and aircraft had been replaced several times.

They had begun their service flying Curtis P40s with a role of defeating the Luftwaffe and isolating the battlefield. As they succeeded in their work their role changed to one of keeping what remained of Jerry's air arm off the backs of the GIs and supplementing heavy artillery. P40s had shortcomings, their load carrying capacity was low and with in line liquid cooled engines they were vulnerable to ground fire.

Pilots soon overcame their distaste for the Thunderbolts' clumsier lines when they discovered that the aircraft could withstand having a cylinder or two knocked from their twenty-seven-cylinder engine and still fly.

True, a lot of oil and smoke would mark their flight path. Even if they didn't make it all the way home the ship could be bellied in. That chunk of metal up front in form of an engine would clear the way for the rest of the important parts of the plane, like pilot's seat/w pilot. One bullet in an inline liquid cooled engine could drain the coolant and freeze the engine then the plane ceased flying right now.

Flight characteristics of the Thunderbolt included a tighter turning radius than most of the German planes in service, An advantage that let P47 Pilots take enemy planes head on with eight fifty caliber machine guns while hiding behind the shield of a big engine. As the war wound down there was some envious talk about the sleeker, faster P51 Mustangs now entering service but pilots climbed in their old Bucket of Bolts and went off to the job of killing Germans and breaking up the countryside with reckless abandon confident that they were going to come home that night to eat at their own table and sleep in their own beds. Most did.

31

WWII'S LAST SHOT

As the war neared its end the 324th was within a half hours flight of Russian forces who when the opportunity presented itself fired on American planes. That added a new dimension to American objectives. Flak was easy to avoid, stay away from Russian ground positions. Russian Aircraft that showed fight were disposed of differently, "turn into 'em and take 'em on". Russians mainly broke off the engagement before shots were fired, those who didn't seldom survived, those who did soon convinced their fellows that planes with star markings were not easily intimidated. In deference to the tender sensibilities of our Russian Allies, pilots were not allowed to count or paint a scythe and sickle on their planes as an icon of victory over our Russian friends although some were claimed.

Returning from dinner at the U.S. Military Government open mess in Heidelberg one evening Tony and I tooled along the Autobahn, jeep lights ablaze as though we were on the Santa Monaco Freeway. We were jolted out of our reverie by a sustained burst of machine gun fire from overhead that kicked sparks out of the concrete as tracers ricocheted out of our light beam.

As the pilot shooting at us pulled out of his dive, Tony said; "Jesus, now what?" I said; "Let's go home." Tony turned off the jeep lights and floor boarded the go pedal giving me a thrill equal to that just received from Jerry. Or was it Ivan? Perhaps conscientious GI Joe enforcing blackout regulations? Who knows? He never came back and Tony drove the rest of the way home very carefully, using only his blackout lights for illumination.

Mid morning, sixth of May, Andy and I with feet propped on the window sill overlooking the airfield were in deep conversation about something important when a low rumble deepened into a roar driven by a shrieking wind punctuated by a steady paced thump of twin forty antiaircraft fire. A blurred plane, spouting fire from beneath its wings streaked past barely off the runway. We had seen our first jet aircraft. The pilot continued past the second forty millimeter gun emplacement, that also took him under fire much too late. He was nearly out of sight when he pulled up in a steep climb, reversed direction in a classic Immelmann, dropped, his wheels and flaps in the universally recognized signal of aircraft surrender and landed.

Several jeeps loaded with pilots pistols drawn, dashed down the runway intent on capturing an enemy pilot. They surrounded the plane as soon as the pilot cut his engine. He slid back the canopy and emerged from the cockpit hands first and elevated. By this time the word of the capture of a German plane had spread and a crowd gathered. About half (maintenance crews) swarmed over the plane and the rest nearly mobbed the pilot out of curiosity. In due time we learned that the plane was a Messerschmitt 209, the first operational jet plane in the German arsenal.

The pilot, a member of a squadron recently equipped and trained with ME209s had been engaged with the Russians on the Eastern Front, seized an opportunity to revisit his old training school and just incidentally surrender to Americans than Russians. After lunch and a lengthy interrogation including a minute examination of the plane conducted by the pilot, everyone repaired to the bar for a more intimate debriefing conducted by American pilots.

Interesting to watch due to personal demonstrations of simulated combat tactics and techniques that nearly demolished the place as the alcohol mists thickened. The next morning the Group Commander called Air Force Headquarters to notify them of his good fortune. Shortly an intelligence Officer, Military Police detail and crew of mechanics arrived to collect a shaken, badly hung over Prisoner of War and disassemble a valuable piece of loot for detailed examination.

On V.E. Day Major Andrew Sanders, the group Operations Officer, his assistant, Captain Steve Nemocek, Lieutenant Lloyd Martin and I were passing a bottle of sour mash bourbon back and forth in my barracks room. The bourbon had been carefully concealed for this occasion from my cohorts of the A/GLO school who accompanied me across the Atlantic and Europe. Obviously, if they had known I had it they would have drunk it. In the room above us a group of pilots were celebrating the same event in the same manner. They might have been a drink or two ahead of us. Over the more or less normal din someone loudly announced;" I've carried this S O B for the past six months and haven't fired it yet." "POW! POW! POW!" Three .45 caliber pistol rounds anointed us with plaster dust from the ceiling and dug into the floor, without touching nary a hair of a single head below. Indeed a fitting end of WWII.

32

WAGON LITS

Lieutenant Martin's TDY orders from the 45th Division were rescinded and Lloyd returned to his parent unit. Our Signal Corps radio station returned to their unit, Tony went back to 7th Army and suddenly I was the lone survivor of the 7th Army G 3 air section left with the 324th Fighter/Bomber Group U.S. Army Air Force. With no specific assignment and not a member of the organization for the next ten days I helped edit some of the group's historic files and became a regular passenger on flights to USO Rest and Recreation Centers in Paris, Brussels and London.

The Group acquired a B26 light bomber and a B25 medium bomber that they converted to passenger planes by removing their armament and installing seats in their bomb bays. Riding the nose gunner's station in either was a great way to enjoy Europe's Geography. It was wise to return to the main cabin before the pilot began the approach and lowered the plane's landing gear. On both planes the nose wheel came down through the crawlway to the nose gunner's station. The only way out of the plane on the ground was by lifting the planes Plexiglas nose cone, something that had to be done from the outside. One experience of the ground approaching at a hundred and sixty miles an hour lasted a lifetime.

The old part of Paris featuring winding streets and ancient buildings with buttressed stonewalls had an unusual artifact of its liberation by the Americans. On a street that narrowed to a passage barely accommodating two very close pedestrians an American jeep had entered the gap at rate of speed sufficient to ride up the buttressed walls on both sides and wedge fast with its wheels about five feet above the pavement. Pedestrians were forced to stoop to a GI's confidence in his vehicles ability to surmount obstacles.

The 324th's flight schedule limited my travel options. I had to check at least once a day with the message center for instructions from my bosses at 7th Army Headquarters. I could fly to any of the three cities and return the next day or I could fly to Paris and return the same day, so I tried all four but ran out of options before completing a full cycle.

During this period the Airfield at Sandhoffen took on the appearance of a cross between a used car lot and a Storch Rookery. Storch may be a German spelling of stork, no matter since it was the nomenclature of the Luftwaffe's light single engine reconnaissance plane. Storches sported an exceptionally long wooden propeller that forced its maker to equip the plane with a very high fixed landing gear that gave this bird a passing resemblance to a stork about to touch his feet to Mother Earth.

International Law gave conquering commanders authority to confiscate military equipment for use of his command. Pilot's creative interpretation of the Geneva Accord assumed this fiat delegated them authority to collect Storches and ground crews to collect Daimlers and Mercedes. After all, Nazis who wore military uniforms exclusively used all the latter two, ordinary Germans had cool Volkswagons.

Tragedy struck In the midst of this collection frenzy. The group commander collected an American Red Cross Girl; at least it seemed that was the case. He was very possessive and they seldom were seen apart. A great deal of their time was spent touring. One of their expeditions took them into the Free French Army Sector just to the south of us. A French Colonial unit recruited in Algeria occupied it. They passed through a checkpoint without stopping obvious of the sentry's challenge. The sentry shot and killed the twenty-six years old Colonel, an Ace who had survived over a hundred combat missions.

On return to Army Headquarters Jocko Graves and I were assigned as booking agents for a squadron of L5s (two seat recon planes used as artillery spotters during combat) augmented by about a dozen Storches. That job didn't last long, Major Innes, The C.O. could handle all those details, thank you, and we became tour guides, We were Escort Officers in correct military terms. Our charges varied from groups of rear echelon GIs to stateside VIPs intent on sharing the fruits of victory. Tour stops included Garmisch-Partenkirchen where the Tenth Division had taken over the ski resort; Oberammergau the site of the Passion play; Berchtesgarden Hitler's Eagles Nest; Dachau's infamous concentration camp; Innsbruck; Alpine resort city and Munich scene of Hitlers take over of the Nazi party. GIs were easy to get along with. They were looking for stories to take home to their friends and neighbors. Above all none had any desire to be left behind; they might miss their rotation ticket. VIPs were more of a problem. Some were looking for a little extra in the way of entertainment and what they were looking for, at the worst could get your throat cut and the best court marshaled if caught.

Not all Germans were convinced that they had lost the war. That attitude changed with time, until it did some mean tricks surfaced. Land mines appeared where none had been before, jeeps drove away leaving a puddle of oil on the pavement below where they had been parked or mysteriously exploded when started.

One of the most popular and nastiest was a strand of number nine wire between two trees on opposite sides of forest roads where jeeps driven in a battle ready mode with windshields down, might pass. The wire strung at a height of a few inches above the top of a jeeps steering wheel decapitated passengers and drivers of jeeps. GIs countered by welding a length of angle iron with notched upper end to the front bumper.

The kids were the first to accept reality. When GIs first encountered German children the kids either ran or stood and stared ready to flee. Not long after the war ended the kinder discovered GIs to be a source of chewing gum, candy and cigarettes then peace began to settle in.

It was most surprising, our forces must have killed, captured or driven all the Nazis out of Germany because none were visible and no German would admit to ever seeing one. They must have passed through, though, there were some jack-boots and armbands with swastikas left by former occupants in the apartment Jocko and I occupied in Augsberg.

Rumor had it that GLOs were in short supply in the Pacific and those in Europe who were recent arrivals would ship through the Suez Canal to ply their trade in the Philippines or other approaches to Japan. Jocko and I talked it over and decided that while we didn't object and couldn't do anything about the prospect if we did, it would be nice to stop in the United States on the way. The 44th Division in Prien Austria had orders to depart for the States, retrain in preparation to be part of First Army that would stage through Hawaii. We requested and received permission to visit Prien for the purpose of negotiating a transfer. Our quest succeeded and we had barely time to return to Augsberg, pick up orders, pack and return to Prien catch the Division and pass through Augsberg en route to Calais via Mannerheim. The journey was an epic.

Orders preceded me and I arrived to find myself commanding E Company 114th Infantry of the 44th Division commanded by Major General Dean. The general later commanded the American 25th Division at the outbreak of the War in Korea. His successful withdrawal of American forces the length of the Korean Peninsula enabled United Nations forces to defend the port city of Pusan was regarded as a classic retrograde maneuver. He successfully led the 44th out of

Europe but it is doubtful that this exercise was studied at U.S. army service schools, as was the case of that of the 25th.

The first stage by truck to Mannheim was routine for the 2nd Battalion of the 114th Infantry, except for an overnight stop near Heilbronn. Two members of Headquarters Company, in the closing days of the war had taken momentary refuge beside a Reichsbank in an unnamed town to escape artillery fire.

The bank was hit and the pair working on unrefuted GI dogma that artillery never lands twice in the same spot moved their safe haven into the ruined bank and found the bank's vault open.

They stuffed their uniforms with valid Reichsmarks before leaving and now were faced with the dilemma of spending several thousand of dollars of German currency that no U.S.Army finance office would accept. The black market was too risky so they treated the Battalion to a huge party. Accomplished without the knowledge of the Battalion Commander or any of his subordinates by bribing the local Burgomaster to host the party as goodwill gesture. It helped that the bribe doubled if the Battalion Commander was kept in the dark about financial details. The full story became known about the time the two conspirators received their "Ruptured Ducks" with honorable discharges at Camp Chaffee Arkansas.

At Ludwishaven, Mannerhiem's twin on the east bank of the Rhine the Battalion boarded a train for Saarbrucken where the German train was traded for a French narrow gauge version of a mixture of WWI "Forty and Eights" and third class coaches.

The French for reasons only known to the French had declined to adapt their railroads to the European standard rail system. Neither did they adapt to the standard automatic coupling system instead they secured one car to the next by parallel three foot lengths of chain bolted to the rear of each car and hooked to the front of the following car.

To prevent the cars from colliding when the engine slowed each car had a pair of spring loaded bumpers on each end that engaged similar bumpers on the adjacent car. In theory train crews would snug up the connecting chains so bumpers would be tight against each other to keep jolting at a minimum during stops and starts. In practice they hooked up in the last link to guaranty a maximum of jolting.

Third class coaches had seats, unupholstered wooden seats but seats. "Forty and Eights" gained their name from WWI Doughboys because these boxcars were routinely loaded with forty men or eight horses interchangeably; sometimes they were cleaned between changes. Fortunately the 2nd Battalion 114th Infantry was without horses. We used them for baggage and kitchens.

The locomotive was steam driven with a top speed of about twenty miles an hour and it seemed that the train crew had business connections in every town and village they passed through. They stopped and disappeared in each for at least a half hour. In all it took two days, stops included, to make a trip of some thing less than three hundred miles. As the train gained earshot of a village the engineer laid on the whistle cord for one long toot. At the outskirts of the village he repeated the signal.

Reaching the station he stopped the train; that is he stopped the engine. Each car closed the slack in their connecting chain and collided with the next forward car. When the length of the train was fully compressed the tension on the bumper springs reversed the movement and sent each car to the length of its bumper chains.

By the time the cars stopped yo-yoing the crew had disappeared. Train and occupants were under siege by twin armies of kids and entrepreneurs. Kids caging "choc-o-let, chewing gum and cigarettes". Entrepreneurs buying any thing GIs would sell for the black market.

That continued until the train crew returned and the engineer blew a short toot on the whistle followed in five minutes by a long blast, two minutes later two short toots and the train began to move, slowly, ever so slowly. Kids and entrepreneurs redoubled their sales pitch running along the tracks with the moving train until the train gained enough speed to outdistance its pursuers.

By the third stop the GIs had this figured out, they sold their shoes to the black marketers who knotted the laces and draped newly acquired bounty around their necks as an easy means of transporting their loot. Boots brought five to ten times the paying price on France's thriving Black Market.

As the train began to move squads of GIs wearing make shift MP arm bands jumped off the train stripped the Frenchmen of their garlands of boots, threw the boots back on the train willy nilly and climbed back on the train. This exercise continued several times before the Battalion's officers could regain control of the train's passengers.

After a week the Division closed in on Calais to ship across the Channel to England. Two weeks later in England the Division traveled by train north across England to Scotland and the Firth of Clyde where they embarked on the Queen Elizabeth for a hot bunk trip to the United States and home. All members received delay en route orders, with train reservations through their hometowns, destination Camp Chaffee. We were at home when the Japanese surrendered.

33

HOME SWEET HOME

Troops returning to the Division from their brief respite at home found a changed organization. General Dean and many of the senior officers had moved on to other assignments. Those remaining officers who were regular army or wannabes turned fishermen and were busy casting their lines into the sea of opportunity.

As one of the latter I had a strike on my first cast. The US Army Air Force, soon to be the U.S. Air Force, the Marine Corps and The Navy were establishing a joint Air/Ground Liaison school at Coronado Marine Air Base in San Diego California. The pentagon was searching for qualified instructors. I qualified and applied for a transfer without bothering to ask for clearance from the 114th Infantry regiment.

In due time a letter order from the Pentagon hit regimental headquarters not long after that I was standing tall in front of the regimental commander. For the second time I had hooked a snag in the form of a Lieutenant Colonel who had an earlier Regular Army date of commission than General Eisenhower.

My hook was deeply embedded in his prerogatives. We had a discussion during which we each stated strongly held positions. His was that no civilian posing as an officer in the Army of the United States who ignored long standing United States Army protocol of contacting higher headquarters without his commander's permission would escape his jurisdiction as long as he could prevent it. Mine was that if I could not transfer out from under his command he could take his United States Army's protocol AND tradition and shove it. I had a hundred and thirty-five points toward discharge and needed only eighty-five for mandatory release. He could not by God stop me. We parted in agreement and I began the separation process the following day.

At the separation center I ran into a Captain Frank Bland whose father owned the Oldsmobile dealership in Lexington KY. Just to guarantee that Frank would return from the war in one piece he stored the last sedan he received at the beginning of the war for him. Frank picked the car up while home on leave. Lexington was closer to Norwalk than Fort Smith Arkansas so I accepted Frank's invitation to ride that far with him. Frank was in no hurry. We wandered around a bit and took a mite longer to reach Lexington than planned. From Lexington, I caught a bus to Cleveland Ohio where Betty picked me up some four days later than she planned. In spite of the date being late August the ride from Cleveland to Norwalk was decidedly chilly.

Tom Battles arrived home about the same time, just a few days before his father died. After the funeral guests had departed Tom and his mother, better known by Tom's friends as "Mother B", decided to put memories in their proper niche. A trip to their camp in the Quebec woods would be appropriate for that task. They asked Betty and me to go along. We accepted and after a long and arduous trip spent the next three weeks relaxing in the Canadian bush.

34

DEJU VU

Soon after our return from Canada Betty and I moved to my parents' old home in Milan Ohio. There we remained until the fall of nineteen-fifty-one. During this period our daughter Bette Alice and son Tod were born. I went to work for the Ohio Division of Wildlife as a county game protector and learned to fly. I rejoined my former battalion commander LTC Russell Ramsey now Major General Russell Ramsey CG 83rd Infantry Division, USAR as his G-3 Air then resigned to join the 37th Infantry Division when it was reactivated as part of the Ohio National Guard.

There as executive officer of the 2nd Bn 145th Inf. I was reunited with many of my wartime compatriots including Bill Morr who now was my battalion commander. Our best efforts failed to recruit Ralph "Ripper" Riley. Who was basking in the glory as a surviving warrior.

The mix of duties, responsibilities, public relations and independence of my job suited me well. By the end of the period I was Supervisor of the Lake Erie District of the Ohio Division of Wildlife. Betty and I also cultivated a whole new coterie of friends, virtually all veterans and their spouses. Between a state job, part time soldier, part time farmer there still was time for play.

Clouds gathered on our horizon in 1950 when the North Koreans crossed the thirty-eighth parallel and drove the South Koreans and our occupation forces into a small enclave surrounding Pusan on the southern tip of the peninsula. National Guard training took on a new urgency and the conventional wisdom among Veteran members of the guard was that we soon would be wearing army green full time.

A year later this peacetime phase of my life came full cycle. I was in Quebec, fishing on a lake having killed a moose the day before. A floatplane circled my canoe, landed and taxied over to me. The pilot leaned out of the cockpit window and shouted; "Is your name Morrow?" then to my admission, "Your wife called

Garfield Jones in Kipewa and said that you are back in the Army and have to report to Fort Benning on Sunday."

In preparation for returning to active duty with the 37th Division I had applied for TIS advanced course in August. By September I had given up hope of being accepted. Agreed to join friends on a moose hunting trip in Canada. Now early in October we were there. Garfield Jones was the outfitter in Kipewa who had arranged our party's moose hunt. This was Friday. Kipewa Quebec is maybe two thousand miles due north of Columbus Georgia as a crow flies and there were no crows flying south that day.

The pilot agreed to return the next day and fly me out to North Bay Ontario where I might make commercial connections south. By seven the following morning we were airborne, an hour and a half later in North Bay I caught a bus for Toronto Ontario. Then I caught a plane for Cleveland Ohio, arriving too late to make connections for Columbus Georgia. Betty met me at the airport and we returned home with reservations for a flight the following day. I arrived at TIS after duty hours Monday with Quebec hunting license in hand to prove my alibi and found the opening date for my class moved to Wednesday.

The Infantry School in 1951 was Deja Vu all over again, once more a second lieutenant lecturing on Military Law surveyed the sea of balding heads, graying temples and gold adorned collars facing him and announced; "Undoubtedly there are hundreds of officers in the United States Army who know more about Military Law than I do" paused, scanned his audience, and continued; "But I don't see any of them here. Gentlemen shall we get on with the business at hand?"

Coats Brown was back assigned to the Rifle Committee only now he was a Warrant Officer Senior Grade and we could talk as equals. As a Major, I had moved up a step on TIS status scale, I was enrolled in the Senior Officers course better known at the school as the metallic class; Gold on their collars, Iron in their skulls and Lead in their butts.

The map course was still mandatory and some of my classmates were lost on the night exercise. This time no wild horsewoman rode through a crowd of senior officer waiting to load a bus for their next instruction site. The "Mad Minute" and "River Crossing" demonstrations were still there but no longer awe inspiring.

This time the best remembered event was a Chemical Warfare class wherein the practical exercise included a requirement that each class member inject himself with a syringe of simulated nerve gas antidote, actually distilled water.

The approved procedure was to grasp the package needle end extending from the little finger side of the right fist, remove the cover and jam the needle into ones thigh with a quick blow injecting the antidote. A relatively painless process if executed forcibly. This was a voluntary exercise and professional pride was a powerful incentive to participate. The antics of the squeamish to avoid the trauma of this apparent self-wounding disrupted the class in hilarious uproar.

A common maneuver was to ignore the prescribed procedure, remove the syringe's cover and grasp with thumb and fore finger at the tip of the reservoir and attempt to gently push the needle through the fabric of the pants leg into the flesh below while averting ones eyes from this scene of horror. This technique never worked the soft reservoir buckled invariably squirting the water down the victims pant's leg. Ten years earlier TIS had been adventure now it was a review of history.

Off Post life too, had changed. No longer was Betty courted by local belles because; "You can get us into the Officer's Club where all those single Lieutenants are, can't you, dear?" No more Johnny Norris, Pat Patterson, Rip Russell and their wives to party with. No more chaperoning seashore weekends. It was hard to accept but time had caught up with us. By Army standards we were on the threshold of middle age. We were a stodgy major and wife with a pair of rug rats.

Those facts became obvious shortly after Betty arrived at Fort Benning. However we had Bill and Anne Sulcebarger to commiserate with. They too were from Ohio and would join the 37th Division at Camp Polk on completion of school. Bill's and my paths had crossed during WWII.

Betty, almost four-year-old Bette Alice ("Kay"), three months old Tod, our Irish Setter Mickey Finn and close family friend Helen Livengood, joined me in early November. Like all good Army wives Betty had closed our home in Milan Ohio to set up temporary residence in Columbus Georgia without the foggiest notion of what fate had in store for her.

We had reservations at the post kennels for Mickey Finn and at the Officers Club Guest House for the rest of us. The first evening we were together at Fort Benning we dined at the Officer's Club. We had been seated in the dining room only a short time when an elderly retired Colonel (?) General (?) and wife wearing a fox fur entered the room and were seated by the Maitre'D at table in Kay's full view. The lady removed and fluffed out her fur as she draped it over her chair. Kay watched the performance intently. When the lady was seated, in a moment that the dining room was absolutely silent, Kay with all the four year old wisdom and knowledge of my civilian occupation as a wildlife specialist announced in a voice that penetrated the room; "Look Daddy, that lady has a coon." Silence reigned and before I could react the lady and her escort got up and departed, noses held high. As they left a captain at the next table to ours leaned toward us and said; "That's what I thought."

Before our five day limit expired at the Officer's Club Betty found an opening in a wartime housing project in Columbus and we moved into a furnished (not too well) row house in the middle of a block. Helen flew home.

The project was organized in blocks with similar rows of houses on all four sides of the block. Each unit had an identical narrow porch in front and was occupied by the family of a soldier assigned to Fort Benning. It behooved residents to memorize their streets and house numbers, otherwise one might find himself knocking on doors inquiring where he lived. Back doors opened out on a not very grassy common, owned by the neighborhood kids. Soldiers are a prolific lot so there were a lot of kids. Our unit was in the middle of a block.

The first Saturday of our occupancy we were sitting down to a late breakfast when a knock on the front door prompted me to open the front door and about a dozen kids, all Kay's cohorts filed through the house and out the back door. Kay wiggled out of her chair and fell in on the rear of the file. That's when we learned that we had rented the short cut to the playground.

When Christmas break came we stashed our kids with the lady who ran the post nursery, Mickey Finn joined the pack at the post kennels and I took a short leave to drive to Camp Polk. En route we stopped at Weidman's in Meridian Mississippi for lunch. Hienkel was still there, a little grayer but claimed to still remember us. We took his word for it even though his recollection of past events didn't always match ours.

At Camp Polk we had a choice of house hunting in Leesville or Deridder we chose the latter. Actually it was more like house selection, LTC Erwin Hostetler, 3rd. Bn. 145th. Inf. had earlier in the fall made a trip to Louisiana and reserved a block of homes being built on the Twin Lakes Housing development in Deridder. My Regimental and Battalion Commanders, COL Sylvester DelCorso and LTC Bill Morr respectively, had written and said; "pick me out a house, too." We contacted the developer, selected three houses in a row and returned to Fort Benning, visiting New Orleans and Mobile Alabama on the way home, in time to pick Kay and Tod up on the morning before the nursery closed for the New Years Eve Holiday. This wound down for us and we moved into a second tour of extended active duty.

35

POLIO

After a short leave back home in Milan Ohio we purchased some furniture collected the rest of our belongings and had the Army ship it to our new home in Deridder Louisiana. That is what we thought would happen. When we arrived our "New Home" was an impressive stand of two-by-fours. Bill and Ethel Moor made the same discovery a week or so before and rented an apartment. They put us up for a few days until the local hotel could make room for us. The Army diverted our chattels to the Quartermaster warehouse at Camp Polk. We joined the 37th Division's third tour of Federal Service in the Twentieth Century.

All high hopes for extended service with the division were shattered on April 17 1951 when General Mark Clark Fourth Army Commander visited Camp Polk and let us in on a little Pentagon secret. They really weren't much interested in the 37th as a Combat Division but they were in dire need of the bodies of the thirty one hundred officers and men, many seasoned veterans of WWII to keep an individual replacement rotation system afloat.

Under political pressure, it had been ordained from on high that every soldier's exposure to combat should be limited to one year. The first year of "the Korean Police Action" had long since passed and the Army was running out of bodies. A little later it was discovered that the replacement training centers were unable to keep up with the demand for overseas replacements and the replacements that had taken the place of the Ohio Guardsmen became replacement trainers under a different name and the division became sort of a hybrid. While its designation remained unchanged the mission of training replacements in military basics was added while serving a reservoir for the combat replacement system.

The transition moved slowly. The division was brought to full strength by an influx of Korean vets, reserve and OCS junior officers, specialist school graduates and duty soldiers not yet moved into the replacement pipeline. Initially overseas order arrivals were sparse and by early September the Division had completed a training cycle through division tests.

More than the original division enlisted strength had been levied and there had been nearly a complete turnover of company grade officers. My overseas orders arrived in early October. In the interim I commanded the 2nd Battalion 145th Infantry off and on, trained and coached the Camp Polk Rifle Team winning the Fourth Army Rifle Team Match at Fort Hood, TX.

Early on before the hiatus of officers for Korea began to play, Division Headquarters received word that Colonel Temple G. Holland, Assistant G-3 Fourth Army would visit the division to survey the state of the division's training. Colonel Temple G. Holland had commanded the 145th Infantry during the New Georgia campaign and not conducted himself well in the eyes of his command. In compliance with normal protocol, General Kreber, the Division Commanding General, hosted a reception for Colonel Holland at Division Officer's Open Mess on the evening of his arrival. Declinations from the 145th Infantry outnumbered acceptances from all field grade vets to zip. Colonel Holland returned to Fourth Army Headquarters the following morning without completing his survey.

On Memorial Day weekend Betty and I packed the kids, some food and headed for Port Arthur, TX and the Gulf coast. Betty had been feeling a bit queasy for about week; she assumed that she must be pregnant, naturally. By the time we reached the Gulf she was definitely sick. We found a place to stay and put in for the night, the salt-water shower didn't give her much relief. Before morning she was really sick and ached in every bone of her body. At first light we packed up and headed home virtually nonstop and put her to bed.

Next morning Bill Moor stopped by to pick me up for work (we car pooled). I yelled out the bedroom window; "Betty's really sick I think she has Polio I'm going to drop her off at the hospital." I left the kids next door with Phoebe Buergel, wife of M/Sgt Günter Buergel, 37th Div Hq. Loaded Betty in the car and left for Camp Polk.

We checked into the hospital during sick call in progress and got Betty into a wheel chair. We waited for something to happen. Nothing happened so I went to the head of the line and asked the nurse in charge very plainly and loudly too; "My wife has every symptom of polio are you going to take her into the examining room or do I?" We both did.

Several doctors looked, listened, poked, questioned her, confirmed what I already knew, loaded her on a gurney and sent her up to the polio ward where she began treatment and was finally released some three months later, to complete her recovery from a severe case of Muscular Polio.

Lieutenant Roy Miller, one of the Platoon Leaders in H Company and his wife Carol a few days after Betty was admitted to the hospital volunteered to take care of our two children. They moved into our house in Deridder and I moved into the regiment's Bachelor Officers Quarters. From then until early September when Betty was discharged from the hospital I spent my free evenings and weekends either with our kids or Betty.

Children were not allowed to visit patients in the Polio ward because of the danger of contracting the virulent disease. Weekends I would bring Kay and Tod out to the hospital grounds so they could at least see their mother. She would have an attendant wheel her bed to the window so she and the kids could wave at each other.

Early on the hospital decided to send Betty to Fort Sam Houston for rehabilitation and she refused opting to suffer through the physical therapy available at the Camp Polk Hospital so she could see her babies once in a while. The hospital allowed visits between twelve and thirteen-thirty on Wednesdays and Sundays, provided, I scrub before and after, wear a surgical mask, sterile gown and booties during each fifteen-minute visit. The command was generous with my time. We saw each other often, as the hospital would allow. Kay and Tod saw their mother from a distance more frequently.

Carol Miller and neighbors Phoebe Buergel, Ethel Morr and Emmy Lou Del Corso saw to that. They took turns bringing the two youngsters out to wave at Mom in the Hospital window. Just before Betty was discharged from the hospital the management at Twin Lakes Housing Development listened to my plea for a larger house and let the Millers and me move into a three-bedroom home to welcome Betty's return but the Millers did not stay long. Roy shipped out to Korea and Carol returned to Warren, Ohio.

During Betty's hospital stay military duty went on. Again the past caught up with me and I trained the Post rifle team for participation in the Fourth Army matches. During our pre-match practice and tryouts Post Headquarters furnished us a pit detail out of the stockade. The detail consisted of a Lieutenant and Sergeant, from the Provost Marshal's Detachment, both armed and twelve residents of the stockade, unarmed and wearing old style blue denim fatigues with yellow "P"s on their back.

Two were telephone operators, the other ten target pullers; all twelve were allergic to work. The first day went well target service was no better or worse than run of the mill service from duty soldiers. Toward the end of the day as I stood near the telephone operator he said, out of the side of his mouth; "Give us a bad report" I ignored him.

The second day was a disaster nothing went right and I gave the detail a very bad report. The third day we had a new detail and good service and I gave them a bad report, same thing the fourth day. The fifth day the original detail was back and the telephone operator, out of the side of his mouth, said to me "See, Major."

A member of the Camp Polk Rifle team was Lt. Trumbull, an Afro-American. The Army during at the end of WWII had been fully integrated. It never crossed my mind that Trumbull's presence on the squad would cause any problems but it did, not with the members of the squad or during the competition but at our first lunch stop in Texas.

We were traveling in an OD government sedan and carryall and were refused service at the roadside "Truck Stop" or rather Trumbull was. I was all for making an issue of the matter but Trumbull said; "No Major, let me take the sedan I can take care of myself, I'll be back in a little bit and pick you up." I said; "We'll go with you." "Major," Trumbull replied; "let it go, you're fixing to get us all thrown in jail." I accepted his advice both going and coming. Texas is a mighty big state and I wasn't the first Yankee to use discretion in place of valor, anyhow we stayed out of jail.

Back with the Regiment, one noon LTC Bill Morr, CPT Tiny Covert, CPT Paul Malarkey and I were seated at a folding field table in the shade of a tent fly eating lunch in the field. I noticed a small (twenty four inch) timber rattlesnake writhing his way between Malarkey's feet under the table towards me. I did what any experienced former conservation officer would do in a like situation, I pulled the .22 caliber pistol loaded with bird shot I carried in lieu of a service pistol and shot the bastard.

I still do not comprehend the uproar from my messmates. They overturned the table spilling food and yelled at me; "Don't you know you might have hit one of us?" after all I was and am a good pistol shot. That little Timber Rattle Snake wasn't more than three feet from the muzzle of the pistol and I could clearly read the intent in his eyes to bite someone, besides I carried that pistol to kill snakes.

Second Lieutenant Snyder in the same training area on a different day elbowed his way through a circle of GIs surrounding an equally small Timber Rattler they were teasing with a stick to get him to strike. Eyeing the situation he said; "Here, I'll show you how to make him strike" and thrust his fore finger toward the snake. He was right. When his finger came close enough the snake struck and left Snyder standing with a snake dangling from a forefinger hooked by his fangs.

Early in August the Division took to the field for Army conducted Combat Readiness evaluation and passed it with flying colors, this was before CPT Paul Malarkey and I nearly scuttled the exercise and then received a Meritorious Mention for a tactical deployment. At the moment I was in command of the 2nd. Bn. 145th Inf and Malarky was the Battalion Operations Officer. Malarky, incidentally, was the person who had told me of the incident of two GIs in waning weeks of the WWII waving a much disliked colonel through a check point into the hands of German outpost.

According to the exercise scenario our battalion was the 145th's reserve Malarky and I were called forward for a briefing on the exercise's scenario. An umpire's jeep pulled up and a mean looking Colonel wearing an umpire's armband debarked. Malarky groaned and said; "Here comes trouble, that's old Roaring Rosy who the Germans captured and we made the mistake of capturing back." Paul was edging behind my back out of sight. The Colonel looked the assembled group of officers over with obvious disdain and proceeded with the briefing. He concluded it by pointing out the initial location of the various combat elements on a map spread out on the hood of his jeep. When Malarky and I stepped up to the map he fixed Malarky with a cold stare without as much as acknowledging Paul's presence and said; "Major, put your Battalion right there", and ground his thumb down on the map as though crushing an errant ant, nearly rubbing the markings of a cross road and surrounding several hundred acres of terrain off the map. I said "Yes, sir" and departed.

Malarky left for the crossroads to select an assembly area. When I arrived with the Battalion he waved us into a wooded area adjacent to the cross roads we organized the assembly area and sent the trucks to be gassed up. When they returned they rejoined their passengers hidden among the trees. In the morning, as soon as the troops were fed they would load their gear, clean up their campsites and stand by to load trucks and move out when ordered without delay.

The next morning the regimental commander called his Battalion commanders forward to receive orders. Malarkey and I arrived at the designated location and were shooting the breeze with other unit commanders and staffs. A small grass fire had started and members of regimental headquarters company had it pretty well under control and were letting it burn out as it burned toward a bare spot. Colonel "Roaring Rosy" drove up, stopped in front of the group and said; "Major, get your men on that fire and put it out." I didn't say anything. Neither did any one else including two or three other Majors in the group nor the Captain commanding Headquarters Company whose men had the fire under control.

Colonel Del Corso arrived and issued his attack order. The 2nd. Battalion's mission was to flank the "enemy's" position and occupy a piece of dominant terrain. When I got back to the assembly area all the Company Commanders were waiting and it took about ten minutes to give them their orders and be under way. We arrived at our destination with the "fustest and mostest" seized our objective throwing the "enemy" into confusion and gained high marks for the 145th Infantry.

Later our regimental commander Colonel Del Corso asked me; "What did you do to upset that old buzzard? He told me he wanted you relieved because he gave you a direct order and you just looked at him and didn't do anything, not only that he couldn't find you or your outfit when he went to check on your assembly area. He paused to let me sweat a little and added; "I told him that I would decide when and which of my officers would be relieved."

At the conclusion of the 37th Division's Combat Readiness Evaluation the Division was designated a training division and the 148th. Infantry Regiment the division's Training Command. In the shuffle I was sent on Temporary Duty (TDY) to the Training Command as Chief of the Weapons Committee. I left the Division in December after we had completed the organizational phase and was in full swing of training replacements.

In December, on the day I cleared the Post to return our family to Ohio for the duration of my tour in Korea Tod came down with measles. Not at all surprising, fifteen month old kids do things like that. Betty's phone call caught me at the regimental dispensary. Captain Bill Blank the Regimental Surgeon and Twin Lakes neighbor said; "Give him this medicine as directed, keep him warm and don't waste any time in getting to Ohio." He neglected to tell me to push Tod's water consumption or perhaps he did and it didn't register with me.

Anyhow, I cleared post in record time and returned home to rig a piece of ply board across the rear seat of our sedan to support the mattress from Tod's crib. In the foot well on the left side of the car, under the platform we stowed Tod's necessities, the right well was reserved as our Irish setter, Mickey Finn's travel kennel. The following morning, car packed, loaded and Tod wearing a night gown with the bottom pinned shut to discourage locomotion we departed. The trip lasted three days and two nights. We were very careful to stop at motels well away from the Office and not to mention that we were transporting a measly kid and a red dog. Tod slept virtually all the way, ate and drank very little. Kay was especially cooperative for a five year old and poor Mickey Finn who had to back into his space never complained once during the trip

36

BON VOYAGE

We hurried Tod to the doctors upon arrival in Norwalk and were severely reprimanded by Mush Patrick the doctor and Tod's grandmother for letting Tod become dehydrated. Tod didn't complain, though, and soon recovered while we were being properly contrite.

The first order of business was to find a place to live. Old friends Peck and Jane Andrews from Ohio Division of Wildlife days had rented our farmhouse and Betty really preferred a more urban setting to weather our forced separation. Fortunately we bought a house in Norwalk just in time to receive our household goods from Camp Polk, courtesy of US Army.

It didn't take long to pick up where we left off with the same crowd a year earlier. As soon as our presence was noticed the Wednesday lunch bunch decided it was their patriotic duty to celebrate my departure. It was indeed a gala affair.

This party shortly after the first of January, 1954 preceded our departure from Gene and Marge Morris' home in Huron Ohio for the Cleveland airport and a flight to San Francisco. Our escort consisted of the Morris' who deserted the caravan after the second stop, Dr. J. Wilson a local dentist and wife Marty and my cousin Bud and his wife Dorothy. The latter pair was along in our family's interest and the former to make certain that I actually left the country. The day was still young, the pace leisurely because we stopped at several watering holes en route.

The receptionist at the airline check-in counter declined to honor my reservation on the grounds that I was a disaster waiting to happen. After appealing the decision to the highest airline authority and pleading dire danger of the army's collapse unless they were reinforced post haste with one battle hardened major we compromised and I accepted a later flight the following morning.

The trip west to San Francisco was much more comfortable, faster, than the troop train excursion of some eleven years earlier. Then too, this time I wasn't worrying about what Betty was going to do with a heavy-duty meat grinder and a five-gallon pan of chow mien.

Two old friends, Majors Fred Pincombe and Ken Norton were at the port of Embarkation waiting to board ship in the morning. Fred had been the 145th Infantry's S-3 at Camp Polk and Ken I knew from pre WW II National Guard days.

The following day we boarded the USS West Point operated by the Army's Transportation Corps, the same ship I had returned on from the Solomon Islands in 1944. We three majors were assigned a cabin on the ship's promenade deck. The troop commander for the voyage LCOL George Maliszeski occupied a cabin on the sun deck with the ship's officers and ate at the Captain's table. We with other transient Army officer were served with the ship's officers. Not that it mattered. except for a half hour conversation with the Colonel when I reported as his deputy I didn't set eye on him again until after reporting to 7th Infantry headquarters in Korea for assignment.

He made it clear that during the voyage that he was not to be bothered with any of the administrative burdens of troop commander and he was not. Twelve uneventful days later we dropped anchor in Tokyo Bay. After two days in the transient officer's quarters of Eighth Army Headquarters in Tokyo, Ken and I left by Japanese high-speed rail to Kobe where we boarded ship for Inchon. Pinky did not come along; he was assigned to Eighth Army headquarters in Tokyo.

At Inchon, our orders were to join the 7th Infantry Division in the vicinity of Yonchon Korea. The three hundred mile trip to Kobe lasted about four hours. Two and a half days later we were anchored off Inchon waiting for the tide to come in so lighters could navigate the channel to put us ashore. The stench of the tidal flats was horrific. The following morning the flats were covered with water. We loaded barges and followed several miles of winding channel through flats that smelled just as bad under water as they had out of water the night before.

As a matter of fact the smell of Korea took a while to get used to. Municipal waste disposal systems consisted of a brigade of "honey" wagons. Some were pulled by horses, oxen or both, others by man (or women) power. All made rounds of residential areas nightly collecting "night soil" from benjos (toilets) for garden fertilizer. Koreans grew beautiful fruit and vegetables that were almost certain to send any foreigner who had the misfortune to consume, handle or otherwise remotely come in contact with, to the hospital with dysentery, hepatitis or other intestinal disease. The sights, sounds and smells of Korea were a new experience as were the people, their culture and this war called "Police Action".

The island hopping campaigns of the South Pacific Theater of WW II had been a series of ferocious and bloody assaults on isolated islands with virtually no resident population to consider. Our enemies the Japanese were determined, tenacious, inured to hardship and implacable in the spirit of sacrifice to their cause. Surrender was not in their vocabulary. In the dense Solomon Island jungles Americans gave the night to the enemy and mopped up Japanese gains by day.

The waning days of WW II in southern France and Germany was a classic conduct of the pursuit of a modern but defeated enemy. The pursuit was over a devastated, heavily populated fertile countryside. The modern infrastructure and massive stone built cities were reduced to rubble the objective was to destroy the enemy's will and ability ever again to wage war against the Allies.

Korea was a purely political war over a mountainous peninsula populated by a people with an agrarian culture that had changed little since the eighth century. At the end of WWII the country had been parceled into Communist Peoples Republic in the north half of the peninsula and a south Republic of Korea. The war began in June of 1950 with the North invading the South to drive South Korean and American forces to Pusan. An allied counter offensive swept the North Koreans back to the Yalu river boundary with China. There the Chinese joined the North Koreans driving the American and Republic of Korea forces back to its starting point at the 38th parallel. By 1953 the war was a stalemate as the two sides haggled over a truce agreement.

From the beginning the United States had been a participant with the Republic of Korea against the Soviet trained forces of North Korea. Under pressure from the United States, the United Nations sanctioned participation of member nations on the side of South Korea. Many U.S. WWII Allies sent at least token forces and at the end of the war's northward surge China joined the North Koreans and the war became one between Koreans and Chinese against Koreans, Americans and Allies. On the North side North Korean and Chinese Divisions were intermingled. To GIs both were Chinese, Chinks or Gooks.

The intervening years between the end of WWII and Korea brought relief from daily casualty reports. Their return had raised the specter of all out war with the Communist Powers. Our political leaders being politicians came up with a political solution of deeming this war we had on our hands a police action with limited objectives. Thus insulting the nation's armed forces by telling them they were not to win. Creating policies that forced tactical blunders and needlessly increased casualties. Limited War is an oxymoron that carries over to defeat.

For me Korea was mixture of old and new. It took time to sort out the differences. In all three theaters we owned the skies although in the Solomons Japanese harassed the troops with ineffective air attacks. I witnessed one friendly attack on enemy positions and that one wasn't very friendly. I was in the beaten zone of the bomb drop. I never saw an enemy plane during my stay in Korea. During my stay in Europe I briefed pilots for hundreds of missions in support of ground operations in Korea as a member of an infantry Battalion on the front line I witnessed three air attacks on enemy ground targets.

In Korea on occasions we fought night and day for dominate terrain on the Main Line of Resistance. Between these fights were long intervals of relative quiet. Most action occurred when patrols from opposite sides ran into each other in no man's land between the two defenses. The exception was when the Chinese decided to intimidate an Allied unit and take the position held on the MLR. They would sacrifice a regiment to wipe out a platoon outpost that had no significant tactical importance. Regardless of the war or theater whatever engagement a soldier was fighting in, at that moment it was the most important event of his life.

Chinese Intelligence that is their knowledge of American battlefield intentions was uncanny at first. The reason they were so well informed was simply that they had agents in virtually every American sector. Each battalion sector had a KSC (Korean Service Corps) unit of about 200 men assigned as laborers who performed all sorts of menial tasks from digging trenches to building bridges plus more. KSCs were men beyond service age who were conscripted for six-month tours. American units carried a ten percent personnel overage in KATUSAs. KATUSA was an acronym for; "Korean Aid To United States Army". ROK (Republic of Korea) soldiers chosen for this program were English-speaking volunteers. Supposed to be, mostly they were recent conscripts. It was easy for the Chinese to plant agents among either KATUSAs or KSC units.

The stories of KATUSAs "bugging out" leaving their GI comrades to their fate were bound in fact, however given the language barrier and the GI's proclivity for considering anyone or thing non-American inferior it was easy to understand that it took a while for Koreans to become part of an American team.

Korea had been occupied by Japan from 1910 until 1945 and then while the south half of the country struggled with their newfound freedom the north half was turned over to a Communist regime trained by the Russians for the single objective of uniting the peninsula as a Soviet Satellite. Our intelligence was comparable; we hired many of the same line crossers as did the Chinese.

The seventy-five mile trip from Inchon to 7th Division Headquarters by truck took nearly five hours. Five hours through war-scarred countryside starting with the port city of Inchon followed by the nations Capitol, Seoul, brooded over by the shot out windows of its capitol building. Over roads clogged by military traffic mixed with pedestrians under A-frames or pulling two wheeled carts piled high with all sorts of saleable items ranging from personal belongings to farm produce and fire wood. It was obvious this was fought over countryside. However, there were no cities reduced to rubble as those of France and Germany of 1945. The simple reason was that this had been a much poorer country to start with.

The farther we traveled through devastated remains of villages the more the traffic mix favored military trucks. Part way to our destination we were reassured that this war was being held in proper prospective by our allies.

We passed under a banner strung over the road and above the reach of the tallest vehicles. The banner marking the location of a division's command post had the 2nd Division Indian Head logo emblazoned on each end. Centered on the banner in foot high letters was; "SECOND INFANTRY DIVISION" below that; "SECOND TO NONE".

A half mile further down the road marking the location of the command post of a British Royal Artillery twenty-five pounder battery was an equally large banner marked in foot high letters; 'NONE". In due time the 2nd Division banner became conspicuous by its absence after an appropriate interval so was "NONE". Cheeky American bastards.

37

I PROBABLY KNOW THAT BUT TELL ME ANYHOW

On arrival at division headquarters I was surprised to learn that Colonel Maliszewski was also there and we were to occupy the same quarters. Not only that but he knew a lot more than I. He knew that we both were being assigned to the 1st Battalion of the 31st Infantry regiment, that the current battalion CO was near the end of his tour and that I would report for duty upon completion of a three-day orientation here at Division. The colonel would arrive later. My hiatus was over, I had a new home with nothing left to do but get used to it.

During the orientation period Colonel Maliszewski and I grew to know each other. We were of about the same age and came from blue-collar depression era backgrounds; his rooted in a Pennsylvania industrial complex mine from a subsistence farm.

Through hard work, perseverance and luck he had graduated from West Point and as a second lieutenant was assigned to an Infantry unit in the Aleutians too late in WW II to see combat, something he took personally. Now a step behind his classmates this likely was his last chance to gain fame and glory. He was not impressed with my view that fame and glory are steps along the route to designation of KIA on a tombstone. Here in the relative comfort of a division headquarters nearly beyond the sound of our artillery, he was limiting himself to one canteen of water to accomplish his daily ablutions. To me it was a little disconcerting. It never appeared to me that practicing for future hardship was particularly helpful, Hardship was tough enough to get used to when it happened.

Major General Wayne Smith who also was enjoying his first combat command wore Paratrooper's wings, as did Maliszewski. Both gained their wings at the end of the same jump class at Fort Bragg, which explained why the Colonel arrived at 7th Division Headquarters ahead of me. The General sent for him.

This association was not without advantages, it gained both of us an invitation to the nightly after dinner General's philosophy seminar since we were to be joined at the same link in the chain of command. Also it gained access to the General's private bar on a limited basis.

The seminar provided the source for a frequently quoted General's favorite response to conversation openers of; "I probably know that already but go ahead and tell me anyhow." The General a rotund 5' 10" out of his earshot was referred to as "Sump Hole Six". This title requires a little explanation; in the army communication system combat units are regularly given code names and prime staff and command positions numbers. The 7th Division's code name was Bayonet thus G-1 (Personnel Officer) was referred to in radio, phone and personally delivered messages as "Bayonet 1", Intelligence "Bayonet 2", Operations "Bayonet 3", Supply "Bayonet 4", Executive "Bayonet 5" and finally the Commanding General "Bayonet 6". GIs being much more of a practical bend changed the system to a more descriptive use to identify individual characteristics thus General Smith became "Sump Hole 6". His exterior dimensions matched a standard kitchen sump hole's interior dimensions. That is the more favorable mention otherwise his 6 appellations was unprintable.

The general's WW II assignment had been that of Quartermaster General of the Department of Hawaii with the responsibility of managing the mountains of supplies that passed through the territory's ports in support of the troops in the Pacific Theater and their creature comforts such as rations, clothing, tentage and letters from home. A position of great importance and fundamental to our victory but one that had little to do with the basic mechanics of a warrior's trade in short fame and glory were not part of the job description. It was a dead end.

Now as a commander of an infantry division engaged in combat his feet were once again on the ladder to high command albeit several rounds below his peers.

A citizen's army had fought WW II. Professionals dominated high level command positions however intermediate through bottom ranks were increasingly citizen soldiers. Many recent U.S. Military Academy graduates found themselves in important administrative assignments during WW II and never escaped to a combat posting, that lead to an interruption of their path to promotions and coveted command slots. True or not it was the perception of most reservists called to active duty for the Korean action that the WPPA (West Point Protective Association) created a priority to use the individual replacement system of this war to rectify the situation by moving as many of their non combat qualified fellows as possible through combat slots in the command structure.

One month was the minimum required for listing as a permanent assignment on which an efficiency report on performance might be filed. Tours of combat duty by veteran civilian component officers were regularly interrupted so Regulars, mainly West Pointers, could meet that requirement. General Smith and Colonel Maliszewski were cases in point. This not to say that West Pointers performed poorly but they were human.

Shortly before our arrival, the 7th Division went through an episode that we latecomers were surreptitiously advised not to mention. Eventually the following account of ":Operation Smack" surfaced from many sources; A small salient projecting into the Allies main line of resistance had long been a literal thorn in General Smith's side. When the 7th division last occupied that sector the General decided to reduce it and directed his staff to put together plans to accomplish his objective. Their main obstacle was the Pentagon imposed mandate that any offensive operation involving a force of more than reinforced infantry company be cleared through channels all the way to and by the pentagon. The purpose of this directive was to avoid casualties. In effect it was counter productive and cost more lives than saved. The policy was politically promoted with the simplistic logic of; "If our boys don't fight they can't get hurt."

General Smith aggressively promoted Operation Smack and eventually succeeded in gaining approval. The longer the plan was in process the more detailed and complex it grew. The final flaw was to milk it for its Public Relations potential. That included building a bunker on prominent terrain overlooking the battle sight for observers including selected reporters. For their information a secret program including the battle scenario was produced for distribution. The plan started the exercise with an air strike and continued with a double envelopment by an infantry battalion reinforced with engineers and tanks. The project was approved; schedule set and guest in place with briefing officers by their sides to explain what they were seeing H-hour arrived without sound of aircraft overhead.

Twenty minutes later a flight of jets arrived to bomb and strafe the wrong target. Artillery preparation began on schedule but lifted before the infantry and tanks were in position. The defenders took advantage of the pause to zero their artillery in on the approaching column of tanks and trucks loaded with infantry. At this point the General had the good sense to order a withdrawal the Chinese shifted their artillery concentrations to pin down the viewing party. Reporters present and excluded wired their versions of the exhibition to state side editors who wrote scathing editorials. The Pentagon stonewalled and General Smith draped a shroud of secrecy over his command.

During our orientation we visited several of the division's front line positions and outposts. One dug into the side of a hill named "Porkchop" a fifty-seven millimeter recoilless rifle crew was engaged in a duel with a Chinese recoilless rifle crew on Hasakkol. The two man crew would load their weapon and move through a connecting trench to one of several vantage points where the gunner would fire at one of the firing ports of the Chinese fighting positions, drop back into the trench and move to a new location. The Chinese crew returned fire at a port where they guessed the Americans had moved. Everyone else in the two positions American and Chinese kept down under cover. We watched the exchange for about a half dozen rounds until I persuaded the Colonel that there was little glory to be gained by casual bystanders carried out on stretchers.

The 7th Division had two Allied Battalions attached. One the Colombian Battalion had a better reputation as lovers than fighters. Their Officer-in-charge, who left command of the Battalion to his deputy, was rumored to have a house and mistress in Tokyo. At least he seldom visited his command except for state occasions such as visits of dignitaries from Colombia or Eighth Army Headquarters.

An MP traffic patrol stopped the Battalion Commander's driver, a young man with an excellent command of English, for doing fifty in a twenty-five mile an hour zone. With no witnesses in view rather than writing a ticket the MP, asked the Colombian; "How fast were you driving?" the reply; "No habla Englis, Senor." MP; "Don't you know the speed limit here is twenty-five miles an hour?" Colombian: "No habla Englis Senor." The Mp spotted a speed limit sign the Colombian had just passed. In desperation he took the young man by arm led him back to the sign to deliver his lecture in what he considered pidgin Spanish, punctuated with gestures. The driver endured the chewing out with much nodding and many; "Si senors." When the sergeant paused, the driver grasped the sign, wiggled the stake out of the ground, carried the stake and sign back, threw both in his jeep and drove off leaving the MP Sergeant open mouthed.

The other was the third Battalion from the all-volunteer Ethiopian Imperial Guard to spend a year's tour in Korea. They came to fight and fight they did with such ferocity that the Chinese avoided them by keeping whatever sector the Eeks (our designation) occupied very quiet. The Eeks objective was to rack up a more prestigious record than their fellow battalions who had preceded them. American Battalions occupying sectors adjacent to the Eeks could count on them to buy into firefights when American patrols became engaged.

Stories had it the Ethiopians enticed Chinese into attacking their positions by building bonfires and holding what in American Indian lore would be called a

Pow-wow, on hills they defended. That is until the Chinese discovered that when they mounted an attack there were more Eeks than they could handle waiting for them at the bottom of the hill. Two examples of the Ethiopian's prowess are related in detail by S.L.A. Marshall in chapters entitled; "Into the Alligator's Jaws" and "The Incredible Patrol" in his book "Pork Chop Hill". The down side of having Eeks as allies was that American units who relieved them were faced with a nasty clean up jobs. Eeks' attitude toward field sanitation was any place outside of where they ate and slept was a suitable sanitary dumpsite. It paid to step gingerly during a stay on the MLR after relieving Emperor Haile Selassie's Finest.

38

BEARCATS

The 7th Division included three Infantry Regiments, 17th (Buffalo), 31st (Bearcat) and 32nd (Buccaneer). In keeping with the Division code of Bayonet all subordinate unit codes began with "B.", Battalions in the infantry regiments were coded by the colors, Red White and Blue. Thus the commander of the 1st Ban 31st Inf. became "Bearcat Red Six" and the regimental CO "Bearcat Six."

Bearcat Headquarters was tucked in a hollow on the south side of a hill near Maktong, a village that no longer existed, victim of the ebb and flow of a war that passed over it three times. A mound of stones marked the site.

Korean legend had it that an adulterous wife was stoned to death in times past and since each virtuous Korean wife who passed by, as a token of fidelity added a stone to the cairn marking the adulteress one's remains. The only pertinence this legend has is rumor had it that this was the third visit the regiment had made to Maktong, once on the way to the Yalu, once on the way back and once again on the way to the truce line. If rumor was true quite likely Colonel William Kern led them all the way, no one ever mentioned there ever being any Bearcat Six other than Colonel Kern.

During the WWII North African campaign the Colonel had commanded an Infantry Battalion, losing an eye in the process. His prosthesis was a good match, it was disconcerting for a GI knowing of his loss but not certain which eye was which, to answer questions during weapons inspection when one of the Colonel's eyes held the soldier's captive and the other peered down the muzzle of his rifle. The popular account of Colonel Kern's recuperation following the combat loss was; following his recovery in an Oran military hospital; he grew impatient with the delay in arrival of prosthesis from the States. During his wait he requested a pass and found a seller of glass eyes in the Casbah. There he purchased a substitute and returned to his battalion to resume command, the hospital commander reported him absent without leave.

The 31st Infantry regiment was deployed on the MLR occupying two battalion sectors with one battalion in reserve. The reserve battalion occupied an assembly area just beyond the reach of Chinese medium artillery. This position was in close proximity to prepared blocking positions to be occupied in case of a Chinese break through. While in reserve a battalion could expect to receive replacements. The 17th and 32nd Infantry regiments were similarly deployed. Once a week a regimental reserve battalions relieved a front line battalion The UN battalions were cycled into the rotation on a regular basis, which made for a two week on the MLR and one in reserve with an occasional longer reserve deployment lasting through one relief cycle. The battalion sectors were organized with fighting positions and connecting trenches on the north facing military crests of hills and ridges. The tactical advantage gained was small since all dominate terrain lie to the north but the dominance of the battlefield by our Air Force diminished the Chinese advantage. The prepared defenses included; mine fields, sector weapons and stockpiled supplies of ammunition and emergency rations. Relief of front line battalions was accomplished at night for security reasons and followed the normal procedure of relieving outposts first, followed by crew served weapons, then riflemen, communications and finally command passed to the relieving unit. Efforts to conceal the date of relief were largely abandoned for the simple reason the Chinese always found out in advance anyhow.

The Chinese weren't alone in the intelligence business the ROKs had their share of agents on the other side and then also there was an abundance of double agents aka; "Line Crossers" who worked both sides for their personal gain. In fact communication between the two sides was quite good although untrustworthy since both sides continually planted false information with line crossers. Americans had an advantage in that we controlled the skies and could verify much of the information received by air observation and photos. The Chinese countered by constructing a much more sophisticated defensive system. Their fighting positions occupied only by sentries were on the forward slope of dominant terrain that looked down on the Americans and were backed by caves dug into the hill where the bulk of the Chinese troops remained safe from American observation and artillery fire. The caves were connected by tunnels to the rear slope of an occupied ridge, The Chinese reinforced and re-supplied their positions by night when they were less likely to be seen and harassed by the Allies. Chinese were creatures of the night and seldom ventured out during daylight hours but they did keep us alert by with harassing artillery fire.

During the late winter and spring of 1953 our forces were denied offensive action except in case of a counter attack to restore a position seized by the Chinese and then not in strength of more than a reinforced company. That restriction left pursuit of the war up to the Chinese and American's ingenuity. Both sides continually worked at improving their defenses, however the Chinese were a bit more discrete or perhaps they were more dedicated to tunneling while Americans were bigger on working above ground. On a ridge called Pokae overlooking Pork chop in the Maktong sector the Chinese were busy carving the heart out of the hill. We could tell because from one of our observation posts some two thousand yards away we would observe a Chinaman, regularly at about five minute intervals, heave a basket of fresh dirt over a parapet onto the slope below. It grated on our professional pride to have an insignificant Chinaman thus step out into the open and gaze on our hill. Through our spotting scope we could see the heaver throw his load and rest his basket on the parapet for a moment while he caught his breath and enjoyed the view. He was beyond small arms range. We tried adjusting artillery fire on the position without much success, it would take a first round hit to get the dirt thrower and artillery men are not much good at hitting the target on the first try. Then too, our artillery forward observer was becoming more jealous of his credibility and fire control more suspicious of his technically correct call of; "Troops" in the open. It was against policy to waste artillery shells on a single man even if he was, allegorically speaking, thumbing his nose at the American Army. Finally we dug a fifty-caliber machine gun in next to the OP, and sand bagged the tripod for maximum stability. The next time the dirt thrower came out we waited until he disappeared into the tunnel then we adjusted fire on the spoil bank below, careful not to fire when he returned. Finally when the fifty-caliber gunner was satisfied with his calibration he raised his sights onto the parapet above and waited. The observer at the scope watched and when the dirt thrower appeared and tossed his basket of dirt he said; "Fire". The gunner did with a long burst, about two seconds later the basket flew in the air and the dirt thrower disappeared from view. The net result was that dirt throwers at that location no longer tarried at their task to enjoy the view. There was speculation among the observers if the Chinese Noncom in charge of the tunneling detail would send us a message of thanks for invigorating his detail not to waist time looking at the scenery but he never did, unappreciative Bastard.

We had other games. Someone discovered that from one of the battalion OPs that at night when a searchlight in an adjacent sector happened to cross a ridge running at an angle from the front, the light silhouetted a Chinese trail running along the back side of the ridge making visible shadows of troops moving on the trail. It was incidental that we had a twin forty-millimeter gun dug in that could enfilade the trail that is; cover it from front to back. After much coordinating with the searchlight and twin forty, a regular shoot was set up. The OP laid its spotting scope on the ridge, the twin forty set its sights on the near end of the ridge and the searchlight agreed on request to begin its sweep just beyond the ridge. If shadows showed troops our OP called the gun. The crew walked bursts of forty millimeter fire, placing shells about five yards apart, the length of the trail. About ten minutes later the searchlight started another sweep and if shadows in twosomes showed, the process was repeated. That way we hit either a Chinese unit reinforcing a front line position, a supply party or stretcher-bearers coming to pick up casualties.

The Chinese countered with a mortar barrage on the forty-millimeter's position but the crew buttoned up their vehicle and rode it out without damage. The next day they began modification on their position so as soon as the fire mission was complete they could pull out and hide behind the hill. That tactic was repeated several times before the Chinese either gave that route up or camouflaged the trail.

39

OLD BALDY

S.L.A. Marshall in his book "Pork Chop Hill" applies these words to Old Baldy; "scabrous after months of battle, a mountain looking more like a refuse dump, more cheated by nature than abused by man". Old Baldy was stage and backdrop for some of the most vicious and bitter fighting in Korea's spring of 1953. The 7th division bore the brunt of the battle in Marshall's description. The shadow of Old Baldy looms over this battle and Bearcats hold center stage.

Early in March MG Arthur G. Trudeau who had commanded engineer units during WWII replaced MG Wayne Smith as Bayonet Six. At the end of our weeklong stint as regimental reserve we relieved the 2nd Bn on Pork Chop, Old Baldy and a third hill for some unknown reason called "George."

For the next two weeks Baker Company on Old Baldy and Charley Company on Pork Chop received a lot of pressure from nighttime Chinese patrols and daytime incoming artillery. The patrol actions were in the nature of probes where the Chinese showed less stomach for sustained firefights than a desire to draw fire from our position. Hindsight proved this to be the case.

At the end of our stint the Colombian Battalion relieved us without incident. In fact the calm during the relief was so intense it was as though the Chinese had called a time out in our favor so we could make the change as expeditiously as possible. That might have been the case.

The 3rd Battalion who normally would have relieved us shifted to a blocking position further to the east. We occupied an assembly area out of the reach of Chinese artillery fire back of the Colombians ready to either reinforce MLR positions or move to blocking positions in the Bearcat sector. The relief followed a plan that was very much like removing a sock from one's foot by peeling it off inside out heel first.

Early on Saturday morning the Colombian Battalion Commander, his Company Commanders, Platoon Leaders and leaders of squads who would initially man outposts reported to our battalion command post and were briefed on the current situation. This was a slow process, because of the language barrier required the use of an interrupter.

Most of the Colombians had been through this exercise before. Between the de facto Battalion Commander (the figure head commander was busy enjoying the good life in Tokyo) and his driver both of who were fluent in English; the ground rules of the exchange were established.

Our three rifle company commanders, 1st LTs all; Jerry Morse from the State of Maine and late of the Maine National Guard commanded Able Company on George Hill. Jack Patterson from the Commonwealth of Virginia and VMI commanded Baker Company on Old Baldy. Roscoe (Robby) Robinson from St Louis Missouri and USA Military Academy commanded Charley Company on Pork Chop. They led their Colombian counterparts to the appropriate front line positions to continue their briefing. LTC Maliszewski and the Colombian Battalion Commander left to tour our sector MLR positions. I went back to the assembly area with the non-tactical elements of the battalion and set up our bivouac for the next week.

At nine that evening the relief began with the Colombians appearing and occupying the fighting positions. Crew served weapons remained manned by our people until our riflemen were relieved and safely off the hill only then did the Colombians begin to replace weapon's crews. Weapon stayed in position and only crews were replaced. Each sector had at least as many crew served weapons over the number authorized by the Tables of Organization and Equipment (TO&E) as authorized. In addition there was a light tank from the 31st Tank Company dug in on Old Baldy whose crew was relieved on a different schedule.

Finally outposts were relieved and by 0300 hours Sunday LTC. Maliszewski turned responsibility for the sector over, the last of our Battalion checked in, and the Colombians were on their own.

After breakfast and church services trucks from service Company reported in and picked up half the command and took them to a quartermaster bath unit some twenty miles to the rear and returned for the remainder of the men, trucked them to the showers and picked up the freshly scrubbed and outfitted first contingent and returned them to their home away from home. Going through Quartermaster showers is an experience to be remembered if not all together happy.

It started with a line of GIs being led through a reception tent where they were given numbered ammunition can with a correspondingly numbered tag. Then they were instructed; "put the tag around yew-ar neck, place yew-ar valuables in the can, take off yew-ar shoes, tie them to yew-ar can and pass them back over the counter to the ay-tendant and exit to yew-ar right." Those instructions left first time literally minded GIs in a quandary as to how to tie ammunition can to their butt and if they ever again would see their valuables. In the next tent they were equally explicitly instructed to remove their clothes and hand them over to attendants who sorted and threw them in a pile. The buck-naked GIs were handed a sliver of soap, about forty square inches of towel and showed the exit. The exit was also the entrance to a shower rigged forty-man hospital tent.

Those who have used Quartermaster Showers will testify that were designed by a plumber from Hell. The floor was a waterproof, by dictum, ground cloth under duckboards. Overhead, the shower, running the length of the tent, was a bank of shower heads mounted on the underside of inch and a quarter pipes, supported on bipods. The pipes were connected to a water heater under a fly outside the tent. This was good since the heater, fueled by diesel fuel, was adjusted to the maximum fume rate. A thermostat allegedly controlled the heater and a valve was turned on in ten-minute cycles. The plan was for the shower heads to produce a soothing flow of warm water for five minutes, shut down for five minutes and repeat the process so that one could step into the spray get thoroughly wet step out during the pause and soap up, step back in rinse off, step out towel down. They produced instead a two-minute spray of icy cold, one minute of tepid and two minutes of scalding hot.

Then there was the quandary of what to do with forty square inches of towel, there were no towel racks, and in fact there were no pieces of furniture in the tent. Towels were supposed to be draped over the shower pipe between heads a solution that worked well for seven footers but left lesser mortals a mite short. Mostly dripping wet, mostly soapy GIs emerged into the dressing tent where they received a clean set of uncertain sized clothing from the skin out, before returning to the reception tent to retrieve shoes and valuables. Then, fresh and clean, they faced a dusty twenty-mile ride to their home away from home.

In midweek the Colombians, a four-company battalion, decided to replace the company on Old Baldy with their reserve company. Instead of the proven tactic of keeping their outposts in place they pulled them in to the main position. The Chinese followed and were in the main trenches of Old Baldy without firing a shot along with two companies of Colombians who panicked in face of the slaughter that followed. Those who survived and were able fled some were found twenty miles behind the MLR near Division Headquarters. Simultaneously the Chinese attacked Pork Chop. Here the Colombians held and limited the Chinese penetration.

Regiment's first word of the debacle came from the artillery forward observers. Word soon followed from the tank dug in on Old Baldy that they were engaged in an intense firefight with the Chinese and the Colombians were bugging out. Colonel Kern directed the tank crew to cover the Colombians the best they could then pull out.

They stayed in place until their ammunition ran out then moved back only to take a hit and lose a tread coming off the crest of the hill. Chinese small arms fire kept them buttoned in the tank At this point artillery "flashed" Old Baldy. Flash fires were a last resort to save a position and consisted of concentrations of VT fire on a position and approaches. "VT" is timed to explode shells a few feet above ground raining shell fragments on anything and anyone exposed above the surface. About the same time trucks pulled into our assembly area to take Baker and Charley companies to a pre selected departure points in preparation for a counter attacks to drive the Chinks off Old Baldy and Pork Chop. Orders for both companies to attack as soon as possible were received en route. Charley Company had loaded and left the assembly area minutes before. Baker with less distance to travel arrived at their IP first and preceded by intense artillery fire launched their attack and by daybreak had regained about a third of old Baldy.

Charley succeeded in reinforcing Pork Cop's defenses and in beating back the Chinese. Baker's attack bogged down after losing its two leading platoon leaders, company commander and executive officer. Daylight and artillery fire helped them hold the ground gained until Bearcat Blue moved in and secured hill 347 behind them.

By nightfall remnants of the Colombian Battalion on Pork Chop and George Hill were replaced by the 3rd Bn. 31st Infantry and the Battalion had organized their defenses of Hill 347 in the prepared blocking positions already there. Bearcat Red was back in reserve ready to receive replacements in the morning.

The following Saturday and Sunday we moved back onto George Hill and Hill 347 while the 3rd Battalion shifted east to Pork Chop and Hill 327 as division realigned its defensive sectors. Lieutenants Patterson and Pedrick, Company commander and executive Officer of Baker Company were released back to duty in a matter of days. Lieutenant Bressler the wounded platoon leaders returned in about a week and Lieutenant Yocum replaced Lieutenant Dale the platoon leader killed in action.

The First Battalion's objective was to restore the breached MLR to its former strength. Old Baldy no longer was ours and adjacent Pork Chop was a salient thrust into the Chinese line. Restoration of the MLR meant a lot of digging, a Hell of a lot of digging. During daylight hours line company members not on outposts or patrol were busy digging. So was the Battalion pioneer platoon. So was the regiments attached KSC Company.

KSCs were the Republic of Korea Army's answer to American bulldozers. Korean men, forty plus years of age no longer needed as armed force replacements were drafted (rounded up by press gangs) from the villages for six month stints in the Korean Service Corps.

They were armed with picks and shovels and organized in hundred man companies. Companies were assigned to MLR regiments as labor pools and were used to build fortifications, pack supplies and as laborers in general. Their uniforms were hand me downs that had already been through the war at least once but these middle-aged men were exceedingly hardy. They really showed young, healthy Americans up.

When Americans passed a contingent of KSCs at the base of a hill resting before they began a climb the GIs could expect the KSCs to pass them half way up the hill while the Americans were taking a five minute breath break. The KSCs chogied their loads to the top without a break. Chogi was pidgin Korean for going from here to there on foot. KSCs did a lot of chogieing. Their units also were haven for Chinese agents.

The scheme of defense included construction of two fortified outposts on separate ridges running toward Chink country from Hill 347. The easternmost aptly named Westview because it provided an unobstructed view of Old Baldy's west slope, the other further south and west was named for Lieutenant Dale who died in action during Baker Company's aborted attempt to retake old Baldy. Dale the larger of the two had scant room for a platoon. A deep trench with mutually supporting, over headed fighting bays circled Dale. Westview perched on a rocky crag was the higher and smaller of the two was in affect a single squad fighting position reinforced with several machine guns sighted to give all around coverage including the nearly vertical walls. Both were connected to MLR positions on the hill by deep narrow trenches.

Telephone lines were pegged into the sides of the trenches for a reliable communication link to main positions. In the trench leading to Westview a ground return telephone wire of the type used by the Chinese was discovered behind a partially filled sand bag. It was obvious that not all the KSCs working on that trench were working for us. GIs worked alone on that project for a few days while the ROK CID (Republic Of Korea Criminal Investigation Division) interviewed the KSC Company. In due course the CID boys left with two KSCs who never returned. The remaining KSCs returned to work much relieved but somewhat bruised.

The Chinese were detected digging beneath the abandoned tank on Baldy's slope well in small arms range of Westview whose garrison discouraged the effort by taking turns sharpening their marksmanship on the burrow. There was no way for them to separate casualties claimed from those inflicted. The CID destroyed the communication link with their target.

Nervous over the lack of reports of Chinese activity on the visible face of Baldy Bearcat 2 (Intelligence Officer) scheduled a daylight patrol to the base of the hill Lieutenant Short drew the assignment. Reaching his destination he radioed the information to regiment.

Regiment sharply questioned his report since the map coordinates he reported indicated that he had crossed the face of Old Baldy with his patrol. Stung to the quick, by regiment's question Short radioed back; "Put your glasses on Old Baldy, out" and proceeded alone to retrace his steps all the way across hill and returned, pausing midway on the return trip to thumb his nose in the direction of the observer. He and his patrol completed their mission and he filed his report. The whole regiment waited while the word spread for Colonel Kern to explode. Bearcat Six remained silent.

Short was interviewed by a correspondent about the incident; during the interview he was asked if he was nervous during his jaunt. Short replied; "Sure was, I chewed two packs, my total supply of Wriggley's Double Mint Gum, Double Mint soothes my nerves." Less than two weeks later Wriggley sent him a case of Double Mint gum.

40

THREE POINTS A MONTH FOR CHRISSAKES

Chinese pressure on the Old Baldy, now Hill 347 sector eased back in intensity to occasional patrol contact and unpredictable shelling. Some nights patrol contact might be lacking, other times there might be several contacts without follow-up or perhaps a burst of fire followed by a quick withdrawal on the part of the Chinese. They never let us forget they were there. On some days we could run a convoy of trucks over a stretch of road exposed to Chinese observation and artillery as peacefully as though they were on a Sunday afternoon drive, again a lone jeep might receive a salvo. The road in question ran at an angle to the front along a dry streambed protected by a sharp ridge on the side toward the Chink positions. At the point the ridge ended another small valley across the way ran into George Hill.

A combination of terrain features providing a covered approach to our positions covered except for a quarter mile gap at the confluence of the two valleys. Three quarters of a mile of road was exposed to a Chinese observation post in the next sector. That problem was partially solved by a fuel oil smoke generator in a sand bagged position dug in behind the tip of the ridge. The gap could only be filled with smoke if Mother Nature was willing and blessed us with vagrant zephyrs rather than the Chinese with howling gales.

The smoke generator was operated by a two GIs from a Chemical Warfare Company located in rear of Division Headquarters. They commuted daily by jeep loaded with jerry cans full of oil to and empty from the generator. They were the two most disgruntled GIs in Uncle Sam's Army. Not that they were much bothered by being closer to the Chinese than the defenders of the hill, they were to busy fighting their generator to keep it operating to speculate fighting the Chinese.

They were unhappy and resentful over the narrow uncompassionate minds of Army Brass who put their assigned duty post ahead of the front lines and their station of record back of the combat zone. GIs on the hill behind them got FOUR POINTS and THEY only got THREE POINTS A MONTH FOR CHRISSAKES. Every morning before daybreak they stopped by Battalion Command Post and said; "Smokey goin' in." every night after dark they stopped and said; "Smokey goin' out."

Tired of getting shot at on the way to Able Company we requested and received an air strike on Chinese positions causing the problem. The first two planes of the flight bombed and strafed the target, the second pair bombed and strafed into the smoke raised by the first pair's bombs. The third pair bombed and strafed "Smokey."

Minutes later our Battalion Command Post played host to the two grimiest, greasy, disgruntled raging GIs in Uncle Sam's Army and they still were only getting "THREE POINTS FOR CHRISSAKES."

Taking a shortcut from one of our outpost to another I came on three men forty or so yards off the trail loading a fourth on a stretcher and out of curiosity started to walk over to them. One of them noticed me and waved me back. It dawned on me what I was witnessing and gingerly turned around to retrace my steps.

In the next footprint on the way back, like first daffodil shoots of spring, sprouted four steel prongs of a Bouncing Betty land mine. I knew then that I had my first encounter with members of the Division's Grave Registration unit at work. Very gingerly I made my way back to the trail carefully avoiding that last footprint thankful it was not my last and stepping in each of the rest. The Grave Registration people were recovering bodies of Colombians who perished in an unmarked mine field while fleeing the Chinese on Old Baldy a few weeks earlier.

Bearcat Red had another unsung and unnamed hero. Unlike Lieutenant Short he remains unnamed not only due to memory lapse but also because his exploit was sensitive to exposure. The Battalions Communications Officer, an outstanding one I might ad, a first lieutenant with a North Carolina accent and a monkey on his back the size of King Kong in the form of an electric generator well past prime.

Generators were not on Infantry Battalion's table of equipment but every Infantry Battalion in Korea had one. They were acquired, scrounged, liberated. Moonlight requisitioned and come by devious means all common in the underground supply system of military units. In WWII Solomon Islands jeeps were the prize in Korea generators. In Korea we mainly fought at night. Without light in battalion command posts not much commanding could take place. Our generator wheezed, groaned, flickered and failed at crucial moments and our Communication Officer unjustly shouldered the blame. Officially we weren't authorized one, officially we didn't have a generator and as long as we did not have an official generator our CommO officially couldn't get parts to repair our unofficial generator. He faced every night with high resolve and low hopes, every morning with low esteem and high dudgeon.

One morning our CommO wore a mantle of smugness with the grace of a Cheshire cat. About three the next morning the Command Post's lights failed and before the emergency Coleman lantern could be turned up, came back on with a new brightness. At breakfast our newly smug CommO angled for recognition of his labor with; "How y'all like how ah fixed that ole generator?" No one fell on his knees in adulation but appreciation was expressed for being back in the light of things. Pressed the source of our brightness became increasingly vague about his mechanical prowess. Eventually word over the grapevine told of misfortune that struck the division ordnance battalion.

A new Table of Organization and Equipment recently distributed authorized Infantry Division Ordnance Battalions a trailer-mounted generator and in due time the 7th Division's battalion requisitioned and received one. Less than a week later it was gone.

The gate sentry on duty could not remember exactly but around two hundred hours a grungy three quarter ton driven by a grungy captain wearing sun glasses drove up performed the sign-countersign procedure correctly and was waved through. Short time later the same vehicle and captain returned and performed the exit sign-countersign procedure correctly and was waved through the gate. The ¾ ton was pulling a trailer carrying a tarp-covered load.

Asked if he had recorded the vehicles identification numbers and if he thought a captain wearing sun glasses in the middle of the night was unusual replied; "No sir, that three quarter ton was too muddy" and "Sir, I don't think anything a captain does in the middle of the night is unusual." His questioner was a captain. Later that morning our CommO supervised the washing of the Communication Section vehicles and if one was curious enough to inspect our newly repaired generator closely he would discover the grime that covered it was undisturbed by repair and seemed to be made up more of mud than grease.

41

BATTLE FOR DALE

In early April line crossers brought the word that the Chinese were planning something big in our sector and we doubled our efforts to strengthen our most vulnerable position, Dale Outpost.

During the construction work a rifle platoon occupied Dale working on the construction by day and standing ready in fighting positions by night. By the middle of April, the encircling trench with additional fighting positions improvised by overhead portions of the trench with timber and sandbags was in place. The trench leading back to the main ridge was deepened. Baker Company's third platoon lead by Lieutenant Bressler occupied Dale. Our battalion's pioneer platoon and about 30 KSCs were working regularly on the project. An engineer platoon had completed two bands of concertina wire around the position and were working on the third when disaster struck The pioneer Platoon and KSCs had completed their assignment for the day and left the hill. The Engineer Platoon was within hours of completing the third band of concertina wire decided to spend the night and complete their task at first light. At 2300 hours a wave of Chinese swept up a finger leading to the ridge, in rear of the outpost.

They were into the trench before the defenders knew it. A second wave followed and was on the top of the central knob before Lt. Bressler could get word back to his company commander. The duty officer at Battalion CP got word that Dale was under attack sounded the alarm and opened the phone loop to regiment.

By the time I got to the Operations bunker minutes later Lt. Patterson was calling for "Flash Dale" the signal to place VT fire on his own troops. I asked; "Do you want a flare?" He said; "No" then "Yes, but push the VT the bastards are all over the place." The artillery liaison officer who had monitored the call looked at me. I nodded yes, about that time Col. Kern came on the phone and said; "Hold flash Dale, you'll kill your own men." Impressed by the anguish in Patterson's voice I replied; "Goddamit, Colonel, I was out there today and our men have some overheading to get under and the Chinks don't!" He said; "Flash Dale."

About that time LTC Maliszewski walked into the bunker and yelled; "Morrow get off that phone who in hell do you think you are trying to take away my command?" Then spent the next five minutes of giving me the worst tongue lashing of my life before stamping out of the bunker without a word to any one else. Captain Preston the Battalion Ops Officer looked at me and grinned; "I never liked that son of a bitch either." Shortly the Battalion commander with Sgt Kim, his KATUSA body guard, was in Patterson's CP saying; "I'll take over, you stay here."

When he left it was my distinct impression that Lieutenant Colonel Maliszewski, George L. had seized on the moment of his fame and glory. The battle for Dale continued into the morning, finally a counter attack by the second platoon of Baker Company pulled out of their MLR positions and a platoon from Item Company cleared the hill of Chinese.

About 0400 hours Sgt Kim burst into CP bunker yelling; "Colonel Mal's foot all f—kd up, throw grenade uphill, step on grenade, foot all f—kd up." Before I could report to regiment that Maliszewski was out and I was in Colonel Kern called and told me so. I left with Hamilton to join Patterson. With a squad hastily gathered from his headquarters people we went out the trench to Dale where all was quiet, we met Lts. Collins, Yocum, Hemphill and other survivors. There were none from the engineer platoon trapped on the hill. The body of Lt. Bressler, leader and thirty-five of those of his forty-two-man platoon were mingled with the hundred and thirty-six Chinese corpse found inside of Dales defenses. A great many of them were in the trenches. So many that in places we walked on them in order to navigate the trench.

Collin's and Yocum's platoons combined had been reduced to less than a twelve-man squad. Hemphill's platoon lost more than half its members. Chinese bodies out side Dales wire were not counted. The single badly wounded Chinese left behind by his compatriots was carried off the hill with the American wounded. Division's Order of Battle section identified bodies from three battalions and two regiments among the Chinese dead. Stateside newspaper battle reports for that night were; "No major contact, light casualties."

A couple of weeks later when again the battalion was in reserve Brigadier S.L.A. Marshall came to the CP to record the battle for the Army's History section. Marshall an uncommon figure for a U.S. Army General Officer, was of medium stature, overweight, soft spoken, wearing a rumpled uniform and armed with a stack of yellow foolscap and handful of freshly sharpened lead pencils. If he had been wearing a fedora with press pass stuck in the band there would have been no question that he was who he really was; a police reporter from the Detroit Free Press on loan to the U.S. Army.

He had walked out to Dale and examined the locale, now he was ready to hear the survivors account. For the next three days survivors of the Dale Outpost fight gathered at the battalion CP. By nine, General Marshall would arrive alone in a jeep from Division and the group would disappear into the conference hooch (Korean pidgin for house) to reappear for noon chop (more pidgin for food) and again in the afternoon when the General drove back to Division in time for evening mess.

At the first conferences Marshall started with the man that first spotted the Chinese on the fateful night and by coaxing and prodding drew out his account of the fight until some one else entered in to continue the story. Over the three day period by fading into the background, emerging only to clarify and substantiate details with adroit questioning, the General extracted a comprehensive eye witness account, from the inside of the battle. The remarkable part of the exercise was that he transcribed every word by hand on his stack of legal pads. Out of his laborious effort came his book Pork Chop Hill published in 1956 by William Morrow and Company.

42

BEARCAT RED SIX

The task of clearing Dale of casualties from both sides and repairing its defenses became the first post battle priority. A task complicated by our KSC's refusal to touch dead bodies because of superstitions. Both Colonel Kern and General Trudeau came up to view the carnage and assess the damage. A platoon from Item Company was temporarily assigned to Baker Company until they could assimilate replacement from the Division pool. Another Engineer platoon repaired the wire and the battalion's Pioneers helped. Artillery re-registered and fired harassing missions on Hill 190 and Chink Baldy. By day's end we were in shape to hold on through another night. The Chinese had enough and didn't return to the ball. In fact we completed our MLR tour without further serious incident.

Dale wasn't the only position enjoying Chinese attention on April 16 1953, further east Arsenal and Porkchop were also hit in a battle that chewed up the 31st Infantry's second and third Battalions plus the 17th Infantry's first Battalion. Including Dale the battle for Porkchop Hill set a record for tonnage of steel and high explosives poured on enemy positions in a single shoot by American Artillery exceeding WWI's Verdun and WWII's Kwajalein. This battle also was the basis for the movie "Porkchop Hill".

In retrospect it was obvious that the Chinese were past Dales listening post without being detected so listening posts' locations were regularly changed from then on. The Battalion had received replacements for its KATUSA contingent and a group of GIs from the 169th Infantry during our last stay in reserve. Baker Company had their share of both and while individuals from the latter group performed well the KATUSAs failed to fight and the Chinese slaughtered them. That posed a two fold problem with no simple answer. None of the battalion staff or company officers had a solution.

Sgt. Chaing, who was in charge of the battalion headquarters' house keeping detail, did. He said; "Korean boy too small, GI rifle too big." and he was right.

M1 rifles were designed for GIs who averaged 5' 9" and many KATUSAS were 5' 2" or less. Weight of the rifle was not a problem but size of the stock was. Small people had to put much more time and effort in becoming proficient marksmen and the Republic of Korea had too little time and not enough trainers to produce the effort. By and large KATUSAS were lousy shots.

Chaing had a clue not an answer. The problem was that were under utilizing our manpower. Koreans had great leg strength. From toddlers on they walked wherever they went carrying loads on their backs. Americans rode in cars with the load in the back seat.

We began shifting KATUSAs to Dog Company the battalion's heavy weapons company and the rifle companies' weapons platoons. They were retrained as machine gunners and mortar men. As it turned out the Koreans had a natural affinity for mortars and machine guns. They also were fascinated with things mechanical and were delighted to take over maintenance of the weapons that suited GIs fine. Koreans kept the weapons clean and in firing condition. The move also helped the personnel system since weapons crewmen were a scarce commodity in the replacement stream.

The 169th Infantry Combat Team was from Puerto Rico with English as a second language. For the Koreans English was a language brought to the peninsula at the end of WWII. During the stress of a firefight communication, particularly within squads broke down because of a three-way language barrier. The effect of the recent integration of blacks into former all white units produced a checkerboard society since blacks gravitated toward their own kind, as did the whites. The Army Chief of Staff didn't consult all ranks before he passed on the integration decision and the Army had a fair share of unreconstructed rebels in its ranks that kept friction between the two races alive and active.

We had an additional factor to consider, a "buddy" system. Every man had a buddy he was responsible for and as far as practical buddies pulled the same duties. They were members of the same squad filling the same slots. During combat they covered each other's back; they went on pass together and pulled KP together. To finish out the rational of fitting personnel into a structure that worked more efficiently we revamped the buddy system by following new rules.

First one of the buddies had to speak English, fluent English. No Korean Pidgin or Spanish Patios qualified. Second, no pair could both be Puerto Rican, Korean or Black. Buddies didn't have to like each other, just be responsible for each other. Once that rule sunk in, typical GI perversity took over and they began to like each other.

Able company had one drastic failure. While in reserve, one morning a white soldier went AWOL to return that evening high on Korean saki and killed his Black squad leader with a single shot. He was convicted of murder.

PFC Hamilton, the battalion commander's driver was the bravest man in the battalion simply because he was the most scared. He drove regardless of danger wherever he was told with great skill and without question. If our direction was away from the MLR he drove with the aplomb of a tour guide, in the other direction with the furtiveness and urgency of a pursued burglar. His particular demons were air burst. Friendly artillery employed a great deal of VT fuses that detonated when in a few feet of another object, sometimes an object unsubstantial as a cloud.

Airbursts usually occurred hundreds or thousands of feet in the air with little or no danger to those below. The explosion had the distinctive crack and tearing sound of any exploding shell. Without the dampening effect of terrain features it gave the impression of detonating just feet from the back of one's neck. On one occasion an airburst left me occupying the passenger's seat of a driverless jeep motoring down the road when PFC Hamilton abandoned jeep in favor of the security of the ditch.

There were many days that the road leading to George Hill was swept clear of Smokey's efforts by unfavorable winds. Those days the trip to that destination was more than interesting; it was on the far side of adventure. First there was a half-mile drive on a very narrow poorly marked lane through a minefield, the last hundred yards under Chinese observation to a point of decision. A decision of whether or not to follow road in clear Chinese view along the right bank of a dry stream bed or opt to dodge boulders in the stream bed and be partially concealed. The Chinese made a real game of it by sometimes completely ignoring George Hill traffic then there were days that a jeep would draw the first round before emerging from the mine field and a half dozen or so more artillery shells spaced to hasten one's trip to George Hill or Nirvana. On one of those days we made that trip Hamilton would be so drained that he could scarcely make it from jeep to hoochie on return to the battalion CP.

The Chinese had a nasty habit of just before dawn sneaking a couple of observers trailing a ground return telephone wire into the blind spot at the base of hills occupied by Americans. Once safely hidden and connected to their own position by telephone they would direct artillery fire on vulnerable parts of the American position directly above them. To discourage this behavior, Americans sent squad sized patrols out every morning to sweep blind spots of this nuisance.

On a particularly foggy morning Able Company sent a patrol to clear one of their vulnerable positions. The patrol dropped down into the valley at the base of the ridge and moved on down intending to cross over the saddle immediately in front of the position and return along the opposite side of the ridge, just as had been done daily since occupying that sector.

Blinded by dense fog, they missed the first saddle and crossed over the second behind instead of in front of the Chinese position. Midway the Chinese discovered them and opened fire killing two and wounding several others. Thinking that his own unit was firing on him the patrol leader radioed Able Company CP to cease-fire. Lt. Jerry Morse the company commander correctly assessed the situation and put mortar and artillery fire missions on the Chinese position and told the patrol to take cover and hang on that help was on the way.

At battalion we called regiment explained the situation and requested an Armored Personnel Carrier to evacuate casualties. Pfc. Hamilton and I took off for Able Company. Jerry Morse had organized a rescue party and left to extricate the trapped patrol. We followed and found Jerry, a jeep ambulance, medics and rescue party tucked into a small draw covered from Chinese observation and fire. Hamilton pulled in behind the ambulance. The fog was beginning to lift so we augmented nature's efforts by having the Artillery smoke the nearest Chinese positions while the rescue party worked its way in and brought out the wounded and returned for the two KIAs. Before they returned with the bodies, the APC arrived and ran over the driver's side of Hamilton's jeep. Hamilton got out of the way barely in time. If nothing has changed, somewhere in Korea a triangular jeep is a monument to Pfc. Hamilton's great adventure.

One afternoon Division called and said they were sending a Psy War (Psychological Warfare) platoon to set up in our sector. Without knowing what we were getting into I said; "Sure, why not, the more the merrier."

The next morning a deuce and a half loaded with a public address system, portable generator and six men arrived. The Second Lieutenant in charge told me that they wanted to set up their equipment within earshot of an occupied Chinese position. Able company had a location that seemed suitable to me so I sent them up to Lt. Rausch who had recently taken over from Jerry Morse thus being junior among the company commanders less likely to object quite as strenuously as the others might. The lieutenant also asked for help in constructing a position from which he could make his unique contribution to the defeat of the Chinese. He was assigned a half dozen KSCs and a lot of sandbags. In a few days he announced they were ready to begin operating. The evening's calm was shattered by Chinese music several decibels above the comfort range and a harangue in

Chinese. The Chinese showed their appreciation by responding with a mortar barrage. However, our side was well dug in and after a brief pause continued the concert. The Chinese conceded victory and gave up the mortaring.

Sporadically over the next few days the Psy War boys repeated the performance. A Chinese Psy War unit took up the challenge and replied in kind with American music, Chinese accent and English harangue. Under a plea for silence so they could get some sleep and threat of mass desertion from Able Company if they didn't. Division agreed to the withdrawal from the battle of Loud Speakers. Recognizing victory the Chinese did too.

One morning shortly after daybreak the platoon sergeant of one of Able company's rifle platoons dozed off in the platoon's CP while his bunker mates were at chow on the back side of the hill. A Chinese Major rudely awakened him with a pistol butt first in one hand and a surrender leaflet in the other. His offer was gratefully accepted and the prisoner was hustled off to division to be interrogated. Eventually the story filtered back from the interpreters. The Chinese Major until recently commanded a battalion. He had been relieved of command for failure of his men to pass their Communist doctrinal exams. He lost face so he quit.

In the middle of May Major Bill Calnan returned to the Battalion and Division assigned me to a temporary duty team responsible for writing a Command Post Exercise Scenario for IX Corps. The first person I ran into when reporting for duty was an old friend, Captain Paul Malarky from Wooster Ohio, the same Malarky who had commanded H Co. 145th INF ONG. I had last seen Paul some time in 1952 at Camp Polk Louisiana. He was nearing the end of his Korean tour with the 3rd Bn 32nd Inf. With several other officers we drove east of Chorwon and spent the next week writing an imaginary sequence of Chinese forces attacking and penetrating the defenses of the Allied Division holding that sector, including "canned" messages from units on the ground. Later another team of officers, over a twenty-four hour period, would test the command and communication network of the division using the messages we had prepared. Before our scenario could be put in play the Chinese put on their own exercise striking at many of the points we had chosen with the object of killing as many ROK Soldiers as possible before truce took effect.

Back at Battalion I had not quite unpacked before General Trudeau called and told me he wanted me to select and train a rifle team representing the 7th Division in the I Corps Matches beginning the next week. When Generals say; "I want", Majors do. In two days time we had about twenty self or otherwise proclaimed expert rifle men and forty ordnance ordained straight shooting rifles assembled at Division's replacement training center. From this combination we developed a twelve man rifle team and rode a deuce-and-a-half to the Marine Corps range where the matches were held. Our team members tried valiantly putting much more effort in than the ordnance ordained straight shooting rifles could put out and placed fourth behind three Marine Corps teams. We had rifles and field glasses. The Marines had a master gunsmith, shooting jackets, spotting scopes, 300mm coaches spotting scopes and a lot of gall to term this competition.

With this hiatus over and back with my Battalion now occupying 7th Divisions westernmost sector Major Bill Calnan finally departed for the states the old familiar routine settled in. By now truce dates had been announced and the Chinese switched to their final objective of destroying the ROK Army. American occupied sectors were strangely quiet. ROK divisions were under all out attack and in retreat. American advisors to ROK units were heading American casualty lists. Experienced American field grade officers we're being transferred to KMAG (Korean Military Advisor Group) in great haste. I was one of them. Three days before the war ended I was sitting on the hill in IX Corps Area as The Regimental Advisor to the 8th ROK Division's 31st Infantry Regiment.

43

GENERAL MOON

Transfer of duty station in the Combat Zone definitely does not follow Permanent Change of Station protocol. My call came at about 0600 via telephone from my Regimental Commander, Colonel William Kern, who said; "You are to report to the Chief of the IX Corps Korean Military Advisory Group as soon as possible today, orders will follow. I'm sorry to lose you and wish you well. I will be glad to have you in my command any time, God Speed." Then he added; "Don't forget to send your jeep and driver back," I said, "Yes, sir, good luck Colonel." In less than an hour Hamilton and I were under way.

Six dusty, back wrenching hours later at IX Corps KMAG headquarters An affable Lieutenant Colonel was telling me he was glad to see me and that I was lucky to be assigned to the ROK 8th Division since, General Moon, the Commanding General was regarded as one of the premier "fighting" Generals in the ROK Army.

On the three hour trip to General Moon's CP I gathered the impression that the LTC considered himself far luckier than me since he was staying in KMAG Headquarters and wasn't an emergency replacement for one of the regimental advisors that the 8th division lost during the past forty-eight hours. He also explained the Chinese during that time had driven the division back a dozen miles but the division's front remained intact in spite of heavy losses including three out of three KMAG regimental advisors.

It was well that PFC Hamilton was on his way back to 1st BN 31st U.S, Infantry and not staying with me to hear this conversation. He may have turned south and drove until his engine drowned in Pusan Harbor.

At division headquarters we were ushered into KMAG Operations where I saluted and shook hands with my new boss, a Colonel whose name is long forgotten but is remembered as saying; "Major, welcome aboard, we better get acquainted fast because as soon as General Moon's briefing is over this evening you will be moving up to the MLR as one of the Infantry regiments' advisor. About the briefing, You will meet General Moon the Division's Commanding General, don't be surprised by anything he might say."

Over evening mess with Col. Long Forgotten and assorted lesser ranks serving as staff advisors I learned a lot about General Moon. He had served in China as a Sergeant Major. Sergeant Major was the highest rank attainable for Korean Nationals in the Imperial Japanese Army. No one could say whether or not he had served with the Japanese Sixth Division, responsible for "The Rape of Nanking" and erased from the Imperial Army's roll in WWII on the Island of Bougainville but he fit the profile. He had gained his reputation in the ROK Army by summarily executing officers of his command for cowardliness in the face of Chinese attacks. The General's reply to the questions, why? "Everyone knew they cowards, all run away from enemy, why waste time?" At that evening's briefing, after all others were assembled he and his staff made an entrance.

The general was, perhaps 5'5" and looked as though he had been carved out of native granite. His uniform, freshly starched, fit him without a wrinkle, his head seemed to grow out of his shoulders without the benefit of neck and his countenance was an impassive mask. His Chief of Staff arose, made a slight bow to the general who answered with a nod then turned and addressed the audience. Including besides the KMAG contingent the divisions principal commanders and key staff members.

The Chief spoke briefly in Korean and interpreter translated; "Colonel Kim, Chief of Staff, say; General Moon wish to give greetings to commanders and American guests, now we hear from staff what today's operation do." Colonel Kim, his name may not have been Kim but that is as good a guess as Lee or any other of the some two dozen or so Korean surnames.

The briefing continued with Colonel Kim introducing 8th Division staff officers who using a map outlined the past twenty four hours of combat and the English speaking ROK Captain interpreting the conversation into fractured English.

The operation had not gone well for the Koreans. During the course of the night long battle they had pulled back some twelve miles to more favorable and higher terrain before stopping the Chinese assault. The sole positive note was that at the end of the night the Chinese had not succeeded in penetrating the division's front.

General Moon sat through the presentation without comment or show of emotion. At the conclusion he got up, walked to the map, using his swagger stick as a pointer critiqued the operation sometimes pointing, gesturing, threatening and sometimes beating the map with his stick. The general concluded his lecture and sat down.

The interpreter stood up and said; "General Moon say soldiers in Division fight hard but leaders lead backward away from enemy not forward against enemy, lose much ground. Twenty-seven regiment Commander Colonel Pak not stop his first battalion from letting enemy go behind position make whole division back up to stop enemy from taking high ground in rear. Colonel Pak must go back to regiment and make new first battalion commander." The interpreter sat down and General Moon stood up this time showing much emotion, all rage and uttered a staccato burst of Korean at the interpreter who visibly shaken turned to the audience and said; "I make big mistake, General Moon say to tell what he say, not lie. He say Colonel Pak go back to twenty-seven Regiment and shoot first Battalion Commander then make new Commander", a very delicate distinction, indeed.

We left the briefing and Colonel Long Forgotten introduced me to Sergeant Blank who would double as my sole American companion and jeep driver, ROK Lieutenant Pak who would be my interpreter and a very worried ROK Colonel Commander of the ROK 8th Division, 31st Infantry Regiment whom I would advise as long as either of us lasted.

The Lieutenant, whose name turned out to be Pak, threw his duffel in Sergeant Blank's jeep and we followed the very worried commander's jeep out of the compound headed north. After about an hour and a half of blackout driving among ruts, bumps, stops and starts Pak told me that the ROK Colonel's name was Chang. We reached the end of the road and began a long climb and chogi down a ridge to the regiment's CP. Completing the transfer from U.S. Army 31st Infantry to ROK Army 31st Infantry in one day. In the distance down the ridge we could see the night sky light up with flashes of exploding shells and hear a rattle of small arms fire punctuated by the thump of incoming mortar rounds.

The CP was a huddle of make shift shelters surrounded by partially dug fox holes and hastily constructed weapon's positions. Colonel Chang was no where to be found but his CP was a bustle of activity and the only answer Lieutenant Pak had for my questions was a shrug and "No say". Soon the sound of small arms fire came from behind us. The people in the CP began fading into the darkness.

Pak said; "Come, we must go now." For a fleeting second I considered manning an abandoned machine gun in one of the fighting positions but the second was so fleeting that could not be even considered a thought. Pak handed me a short billed soft cap and motioned me to put it on, he was already wearing one in lieu of his American helmet.

We dropped off the ridge and found a trail part way down that we followed back in the direction we came from earlier that night. Occasionally we saw small groups of men moving around higher on the ridge wearing the same small billed soft caps we were without inquiring directions of them. Eventually we passed the sound of small arms fire that seemed to be concentrated on the opposite side of the ridge and began to see in the growing light of dawn the rounded silhouette of American style helmets.

Pak put his helmet back on and I donned my American style flat topped soft hat and joined the crowd. We continued down the ridge for another couple of miles and ran into Colonel Chang and his command group busy digging in a new CP.

Chang offered no explanation; Pak and I were too beat to ask for one, we slept most of the morning. The following night remained relatively quiet marred only with the sound of distant fire. Mid afternoon of the third day of membership in the Korean Military Advisory Group I came off the hill unwashed, unshaven and unhappy with the hand fate dealt me, and learned that truce was a fact. Back at IX Corps reunited with my duffel, fed, washed and shaved life brightened.

44

TAEGU

A few days of heel cooling at IX Corps brought orders to report to KMAG Headquarters for an orientation and reassignment. With several other late replacements I embarked on a twenty-four hour train ride covering two hundred plus miles to Taegu. The first class section of the train where we officers rode had curved wooden seat backs, the rest of the train didn't, just wooden seats, straight backs. At its rattling, jolting, jerking best the train might get over fifteen miles an hour but not often, the road bed couldn't stand the pounding. We had K rations to see us through.

The train ride was interesting but uncomfortable, very uncomfortable; the seats were constructed of wooden slats over contoured uprights, contoured to fit Korean not American frames. The non adjustable seats were too close to the floor and the space between them too short. Americans fit into them like crows perched on a fence rail.

No two rails in the roadbed were on the same level and the cars were hooked up European style with chains and separated by bumpers. When trains departed the station there was a measurable pause between that of the engine and caboose. When the engine left and the slack in the connecting chain was expended the first car started with a jerk, when the slack between it and the second car was gone it stopped with a jerk. The oscillation punctuated by bumps as the car wheels passed over misaligned rails continued down the string of cars well past the time the full train was underway and repeated in reverse when the train counted down for the next stop. Not a pleasant trip at all.

The panorama that unfolded as the train huffed its way through Korea was interesting. The roadbed like water sought its own level and meandered down valleys seeking saddles to cross into the next. Valley floors were latticed with uniformly green rice paddies climbing like stair steps up tributary watersheds. Intervening hills and ridges were sparsely vegetated with low trees. At the base of the hills and between rice paddies every few miles rested a village or occasionally a small city.

Building construction in the villages was typically oriental style thatched roof with flaring overhang and mud and wattle walls. Houses were easy to distinguish from utilitarian buildings, houses had chimneys. In Korean villages central heating was a reality when European Royalty was still huddled before chimney grates in stone walled bed chambers. The village fixture was a "hot floor" in every home.

Koreans prepared a house site by digging a ditch the length of the planned building and laying up a stone arch in the ditch. The next step was to tamp a dirt floor over the arch. The house was built over the floor with a chimney at one end a hearth outside the house at the other. Smoke and hot gases from a fire in the hearth heated the floor and house built over it. In a way this construction technique accounted for the sparseness of vegetation on the hills. South Korea was a fuel poor nation that had consumed most of its timber supply and the villages now depended on rice straw and spare branches gleaned from fruit and nut trees on the slopes for fuel.

Footpaths and narrow lanes connected villages. Dirt roads and railway netted the cities. A frames and an occasional ox cart moved loads between villages. An A frame was an ingenious extension of a pack frame. Built to individual specifications, an A frame consisted of two sturdy poles fastened together at the top well above the users head and separated by a crossbar at hip height. On the front of an A frame, six inches or so below the top of the users' shoulders on each pole was secured a curved shoulder piece On the back of each at hip height extended a short perpendicular load bearing member. The frame was built to suit the users shoulder breadth that width separated the base of the A enough to permit the user to walk without interference. The final element of this device was a separate pole that served as a walking staff and prop when at rest, thus converting the A frame to a stable tripod so a load could be lashed to back of the frame. With a propped A frame loaded the bearer bent his knees and backed under the shoulder piece, grasped the walking staff, straightened his legs and walked off with an incredible load. From the back a Korean farmer with an A frame load of bundled rice straw looked like a walking hay mow.

Taegu was a bustling city of single storied, tin roofed buildings crowded together on both sides of winding dirt streets. At the edge of the town ran a rocky river that housed the cities laundry and silk dyeing industries. Other industries conducted under the overhanging eaves of the owner's establishments included shoe making from discarded GI tires. (Drivers keep your spare tires chained and locked to your vehicle and never leave it parked unattended outside the military compound). Light bulb rehab, replacing burned out filaments in GI discarded light bulbs. Sheet metal manufacturing from GI discarded tin cans.

There was a gold mine of tin cans waiting some Korean entrepreneur in the barbed wire entanglements left by American units. GIs threw their empty c-ration cans into the wire as an impediment to adventure minded Chinese who might try to crawl under the wire. These are only samples of the conversion of GI discards to wealth. Bicycles and pedestrians filled the main streets flowing in opposite directions at the same time. Life in the military compound that housed both ROK Army and KMAG Headquarters was much more ordered and serene.

There I learned that I was scheduled out on the morning's flight to Osaka Japan for a five days rest and recreation leave but it was raining. On return, they would have orders cut for my next assignment. Then I drew the three months back pay all ninety dollars of it bought some clean underwear and socks at the Post Exchange, paid a Korean orderly a quarter to shine my second pair of shoes and press my spare uniform. Showered, shaved clean from the skin out, went to the Officers Open Mess had a drink at the bar and a steak to order dinner. This was civilized living almost worth leaving my beloved U.S.A. First Battalion, Thirty First Infantry.

Looking for something to do I kibitzed a poker game in the lounge. It was very interesting. The participants were two old timers a Captain and Lieutenant Colonel and four transients Two Lieutenants, a Captain and Major. The longer I watched the more it became obvious that this game wasn't "Poker", it was "Fleece the Lambs", the old timers were playing sides. I went to bed bemused by the gullibility of some people.

In the morning it was still raining and my flight was canceled. During the day I concluded that by judiciously applying my new found knowledge of a certain game of chance I might turn an extra buck or two. My seventy plus dollars and change could use reinforcement.

After dinner I wandered over to the Poker table as the two sharks were looking for likely victims. Looking my most likely I was invited in. Lady luck smiled when the club closed my seventy plus change was within shouting distance of seven hundred. In the morning it was raining and my flight was canceled. That evening leaving the dinning hall two of my companions of the night before were waiting for me, they wanted their money back.

I had faint prior inkling of this possibility and had the really big bills from the night before stashed in my shoes so when my bankroll shrunk to that point I could turn my pockets inside out to back a story that the rest had already been sent home to an ailing wife. Lady Luck didn't smile, she grinned from ear to ear, when the game ended at three the following morning, in the latrine, after the club closed. I had prospered twice. Last night's seven hundred was almost fourteen hundred. In the morning the clouds parted, the sun came out, smiled and I went to Japan.

Aboard the flight was another major who looked vaguely familiar and turned out to be Major "Rudy" Rudolph from 147th Infantry and Cincinnati OH whom I had known casually at Camp Polk. Landing at Osaka we checked into the USO hotel then visited the PX. Feeling very rich, I purchased a sports jacket, slacks, shirts, ties, underwear, socks and shoes. Back at the hotel dressed in my new finery Rudy and I descended to the lounge and had several drinks at the bar one or two included the "house." At dinner our party included some new acquaintances and some we had yet to meet. As a token of our successful Trans Sea of Korea flight we toasted the house in champagne and a fog drifted in that never fully dissipated for the next seven days, the monsoon had settled in, it was raining and our return flight to Taegu was also twice canceled.

We gathered culture touring Osaka, Otsu and Kyoto, mainly Otsu's Officer's Club where we could wallow in nostalgia under the spell of an all Japanese American style swing band We also shopped and haggled with Japanese merchants who ignored the American one price take it or leave it sales system. I bought Betty Miki Moto cultured pearls, damascene jewelry and tried on a trans—Pacific phone hook up to talk her into a twelve place setting set of Noritake dinnerware. She would have none of it. Finally the fantasy ended. I packed my sports clothes, sent them home, put on my uniform and headed for the hill.

45

COLONEL CHOI

The train taking me back to the MLR had not mellowed nor had the distance shrunk. Colonel Long Forgotten said; "You're in luck you're being assigned to the top division in the ROK Army, the Cap ROKs." Having met the premier fighting general in the ROK Army there was no reason to explore the subject further. He also got me a jeep with a driver, one Sergeant O'Rourke, who knew his way to the Capitol ROKS.

I reported to the KMAG Chief who invited me into his office, closed the door, and informed me my assignment was advisor to the 1st ROK Infantry Regiment commanded by Colonel Choi (pronounced Shay) then outlined a litany of Colonel Choi's character flaws, high crimes and misdemeanors. The Chief made it clear that my mission was to report substantiating evidence directly to him so the Division Commander, a Brigadier General, could get rid of Choi. That didn't quite clear with what had been explained to me at KMAG Headquarters as KMAG's role.

The Chief may thought I agreed whole heartedly with his instructions but he was wrong. What I agreed to do was to discover all the dirt I could. He continued the briefing with the Divisions current situation, introductions to his staff and my interpreter a ROK Lieutenant named Chaing. Then he shook my hand and wished me Godspeed.

Chaing took me to the motor pool where I signed for a 3/4 ton and equipment. Met truck driver Pak and a sixteen-year-old former line crosser named Kim. Who gave up his career and turned orderly, cook/handy man because the communists suspected his sympathies ran deeper south than north. Kim completed my detachment.

The Division had been badly mauled but not broken in the Chinese final drive to kill as many ROKs as possible. By the time the war wound down and the cease-fire took effect the 1st Regiment had lost its entire 3rd Battalion, from LTC Alpha to Pvt. Zed, all, entire, lock, stock and barrel. The first two Battalions and regimental special units were reduced to cadres but the regiment was on its feet and killing Chinese at the bell. The 3rd Battalion had been replaced with a battalion from the ROK Interior Defense Force (IDF).

The IDF was made up of separate light infantry battalions. Their TO&E did not include a heavy weapons company. Their roles were to keep lines of communication open, fight delaying actions and in their spare time serve as the National Police Force. The ROK Infantry Replacement Training Centers were drained of replacements to bring the battered divisions to strength. IDF battalions became the main source of replacements.

When I joined the regiment it had just arrived at a training area to begin basic training, an area that was an extended collection of abandoned rice paddies in typical broken Korean terrain. Rather than face the inevitable of a long haggle in getting new home set up I told my interpreter; "You do." The implacable veneer of Chaing Il Suk, 1sr Lt ROK mask cracked a little at this opportunity, He saluted and said; "Yes, Sah, Colonel". I shook my head and pointed to my gold oak leaves; "Major" "Majah" he corrected. I rejoined Sergeant O'Rourke my jeep driver and sole link to the United States Army to observe the efficiency with which Lt Chaing dispatched his first assignment. Chaing walked back to the 3/4 ton and engaged Orderly Pak and Cook/Handyman Kim in conversation, they departed. Chaing joined O'Rourke and me at the jeep. The 3/4 ton with Pak and Kim returned followed by two files of about a dozen each of ROK soldiers. Pak took charge of one file Kim the other and a volcano of activity erupted. I had planned well, I had directed well now I would sit back and supervise well. I was happy with my new command.

Before completion of my supervisory chore a ROK jeep showed up, the driver talked to Chaing, Chaing talked to me and we went to meet Colonel Choi. The Colonel received us ceremoniously at his headquarters. He was tall for a Korean, perhaps 5' 10", slender and very much in charge of the situation, His words, at least Chaing's delivery of them, were well chosen but empty. It was obvious that he disliked Chaing and his understanding of English was better than he let on. He cut off Chaing's delivery of my reply well before the end with; "We have tea now." we drank our tea and came home. My gut reaction was that this was going to be a cool dry summer.

The following morning Col. Choi showed up just as I was finishing breakfast. Following his jeep a deuce-and-a-half loaded with a dozen ROK soldiers. I saluted and said; "Good morning Colonel." He answered my salute and spoke in length to Chaing who interpreted; "Colonel say he hope the Majah have good night sleep now he wish to show Majah new training area while his soldjahs move

Majah's tent to bettah place. This place no good bullets from rifle range land heah when we do rifle training. Majah's sahgeant can stay watch ROK soldjahs see they do good work." I told O'Rourke what was happening Chaing and I climbed in the back of Choi's jeep.

Our first stop was regimental Head quarters where Choi introduced his Battalion Commanders, principal Staff Officers and showed off the major installations under construction.

The first was a large open sided pavilion whose centerpiece was a six by twelve foot sand table scale model of the regiment's current training area the quality of work was impressive. We spent the rest of the day touring and in a three-way discussion of the training facility under construction. Some of our discussions were pretty heated but usually at the end of the day we both would agree on a position. I developed a genuine liking for Choi.

There came a morning that Choi showed up alone in his jeep and said; "Get in." I stood aside to let Chaing in the back seat and Choi said something in Korean to Chaing then turned to me grinned and said; "We don't need him I talk pretty good English." He was right he talked much better English than Chaing. Later on I asked Choi why he waited so long to decide we didn't need Chaing's interpretations of our conversation, he said: "I wait to see if you make mistake that tell me you are not okay guy. You do not make mistake, you okay. Besides Chaing Japanese I do not trust Japanese." He was right Chaing was born in Japan of Korean parents Just as a side bar and a matter of fact Chaing had been in Hiroshima on the day the first atomic bomb fell. He was a student at the time leaving the city with a group of friends and only remembered a huge explosion of orange light before losing consciousness. He awoke on a makeshift bed in an open air hospital with the back of his neck badly burned and his back burned to a lesser degree. He never saw any of his friends he had been with again.

He attributed his survival to the fact he was wearing light colored clothing that reflected much of his exposure to radiation. He had the scars to back up his story. That didn't cut any ice with Choi, Chaing was Japanese and Choi did not trust Japanese. Choi occasionally chided me; "You leave too many Japanese alive in big war."

At the end of WWII Choi second son of a schoolteacher in a small North Korean village had just embarked on career of teaching school when Communist trained governing cadres returned to Korea from Russia. Their mission to impose a Red Regime on the Russian occupied zone. Choi, senior, was arrested and was never heard of again. Choi's elder brother escaped to South Korea and began a career with the Korean State department.

Choi, his mother, sister and younger brother abandoned their home and took up residence in the slums of a larger city. There they eked out a hand to mouth existence until the day his sister failed to return home from shopping for rice.

They learned that the police had picked her up. A common fate for many young North Korean girls. Conventional wisdom had it that the police sold them to brothels since they never returned. The three remaining Chois decided that night to work their way to the coast and use the small amount of gold they had been hoarding to bribe a small boat crew to smuggle them into South Korea.

They were successful and Choi's mother now reigned over the household of the older brother, making his wife miserable. She looked forward to the day she reigned over her oldest son's household, making his wife miserable. Choi and his younger brother were both ROK Soldiers, one a Colonel the other a First Lieutenant.

There is absolutely no doubt in my mind that during our brief association that I learned more from Choi than I taught him. He taught me that the human spirit is indestructible and obstacles are there to be overcome. In the process I learned how the ROK Army overcame the challenge of maintaining a modern Army in the field in the face of the country's grinding poverty. The United States helped with the materiel of war and a little more. The Korean government provided a rice ration.

ROK units took it from there, with regiments the mean, that is some smaller some larger, units engaged in a number of entrepreneur enterprises to augment the government's contribution. Not all were nice and some went beyond legal and ethical limits but all were productive.

The 1st.ROK Infantry Regiment acquired several blocks of residences in Seoul, a farm and an operating gold mine. The gold mine, part of the corrections system, was operated by soldiers who didn't want to fight. When a soldier reached a point that he was about to go AWOL he could turn himself in and work the urge out of his system in the gold mine. If he went AWOL and was caught he was likely to be shot. The farm was sort of a convalescent leave center producing rations for the regiment and the rental property a source of income. The Seoul property was the center of the controversy between Choi and the Division Commander who wanted to dump Choi to gain the property.

It was tough to keep the EE8 phone system working among ROK units because beyond an occasional meat animal issued along with the governments rice ration and limited number of meat animals raised on the farms the chief source of additional protein was the small fish that inhabited the rice paddies. The easiest way to catch these minnows was to trail two bare ends of telephone wire through rice paddy ponds while vigorously cranking an EE8 phone attached to the other end of the wires. This operation took three ROK soldiers, one to maneuver the probes, one to crank the phone and one to retrieve the shocked fish with a dip net fashioned out of mosquito netting. This practice quite obviously was "calling up fish".

Choi showed up before breakfast at my quarters one day with a basket of eggs and blandly announced; "Now every day I have breakfast with you American style, more better. Korean style breakfast all same other meals, rice and kimchi, kimchi and rice." From that moment forward Choi was a regular at my Breakfast Board. Quite an outspoken one when Kim's culinary efforts fell short of Fort Benning Officers Open Mess' standards gauged by Choi's recollections.

It was possible but not likely that we both attended TIS at the same time. Our explorations down that trail always came a cropper with; "Do you remember the fat Medical officer who taught how to use a Syringe loaded with an antidote for nerve gas?" "Nah, we had a skinny first lieutenant who showed us that." Choi had been there, he complained bitterly about the inability of the management of the Officer's Mess to keep up with the demand of Korean students for Louisiana Hot Sauce; they ate it on everything not excluding desserts.

He also had an account of his first day in the United States that only could have happened to naive, unworldly Korean. His contingent of newly commissioned second lieutenants bound for TIS arrived in San Fransisco on a troopship under the guidance of an American Escort Officer who had briefed them on the perils of the innocents in the wicked cities of the west. The first day off ship they were housed in a downtown hotel. Choi discovered the telephone in his room and with a little experimenting discovered he could talk to his compatriots in a room a couple of floors beneath his. Dressed in his skivvies he decided to call on them. He didn't bother to take a room key. He stepped out of his room the door closed behind him. He realized he was in a public area scanty clad he tried to get back into his room the door would not open. He spotted the door to the fire escape that opened but closed behind him and would not open again. He went up a flight. That door didn't open nor did the one two floors down. He descended to the bottom of the stair well and found a door that did open but when he stepped through, it closed behind him and would not open to let him back in the hotel. Not only that the street was full of cars and the sidewalk full of people who stared at him. An understanding policeman discovered him, escorted him around to the lobby and presented him to the front desk. He was put in the hands of a bellhop with a master key who escorted him to his room and opened the door for him. Choi was a quick learner; he avoided fire escapes from that time forward.

During my stay with the American 31st infantry it became obvious to me that much of the blame for ROK soldiers' reputation for being untrustworthy lay with GIs' failure to understand the obstacles ROKs had to overcome. American's propensity for jumping to conclusions and stereotyping strangers as inferior added to the impression. My experience was when ROKs were a part of a team, were given instructions and explanations they could understand they stood as tall as GIs. On more than one occasion I lost or inadvertently left an item of personal property behind in our tours of Choi's command and on every occasion it was returned.

My experience with the 8th ROK Division did nothing to bolster my earlier conviction until at the end of the day. Thanks to ROK Lieutenant Pak, I lived to fight another day. Watching Choi rebuild his shattered regiment erased any shadow of doubt about the character of ROK Soldiers that might have remained.

Choi's regiment arrived on site of their new training area on Thursday. I arrived on Friday. Monday morning Choi introduced me to a newly constructed rifle range backed by a Fort Benning style Preliminary Rifle Instruction (PRI) field. There were improvisations never imagined on the shores of the Chattahoochee. Instructor stands were flat topped square mounds of packed earth raising assistant instructors and instructors to commanding views of their sector of responsibility. Targets were made of rice paper on wooden frames hand numbered at the top. Firing points were marked with corresponding numbered stakes. Every thing had been constructed by hand with the simplest of tools. In lieu of conventional pits that targets could be withdrawn into each target had an individual foxhole dug just in front of and a little to the right of the target where a target marker could stay safely hidden during the firing of a string to emerge on signal and score the target with a double ended paddle marked with conventional black on one side disc, indicating two and black on white cross reverse side indicating three, at one end and a red, indicating four disc with a reverse white side, indicating five on the other. Choi and I had quite a discussion over safety precautions on a range with such hazardous conditions as this that he ended with finality by saying; "Soldiers must learn the sound of bullets." If anyone ever was hurt on that range I never learned of it.

Choi and I stopped by the regimental dispensary one afternoon and Choi climbed out of the jeep and confronted a young ROK Lieutenant. The Lieutenant was wearing an American style flat topped stiffened cloth cap, a pistol belt and pistol items of equipment not authorized for ROK company grade officers.

After a short conservation the Lieutenant drew the pistol and held it out to Choi who seized the pistol and hit the Lieutenant a full extended arm blow across the side of the face. knocking him to the ground and cutting a deep gash in his face. Choi yelled something toward the dispensary, unbuckled the Lieutenant's pistol belt, jammed the pistol into the holster, picked up the Lieutenants cap, tossed both side arm and hat in the back of the jeep climbed in and drove off. Two ROK soldiers helped the Lieutenant into the dispensary. A little way down the road I asked; "What was that all about?" Choi still shaking said; "I ask Lieutenant what is his name? He say 'Lieutenant Han' I ask what is his unit? He say 'Charley Company 584th IDF.' He lie make me very angry Charley Company 584th IDF no more now Love Company 3rd Bn 1st ROK Army Infantry Regiment. Now I go sign Court Martial paper."

On another occasion we passed by about a half dozen ROK soldiers lined up and being lectured by a powerfully built ROK Master Sergeant who was carrying a four foot piece of wood two by four. The sergeant stopped, barked out a command and the file faced to the rear and bent over hands on knees. The Sergeant stepped up to the first man and with a baseball swing sent him sprawling with a flat side blow of the two by four and the next, the next, the next, the next, the next and the next. Choi elbowed me, grinned and said; "Company punishment." The ROK version of military justice might have been severe and personal but it was quick.

One evening after chow Choi and LTC Kim, his executive officer drove up and Choi said; "Get in we go bathe." They had towels so I grabbed a towel and bar of soap and joined them. Choi drove us back in the Boonies to a place where a clear mountain stream flowed over a lip of rocks cascading into a shelving pool, a natural reproduction of a Roman Bath. Our trip to the baths became a nightly ritual. Since no one other than those invited by Choi ever put in an appearance I assumed that the word was out that the pool was the old man's private perk.

One morning at breakfast Choi announced; "Soon winter come, this tent too cold. Today we build you house." As we drove off, a truck load of ROK soldiers drove up. When we returned that afternoon, where my A tent once stood, was a new mansion. The house, mounted on rock piers, was about 10' X 12' X 7' divided into two equal rooms. The wall dividing the two rooms had a 5' X 2' doorway, no door, cut in one end. The bed room had been built around my meager bed room furniture. Each room had two windows, two foot square holes covered with rice paper on the inside and a solid hinged at the top shutter on the outside. The living room was furnished with the same two folding chairs and table my tent had been. My living room had 5' X 2" doorway/with door and a slanted drip guard over it. Both rooms were papered with plain rice paper. The amazing thing was that it was constructed of dismembered ammunition boxes. Pieces of board 18" long and varying in width between 6 and 12 inches cut from standard three quarter inch stock. By overlapping these boards the carpenters turned them into one and a half inch planks with lap edges. The house was put together without beams or pillars in about eight hours time. Oh yes, I nearly forgot it was floored with a herringbone weave of ammunition box lids and shingled with flattened c-ration cans.

My residency in my new mansion was short lived I came down with hepatitis or something like it or perhaps the Chinese were wrong and Kim's sympathy ran deeper north than south. After three weeks of trying unsuccessfully to get medical help through KMAG channels I had my driver (O'Rourke was gone and I don't remember his replacements name) drive me west into I Corps area and stop at the first Aid Station we found. We found one that belonged to an Artillery unit whose docs agreed that I was no longer fit for duty and shipped me out by air to a General Hospital in Osaka, Japan. The Docs said they knew all about Army regulations and would in due course notify KMAG of my whereabouts.

I'm not too sure that they kept their word because two months later when I returned to KMAG Headquarters it took me about ten days to convince KMAG Personnel that I belonged and they owed me back pay.

46

HELLO KEN

The Admissions room of the hospital in Osaka echoed the sound of a familiar voice. Ken Norton had arrived seconds ahead of me, up front in the plane. I rode in the back section. Now he was trying to talk the admissions clerk into something of which I had no idea, one thing was certain if he was in it I was going to be too.

As it turned out we didn't have a choice we were both Majors, both had been tentatively diagnosed as having hepatitis and we were about to be assigned the same room. Ken's diagnosis lifted a degree of Kim's suspected guilt since Ken had never dined at Kim's cuisine there was little chance that Kim could be responsible for both our internal problems.

Once we were admitted and assigned to the same room we compared notes and discovered that we shared the same symptoms, low appetites, nausea, low grade fever, low energy but neither of showed any signs of jaundice. The doctors poked probed and pondered then decided maybe yes maybe no we were stricken with hepatitis but at least whatever it was it was close enough to be treated as hepatitis.

First they lectured us on the prospects of permanent liver damage including that never again for the remainder of our lives would we dare the chance of taking even one sip of an alcoholic beverage, it might result in an almost immediate and painful death or possibly a long lingering painful terminal illness whichever displeased us more.

Then they put us on a high-energy diet and a regimen of daily blood chemistry test, one morning we each donated a vial of blood from our right arm and the next from the left. It wasn't long before at the sounds of the blood sucking technician's footsteps our veins retreated behind our elbows.

Smitty, Captain Smith R.N. ANC offered us no sympathy instead regaled us with stories of collapsed veins and veins of last resort from which to draw blood. To make matters worse it seemed as if no matter when we opened our eyes

Smitty or someone else clad in white was by our bedside demanding we drink a milk shake or some other noxious concoction or asking how rare we wanted our steak.

We got even with Smitty. Not long after we arrived we were labeled Ambulatory patients and allowed to use the hospitals day room and Post Exchange. In the PX we discovered a stateside fad that was sweeping American Occupation Forces in Japan, three-dimensional comic books.

Some one in the film industry discovered by separating green from red tones on a film and printing the two colors on the same film offset from each other, when viewed through one red and one green lens the image appeared to add depth to its dimensions.

We purchased red and green glasses and a supply of three D comic books and waited for Saturday. Smitty had been brainwashing us to be on our very best behavior for next Saturday's command inspection. She forewarned us that the Hospital's Commanding Officer was an absolute bear, a Bird Colonel who was bucking for a star in a field of many applicants.

We were most cooperative, on Saturday morning we had our belongings neatly arranged, were freshly scrubbed and shaven, lying in un-wrinkled beds with the same amount of sheet showing on each side. When Smitty after a final check and departed down the hall to the end of the corridor of her ward we donned our red and green glasses, opened our comic books to the middle pages and turned them upside down and assumed a reclining position of attention, as near as possible.

Shortly we heard footsteps and muffled voices in the hall then Smitty opened our door stepped inside and commanded; "Atten-ah-er-Oh My God." The Two Star General, obviously the department commander, accompanied by a full Colonel, snorted coughed and said; "At ease, Gentlemen I presume." and led the inspecting party down the hall. Later Smitty admitted that was the easiest Command Inspection she had ever survived.

After two weeks of blood letting the Doctors deemed us well enough to have a six hour pass. We accepted the opportunity and caught the local train for Otsu the headquarters of the US Army Southern Honshu Department and the home of one of the finest Officer clubs in Japan. Ken and I had been looking forward to this occasion for several days not only for the welcome escape from hospital routine but also to test the medical theory so adamantly articulated by the hospital staff that in our case any intake of alcohol would prove fatal.

We went to Otsu determined to scientifically test that theory by taking small alternate sips of a martini waiting to observe the effect on the first sipper before moving to the next. The first martinis passed with only a slight aura of a feeling of well being and a small increase in appetite. By the end of the second martinis it was obvious they indeed did improve our appetites to the point we ordered large rare steaks. Convinced we had decisively disproved a seriously flawed medical theory we had another martini while waiting for our steaks.

Ken said; 'You know, Cliff, Smitty and her husband belong to this club and everyone in Japan goes to the club on Saturday night. Why not wait and have dinner with them?" I agreed. Smitty and her husband never showed but we didn't care we discovered that the Otsu Officer's club Square Dancing Society was having a thing.

We stayed for that. The last thing I remember of the occasion was seeing Ken laid out flat and horizontal about four feet off the dance floor on his way down until a Japanese taxi driver and an orderly helped us into the hospital in Osaka.

We proved our theory but they didn't let us out on pass for another two weeks. Some two months later we were discharged from the hospital, rode Japan's Bullet train to Tokyo and returned to Korea, Ken to I Corps Headquarters and me to KMAG Headquarters in Taegu.

At Taegu the same elderly Captain and Lieutenant Colonel were playing sides against new replacements at the poker table but since Taegu was my new home I couldn't waste valuable sleep staying up all night playing poker.

My new assignment was in KMAG Plans and Operations section where with several other staff officers, we were busy reviewing contingency plans for defending South Korea if and when the Chinese decided to move in our direction. As staff jobs go this one wasn't so bad, frequently we got to travel to the MLR to see if the plans being reviewed accurately represented the terrain to be defended.

Our section chief was a Colonel who had a private office and there were other assorted ranks in the section. The action officers and supporting clerical personnel occupied a large room with an open space for administrative people and two man cubicles for the action officers. Each cubicle contained two desks face to face with three chairs, a straight chair beside the desks for a visitor, for multiple visitors borrow chairs from other cubicles, a swivel chair at each desk with a file cabinet against the partition behind it. My desk mate was Major Ray Meyers.

Ray had been with KMAG longer than I but had more three point months. He was embarking on his first winter in Korea, while I had half a winter under my belt and could look forward to returning to the states by early spring.

One day Ray looked up from his desk as a master sergeant grinning from ear to ear entered our cubicle. Ray knocked over his chair in haste to greet the visitor. By the time they reached each other they were laughing to the point of complete incoherence and hanging on to the other with one arm while pounding his back with the other. Pandemonium finally ebbed and the story came out in bits and pieces.

Ray's last state side assignment had been Fort Riley Kansas, an old Cavalry post. The possibility of organizing a Mule Pack Train Battalion was under consideration as a support element for troops fighting in mountainous terrain. Such a provisional unit had been put together in Italy during the late days of WWII with some success.

Ray's best buddy at Riley was a Major who worked in the posts Adjutant General's department. All personnel assignment orders are issued through the Adjutant General's Department. Ray's friend had the misfortune to be caught in one of the Army's reduction in force programs and was given the option of resuming his former enlisted rank of Master Sergeant or leaving the service, he opted for the former. On his last duty day he stayed at his office until every one left then proceeded to cut a set of fictitious orders complete with a Department of Army Message number activating a Mule Pack Train Battalion. He assigned Ray as the Battalion Operations Officer as well as several other choice assignments for other of his friends. He ran enough copies to provide one for each of his buddies and put them in distribution. He overlooked destroying the stencil. The morning crew came on, the stencil ran it and made full distribution of the false order. It took about two days before anyone thought to check the Department of Army Message number. Army's reply to the query was that no such message existed. Ray's buddy had long since departed for his new station and the Post Commandant in a moment of facing reality decided that the best solution to the whole incident was to make believe it never happened and all those who had packed to move to their new non assignment unpacked and pretended to forget it.

There was one other really noteworthy happening during my final stay with KMAG before leaving for the states. ROK Headquarters in keeping with their national traditions honored KMAG with a New Years celebration not on their New Year's Day but on the American's.

It started with a formal reception with all ranks present. After appropriate remarks by the Commanding General Officers retired to their own private affair and enlisted people left for their own club and further celebration Officers were treated to a lavish spread followed by a ball. However, there was a glitch to the proceedings. Koreans followed the Japanese protocol for public entertainment by not including wives but substituting geishas as dinner companions and entertainers. Geishas had been an honored profession in Japan and Korea before the American occupation at the end of WWII but GIs had quickly degraded the profession to prostitutes and American Brass banned the practice for official occasions involving Americans.

For this occasion ROK Headquarters invited a multitude of ROK Women's Army Corps volunteers of all ranks decked out in American mail order finery. These young women who filled clerical and menial post in the ROK Army were the avante garde of liberated Korean women and welcomed the chance to socialize on a formal basis with their superiors and American guests.

The orchestra was a passable substitute for an American swing band. We older guests, most of whom had long since joined the more sedate ranks of would be Fred Astaires, were outstripped by our more energetic and athletic juniors soon gravitated to the role of observers. The center of attention was a very attractive young lady wearing a strapless red evening gown with no obvious means of support, so obvious that she had resorted to artificial means to round out the contours of her costume. The support from below proved adequate to withstand the force of gravity while jitterbugging with a young American Lieutenant however there was nothing to anchor the centrifugal force of their gyrations and her exterior decor shifted moorings so that when she left the dance floor at the end of the number malformed with one bosom in the middle of her chest and the other anchored just below her left armpit. She disappeared into the midst of the pool of her sisters to emerge once again with everything properly balanced. This event indeed left a brief pleasant memory of a war we did not win.

47

HOME AGAIN

In mid February I rode a troop transport from Yokahama Japan to San Fransisco with a brief stop in Guam to pick up more returning servicemen. In San Fransisco I missed my scheduled plane and arrived home a day late. The day before Betty was left waiting at the Cleveland airport with two fretful kids turned demons. They stayed home with their Grandmother on the day of my arrival.

My new duty station was Indiantown Gap Military Reservation, Pennsylvania with a reporting date in late March. Before the expiration of my leave Betty and I drove to Lebanon PA, stopping at Ben and Gladys Kilpers, Rented a house in Lebanon PA before checking in with our new bosses at Headquarters Pennsylvania Military District, returned to Norwalk and packed out for our new home.

PMD's mission was to support the Administrative and logistical needs of Army Reserve units stationed within Pennsylvania while coordinating their training and planning activities, couched in more grandiose and elegant sounding words. It was a mission with much responsibility and little authority. All units had their own chain of command separate from PMD. The main national military concern was a sneak attack by the Soviets; we had entered the cold war and were awash with "what if" scenarios. Army Reserve Units lacked a civil defense mission. The National Guard had one and a chain of command to facilitate its accomplishment.

The Army Reserve was pushed into the position of an eager volunteer whose services nobody wanted. My job in PMD's G-3 section was "Plans Officer" and there were no plans. My boss and I never reached a mutual understanding of what and how we were to accomplish or what to do. If anyone asked me what I did I would have said; "Not much."

Out of this miasma of misunderstanding a lifeline dangled and I grabbed it.

Department of Army had decided as a training incentive to re-enter the competitive marksmanship field by fielding rifle and pistol teams and sponsoring matches from unit to international level. They issued a directive giving participation in the program priority over all other assignments.

I stepped one pace forward saluted and said; "I volunteer". The result was, against the better judgment of my boss. I took a rifle team representing PMD to the 2nd Army matches at Fort Meade, MD. The team didn't fare too well but Captain Lloyd Courtney and I were selected as members of the 2nd Army team to train at Fort Meade and compete in the All Army Matches at Fort Benning GA. My position was made more secure by being appointed team Captain/ Coach.

At Benning I earned my third and final "leg" for Distinguished Marksman designation, having earned my first two "legs" prior to WWII with Ohio National Guard teams at the National Matches. After a stint with the All Army squad I returned to Fort Meade to train and head the 2nd Army team that would compete in the Nationals.

During this time we obtained on post housing in the form of what had been the Post Chaplains quarters. PMD Headquarters had been down sized, withdrawing the Chaplain's slot from the Post's Table of Organization, either because there were no longer enough souls on post worth saving or saving what was left was no longer cost effective or, perhaps a little of both. Anyhow, the place was vacant and we moved in.

The place was strategically located near the post dispensary and movie theater. Three year old Tod became a regular patron of the former, lining up with GIs for shots or sick call. Tod's "shots" were candy kisses and his "sick call" treatment the real thing from Marie, the dispensary nurse. Seven year old Kay became adept at unauthorized entry into the movie theater and soon taught her brother the technique. Both became friendly with the post grounds keeping detail often raiding our refrigerator for soft drinks or other potables in their behalf.

The later lead to near tragedy. One Saturday afternoon while at Benning trying out for the All Army Rifle Team I flew into nearby Harrisburg quite unexpectedly. Betty picked me up at the airport and brought me home for a long leisurely weekend and respite from marksmanship training. About three the following morning I was startled out of a sound sleep, by Betty sitting up in bed screaming. A dark figure was hastily departing our bedroom. I gave chase and lost the intruder when my bare feet hit our cindered driveway. Mickey Finn, didn't help either by getting in my way. The fact we lived in a house with dozens of various types and caliber of firearms with ammunition safely stored out of the reach of our kids had proved no deterrent whatever.

Betty had called the Provost Marshall while I was otherwise engaged and in due course a pair of M.P.s showed up and investigated the situation. Later the Provost Marshall called and asked us to view a line-up of suspects.

The suspects were lined up before a two way mirror to conceal our identity. Betty easily picked out the intruder as one of the grounds keeping detail. She had a good look at him when she first was aware of someone being in our bed room and turned on the lights. I couldn't identify him because the line-up faced us and I only saw our visitor's back as he departed. Mickey Finn might have helped but he wasn't talking.

In due course the suspect was charged and in the preliminary investigation was referred to the Army's Valley Forge Medical Center for evaluation. He later was returned to IGMR for administrative discharge as unfit for military service because of possible psychotic diagnosis. Solved one mystery though, when first apprehended he was in possession of a footlocker full of women's lingerie that a number of the Post's Wives had reported missing from their clotheslines.

While at Fort Benning I ran into now Colonel George Maliszewski, Captains Jerry Morse, Jack Patterson and Roscoe Robinson. Maliszewski, I bumped into in the Mess Hall, or rather our eyes locked across the hall and he left before I could reach his table. I had lunch with Morse and Patterson, a welcome reunion and dinner with Robby and his lovely wife in their home. In Korea, Jerry, Jack, and Robby had been close friends, so close that the first two delayed their R&R leave so all three could go to Japan together.

At Fort Benning old prejudices took over and the first two who were white no longer associated with Robby, a black West Point graduate who later gained four star rank, and had the distinction of being the Army's first black four star general. I prefer to remember all three with great affection as outstanding 1st Lieutenant Company Commanders in an Infantry Battalion I had the good fortune to command for a time.

Back at Fort Meade we were able to assemble a representative rifle team that was competitive with other service teams at the National Matches Camp Perry in August. The Nationals were old home week. Betty and I had been born and raised within thirty-five miles of Camp Perry and Camp Perry belonged to the Ohio's Adjutant Generals Department that was stocked with friends of mine from WWII South Pacific Campaigns. Ben, Gladys and daughter Benita had strong ties to Camp Perry and visited us there several times.

Jim Stitt a teammate on the 1939 Team captained by Perry Swindler was also competing as an individual. Jim had shot for Ben as a PFC on the 1938 Ohio National Guard Rifle Team now a LTC in the U.S. Air Force reserve. As a teenager shooting for Ben in his own words had been; "Scared sh—less of the old Bastard." He ran into Ben and I in the PX one afternoon after the shooting was over. He joined us and learned what I had known all a long, that beneath a crusty exterior, Ben was all heart and lived for his "boys" success. Roughing us up orally, once in a while was just his way of letting us know he cared.

Three going on four Tod and seventy plus year old Ben formed a strong male bond strictly on a first name basis. No "Sonny, Young man, Mister or Uncle" simply Tod and Ben. They valued each other opinions. Approaching Port Clinton on the way to Camp Perry with Ben driving his Packard, Tod perched on the front passenger's seat and his mother, sister Kay, Gladys and Benita in the back the following conversation took place, Ben; "Tod, are you hungry?" Tod; "Yeah, Ben." Pointing; "Pull in over there that looks like a good place to eat." so they did.

At the conclusion of the National Matches the Second Army Rifle team returned to Fort Meade to disband and we returned to IGMR. Over the Thanksgiving Holiday we took a short leave to have Thanksgiving with Betty's family in Norwalk. On the way back we stopped at the Kilpers in Massillon and enjoyed an afternoon and evening with them. After dinner Tod was riding a saddle with wild abandon. Ben converted the saddle into a footstool as a gift for Benita. Ben watched the performance and remarked; "if I had ever had a son I would have wanted him to be exactly like Tod." leaving no doubt of their mutual admiration.

Later in rare form, Ben reminisced over his many years with the Thirty-seventh Division. In particular he accounted for all of 'His Boys" reveling in their successes and commiserating with their disappointments. Shortly before we all retired he said; "I've heard from all my Boys save one and surely I'll hear from him in the next few days." About three the next morning Gladys came to the foot of the stair to our room and called for me to come down stairs, something terrible had happened to Ben.

I pulled on my trousers and went down to the living room to find Gladys in tears and Ben sitting in his favorite rocker dead. He had awakened and come out to sit in his chair and smoke a cigarette before returning to bed. He passed away some two hours before Gladys missed him.

Later in the morning I called PMD Headquarters and extended my leave for another five days so we could help with the military protocol of the funeral. Betty called Helen and Urb Livengood our friends in Milan who drove to Massillon and picked up Kay and Tod to care for them until after the funeral. Ben was buried with Full Military Honors. My Military life from adolescence to middle age under Ben's mentorship had come full cycle.

The end of an Era had begun. I hung on with the Army Competitive Marksmanship program for some time before being caught in a reduction in force. Some seven years later after it became clear to me that I never again would lead men in combat I gave up my affiliation with the Ohio National Guard.

978-0-595-42152-7
0-595-42152-0

www.ingramcontent.com/pod-product-compliance
Ingram Content Group UK Ltd.
Pitfield, Milton Keynes, MK11 3LW, UK
UKHW041431210726
13854UKWH00010B/1844